"The typical primary-school classroom is a bewilder[...]
feelings: hopes, fears, excitement, sorrow, hates and lo[...]
with the teacher is central to their happiness and succ[...]
Hilary Smith draw upon their vast experience as succe[...]ιι ιεαcιιers and school
leaders to guide you in creating the relationships-based approach which is essential
to the learning of every child in your class. But this isn't just a 'how-to-do-it'
handbook. Taking you through every aspect of managing children's experiences
and feelings, their advice is based on sound theoretical principles and data from
recent research to convince you that the key component in primary teaching is
love."

Stephen Ward, Emeritus Professor of Education, Bath Spa University, UK

"Every child has a right to a good education but school and the relationship with the
teacher is so much more than that. Empathy, respect and support that 'sticks with'
children is so important in creating the nurturing and empowering environment
that helps children grow and flourish."

Anne Longfield, OBE, Children's Commissioner (2015–2021)

"This book is about such an important aspect of education. What is good primary
teaching if it isn't done with love, warmth, care and kindness with a passion for the
best outcomes for young people? Without that drive the job is too hard."

Steve Savory, Chief Executive Officer, Gloucestershire Learning Alliance

"As children returned to school following one of the Covid-19 lockdowns and were
interviewed by the BBC, many said they were most looking forward to being with
their friends and teachers again. Some expressed concern about forthcoming SATs.
While assessment and curricular control has obsessed policy-makers for the last
thirty years, some in education may have lost sight of what is really important
in child development. This book would have been timely at any period, but is
especially so as we come to terms with a population of teachers and pupils who have
experienced the challenges of isolation, home-schooling and social-distancing.

Henderson and Smith focus on the human aspect of teaching and learning, and
the importance of relationships, values, positive mental health and well-being.
They provide commentaries on their own perspectives, experiences and values, as
well as exploring a range of relevant research to underpin practical guidance. They
stress the importance of childhood and the ability of children to express opinions
and develop the skills and attributes which will enable them to resolve conflict.
The role and attitude of the teacher is at the heart of the development of what the
authors term *relationship-based pedagogy*.

This is an engaging and thought-provoking book, which should be essential reading for trainee teachers developing their educational philosophies, but it should
also be read and debated by school staff who wish to reassess their ethos and create environments in which children can develop as social beings with ideas to

share. The *Pictures of Practice* case studies alone are ideal material for promoting discussion and reflection. When read in conjunction with the well-articulated discussions about research and the clearly-described ideas for practice, which include developing connectivity with children during and post-lockdown, they provide potent stimuli for reassessing educational priorities."

Professor David Waugh, Author of academic texts, children's author, teacher and lecturer (Durham University)

"This book is essential reading for everyone working in education, especially in a post-pandemic world. We need a relationship-based approach to be central within our schools and now, more than ever, children need loving relationships at the heart of our teaching. This will not only transform our schools but also the lives of our children. I challenge you not to amend your teaching in the light of this book."

Tamsin Grimmer, Early Years Consultant, lecturer, and author of *Developing a Loving Pedagogy in the Early Years*

"Having led for 25 years I know that being loving, and feeling loved, has to be at the heart of an effective and inclusive school culture. We have to embrace affectionate practice as it is only through these authentic connections and trusting relationships that we can truly hold, enable, empower, and ignite our learning communities. This book gives us the confidence to make this happen."

Lucy Driver, Headteacher, St. Paul's Nursery School and Bristol Central Children's Centre, and National Leader of Education

"*Teaching* is a political and passionate profession. *Teachers* empower children to make sense of and take responsibility for their world, and to become future critical agents of change, democracy, and social justice. This book, with the *pedagogy of love* at the core of teaching and learning, offers a new way of affirming and liberating those who teach as well as those who learn."

Pat Black, Head of Teacher Education, School of Education, Bath Spa University, UK

Relationship-Based Pedagogy in Primary Schools

This insightful book shows how prioritising loving relationships in the primary school between practitioners and children helps secure children's emotional well-being, improves behaviour, and leads to more successful learning. It identifies the fundamental values that underpin effective learning encounters and provides the practical tools and language to realise deep connections with children.

Combining theory with personal experience the authors present relationship-based practice as a robust and credible pedagogic approach to teaching and learning. The book offers unique features such as 'Shared language' to support and promote a rich, meaningful dialogue and 'The lens of the authors' offers practical and realistic contexts to help teachers apply theory and ideas from personal experience.

Giving educators the confidence to teach with the relational qualities of love, trust, respect, and empathy, this is essential reading for all teachers wanting to develop authentic relationships with the children they care for.

Nicki Henderson is a former teacher, Local Authority consultant, Lecturer in Early Years and PGCE Programme Leader at Bath Spa University. Her most recent role was headteacher of a nursery and primary school where she used a relationship-based approach to drive positive changes to the school's reputation, experience and outcomes.

Hilary Smith is a retired teacher and lecturer with extensive experience in primary and early years education. She is an education consultant, and Associate with Kate Cairns Associates, providing training for schools and early years settings on attachment, trauma and resilience, and emotion coaching.

Relationship-Based Pedagogy in Primary Schools

Learning with Love

Nicki Henderson and Hilary Smith

Routledge
Taylor & Francis Group

LONDON AND NEW YORK

Cover image: Peter Cade / Getty Images

First published 2022
by Routledge
2 Park Square, Milton Park, Abingdon, Oxon OX14 4RN

and by Routledge
605 Third Avenue, New York, NY 10158

Routledge is an imprint of the Taylor & Francis Group, an informa business

British Library Cataloguing-in-Publication Data
A catalogue record for this book is available from the British Library

Library of Congress Cataloging-in-Publication Data
A catalog record for this book has been requested

ISBN: 978-0-367-63747-7 (hbk)
ISBN: 978-0-367-63748-4 (pbk)
ISBN: 978-1-003-12053-7 (ebk)

DOI: 10.4324/9781003120537

Typeset in Melior
by Apex CoVantage, LLC

For Bradley and for Paul

Contents

Acknowledgements

We would like to thank all those who have contributed to the generation of this book, both in thought and deed. A particular mention to the staff and children at The Mead Academy Trust who inspired the initial MA research proving that a relationship-based approach to teaching can bring about a real and positive change to individuals as well as to the culture of a learning community.

Special thanks also to Stephen Ward, for his attention to detail in the proofreading process. Also to the teachers and children who donated their wonderful pictures and testaments, including Alison, Emma, Georgina, Georgie, Fiona, Isla, Josh, Lucy, Pam and Rosie. Our deep appreciation goes to our friends and colleagues who have, over the years, influenced and inspired our confidence in loving practices including Anne, Becci, Christine, Jenny, Lesley, Lucy, Lyssy, Mary, Pat, Sue, Trish and especially Viki. To Pat Black, Lucy Driver, Tamsin Grimmer, Anne Longfield, OBE, Steve Savory, Emeritus Professor Stephen Ward and Professor David Waugh for taking the time to read and validate our efforts and of course the team at Routledge for enabling them to come to fruition.

And finally, to our families for their patience, kindness and support: Alice, Avis, Damien, Harry, Kieran, Les, Peter, Sarah, Sophia and Theo. We love you.

At the 'heart' of the approach

Teachers have three loves: love of learning, love of learners, and the love of bringing the first two loves together.

(Scott Hayden, 1882–1915)

This book joins a growing body of literature advocating a model of education that emphasises meaningful relationships through a strong emotional connection where reciprocal and authentic relationships with children, characterised by the qualities of love, mutual respect, trust, and empathy, are at the root of effective education. Combining sound theory with authentic experience we present relationship-based practice as a robust and credible pedagogic approach to education, worthy of serious and intellectual consideration. We seek to reconceptualise any condescending connotations associated with the 'soppy, touchy, feely' world of relationship-building, which for too long has been dismissed as merely natural or innate for a predominantly female early years workforce, and often left unrecognised and unvalued in the later phases of education altogether.

Central to the relationship-based approach is a theoretical and clear understanding that children's relationships with those around them are important and, moreover, the way in which children make sense of those relationships is fundamental to how they feel about themselves, their lives and will ultimately drive how well they develop socially, emotionally and cognitively. Put simply, children who are loved do better, in school and in later life.

We urge you at the outset therefore not to be put off by any preconceived ideas about the seemingly sentimental language nor to dismiss this approach as one that is not relevant or appropriate for you; it is! Indeed the evidence suggests that it has to be. The book will help you to understand that the human aspect of your teaching is as important, if not more so, than delivering the curriculum. It will identify the fundamental values that underpin the most effective learning encounters and provide you with the necessary practical tools to secure deep and meaningful connections with the children and young people in your care. It will demonstrate the

DOI: 10.4324/9781003120537-1

impact of a relationship-based approach in transforming a school's culture and its outcomes.

Above all we hope it will give you the confidence to put loving relationships at the heart of your teaching.

The lens of the authors: our values

Life imbues us with values (the things we feel most committed to or passionate about), absorbed wittingly, or sometimes unwittingly, from a melting pot of opinion from a long list of influencers including, family, friends, colleagues, teachers, politicians, the media, and so on. These values help inform who we are, how we interact with others, and ultimately the lens through which we see and judge the world (Hawkes, 2013).

As authors we recognise that the opinions we hold and the experiences we have had will inevitably affect what we choose to discuss and the way the issues are presented. From the outset we believe it is important, therefore, to openly acknowledge our 'positionality' (Thomas, 2017: 152) and to share with you the pivotal experiences and moments in our lives that have shaped our biases or preference for one side of an argument over another. In this way we hope to set into context our understanding of relationship-based practice as well as our 'credibility' and 'competence' (*ibid.*) in promoting the relationship-based approach more widely. Furthermore, in a book that promotes learning in the emotional spaces between people we believe that the more you understand about our backgrounds and experience the more likely you are to be interested in us, and therefore in what we have to say. Our purpose is to inspire you to adopt positive human qualities: to listen, develop empathy and be open to transforming your own practice building on the evidence offered here. If the messages contained in this book are going to resonate with you we need to establish a shared understanding, your respect and trust in the practices we are describing, and a sense of community connection.

The following section highlights how our own experiences have helped to shape and develop our commitment to a relationship-based pedagogy.

Nicki Henderson – 'leading with love'

> Each and every classroom (about 260 children) always has a little bit of Henderson heart to guide them through their big future, waiting a few years ahead of them.
>
> (Child in the school)

My teaching career began 30 years ago and I have always worked hard to secure harmonious working relationships. My first appointment as a reception teacher in a team-teaching context with nine feeder pre-school providers enabled me to understand that the trust and respect of the whole school community, including the parents, was of paramount importance. I was also determined to promote positive and loving relationships with the children in my care as I had observed the negative effects on children (in their confidence, enjoyment and ability to be independent) not only in my own schooling, but also in what I considered to be overly controlling environments witnessed in many of the school placements during my teacher training. I was challenged by practices that involved restricting the children's choices and movements and that seemed to me to be more about the control of the teacher rather than any other aspect of responsible pedagogy. Activities that were described and accepted as necessary supervision (e.g. a school policy that demands that the toilets can only be used at playtimes) fell, I believed, into the realms of unacceptable manipulation or restriction. I resolved, therefore, that I would look differently at the classroom power relations and expectations in my own teaching – aiming to practise power 'with' and not power 'over' the children. Although I did not know it at the time, my values were already beginning to align with the practice of the now renowned early childhood provision in the Italian municipal town of Reggio Emilia. My focus on authentic relationships certainly mirrored the partnerships promoted by Rinaldi (2006) in securing mutual involvement and respect.

My teaching reflected a child-centred constructivist approach to learning characterised by a rights-based discourse, outlined by Nutbrown (1999: xv) and Jones and Welch (2010: 13) who promote practitioners as 'respectful educators' and challenge the ways of living and learning that 'oppress, harm or limit children'. My aim was to provide an ethical service that affirmed the importance of childhood and the enormous capabilities of children. In practice this meant organising a classroom that facilitated independent access to resources, provided learning opportunities centred on the children's fascinations and where we were all motivated to play, to take risks, make mistakes and build relational resilience. The outcome was a happy classroom where the children told me they felt safe, secure and loved. When a supply teacher told me she hated taking my class because the children kept telling her what they should be doing next, what she should be saying and how she was making them feel, I knew that the learning culture was one that the children and I should be proud of!

I maintained a firm belief in these same underpinning principles for teaching, learning and living as I moved to my subsequent role as a consultant in early years for the local authority, delivering training and support to schools and settings often in challenging circumstances. Moving practice and thinking forward demands great diplomacy and sensitivity, and whilst it was my role to ensure the quality of provision improved significantly, this had to be accomplished with the well-being of the staff intact. Central to the success of this role was undoubtedly the need to communicate effectively and the ability to quickly establish a warm rapport and emotional connection. I relied instinctively on humour (a strategy honed as a child) to help people relax, making it easier to engage in difficult and open conversations.

Moving from the local authority to my new roles at Bath Spa University, first as Senior Lecturer in Early Years and then as Programme Leader for the Postgraduate

Certificate in Education (PGCE), offered a privileged opportunity to gain a theoretical base to the innovative philosophy and practice that I had been sharing with others. For example, the importance of establishing a motivating and welcoming environment for learning (Hattie, 2012; Malaguzzi, 1998); authentic communication with parents (Jelley and Sylva, 2017); effective processes for transition (Fabian, 2002; Howe and Richards, 2011); and the importance of shared and sustained thinking in the learning process (Sylva *et al.*, 2004).

It was here too that my eyes were opened to a world of political and social debate, where I found like-minded people (including Hilary Smith) who were comfortable to encourage a positive discourse about feminism, social justice and diversity. These conversations enhanced my awareness and consciousness and helped me to see the world through an adjusted lens, perhaps distorted by a family experience that, although loving and supportive, was based on traditional patriarchal and imperialistic values. Now a passionate advocate for equity and equality, I enjoy engaging in regular challenging conversations with my family!

Working with a creative and dynamic team we set about restructuring the PGCE so that discussion on the rights and image of children were foregrounded with the practices of Reggio Emilia. Our aim was to encourage teacher trainees to embrace an approach where respectful attitudes and reciprocal relationships with children and their families are valued (Rinaldi, *op. cit.*). This direction was warranted. It was clear that many of the trainees and indeed many of the school mentors lacked confidence when it came to dealing with relationship issues in their classrooms. They were either concerned not to appear 'too nice' for fear of 'losing control of the children's behaviour' (echoing a traditional view of teacher training where trainees are warned about the dangers of smiling at the children before Christmas!), or in some cases were worried about developing healthy positive relationships in case they be wrongly misconstrued as crossing safeguarding policies.

I am proud of the many outstanding teachers who emerged from the PGCE, characterised by their commitment to playful learning, creative thinking, risk-taking and innovation. Many too are showing in their practice that it is *who* they are teaching that is as important as *what* they are teaching.

My own subsequent research (Henderson, 2019) and reflection has led me to question, however, why we did not do more to focus on the particular human characteristics or qualities that facilitate and support the relational bond between teachers and children. Loe (2015) found that the subject is largely missing from all professional dialogue and teacher training. He rightly asks why it is an issue left to the personal styles and preferences of teachers, given how crucial it is in determining children's positive experiences and outcomes. We hope this book will open up and help advance this important discourse.

My most recent experience as headteacher of a nursery and primary school further galvanised, and ultimately gave a name to, my interest in this 'relational' aspect of teaching. It was here that I first became aware of the *Relational Schools Foundation* that was formed in 2014 with the aim of encouraging schools to see the connection between relational practice and children's outcomes and achievements (see https://relationalschools.org). This concept of teaching that focuses on the importance of the quality of human interactions between a teacher and the young people in their care seemed to bring together all the individual elements of practice that I had valued and promoted throughout my teaching career. Although it might appear to be at odds and a long way from the dominant paradigm of discipline and data-driven accountability that as a head I perhaps 'should' have been interested in, I was increasingly inspired by the Foundation's growing body of evidence that suggested a tangible link between 'a school that provides a secure base and the achievement of stronger academic outcomes' (Loe, 2017: 106). This claim was relevant for my own school particularly given its social context. The school is in an area of high deprivation, and low aspiration. It has a long history of weak teaching, low expectations, under-performance and a high percentage of children with special educational needs and development. Although the children are wonderful, curious and articulate, many of them are also 'fragile' learners who commonly have difficulty in trusting, lack self-esteem and have home environments that are often chaotic, leading many of them to question the point of education in general and schooling in particular. They certainly showed us in their behaviours that they had issues related to their well-being and/or mental health.

Recognising myself as a 'pastoral leader' (Loe, *ibid*: 82) I sought to improve the practices and reputation of the school with the quality of relationships as a driving imperative. Drawing on my own cherished beliefs, accumulated from 30 years of experience and observation of the most inspiring practice of others, I set about creating a 'school of warm-heartedness' (Boddy, 2017: vi). I drew attention to the personal characteristics or behaviours that teachers needed to employ to secure effective relationships. I wanted all adults in the school community to model and teach children how to show love, care, tolerance, respect, openness and honesty with each other. I was convinced that when the children started to believe that the adults genuinely cared about them they would be more motivated to learn, to feel optimistic and confident; to take risks, make mistakes and build resilience. I hoped the adults would benefit from a similar ethos directed towards and between them.

In order to help us improve our relationship-based pedagogy and skills I developed a 'Framework to Support Relationship-based Practice', outlining the characteristics of teaching and learning to be employed in practice. Many of these strategies were not new to teachers; however, it was the first time we brought them together and introduced them using the collective term 'relationship-based teaching'.

In the Framework I promote the need for authentic connections and describe how practitioners and children should invest time in finding out about the significant events and interests in each other's lives. I consider the possible impact of interruptions in relationships and introduce techniques to help rebuild connections when things go 'wrong' or during periods of separation: e.g. the use of conflict resolution between parties (adult–child, child–child, adult–adult); and the concept of holding children in mind (so that they know that someone cares about them, what they are doing and how they are feeling). I champion a philosophy that seeks to understand the child, their history and the reasons behind their behaviour, and promote strategies that underpin this approach (clear consequences, managing reactions, positive reinforcement, and de-escalation techniques). I advocate the place of effective community conversation where close dialogue with all stakeholders happens regularly, ensuring all views are shared together with honesty and respect. I reinforce my vision of an enabling environment that focuses on the physical (as a home away from home), the emotional (as welcoming and motivating) and the cognitive (with the learning culture recognised as a shared and mutually constructed experience). Analysing the turbulent impact of change on the school community I include effective transition as a key priority and in particular the importance of an extended strategic approach to the end of year (Henderson, *op. cit.*).

This book illustrates the influences and impact of the above strategies and the practical reality of my experience. It shows that when responding to the relational demands of a setting, the clarity, consistency, and above all, the shared language and understanding evidenced in the 'Framework to Support Relationship-based Practice', is needed. Above all it proves that a relationship-based approach to teaching can bring about a real and positive change to individual children as well as to the culture of the learning community as a whole.

The following quotations bear testament to this:

> 'I remember when you pretended to be my grandma when my mum wasn't there when I was star of the week. Thank you for smiling, caring and making the hurt better.'
>
> (Child of the school)

> 'Thank you from the bottom of our hearts for dedicating yourself to our children's futures. You have filled the school with love, laughter and positivity. What you and your dream team have helped them to accomplish is nothing short of magical.'
>
> (Parent of the school)

> 'You have taken on a school at rock bottom and in two years have turned this around. Teaching is now good and progress is accelerating. There is exemplary practice in Early Years and Year 1.'
>
> (Steve Savory, Deputy Director, DfE supporting the Regional Schools Commissioner for the South West)

Hilary Smith – 'love at the heart of learning'

In order to give you insights into my allegiances, assumptions and beliefs, I will begin with my family of origin, an opening statement which in itself reveals my conviction that our upbringing, and the significant adults in our early childhood play a crucial role in the way we view the world. Throughout my childhood, my dad worked as a police officer in the London Metropolitan Police Service and my mum was employed as an audio typist for London County Council. Obedience, honesty and commitment to public service were the values my parents espoused and tried to instil in me and my two brothers; and whilst I rebelled against the first, I have always tried to be truthful and have spent my working life serving, and believing in, public institutions.

As a teenager, my first passion was the theatre and, although I wanted to be an actor, I was encouraged to go to university, and fortunately was accepted to one of the few single honours drama degree courses available at the time. I spent three wonderful years learning not about acting but about the power of creativity, how people communicate and behave, and the value of positive and persuasive interactions. I also learned about group work, about the advantages of collaboration and cooperation, and about the importance of process rather than product. Alongside these exciting revelations, I also cut my political teeth and became an ardent feminist and socialist, staunchly opposed to the prevailing politics at the time of Thatcherism and the increasing prominence of individualism and greed.

Moving from drama into teaching felt like a natural progression, and after qualifying with a PGCE my first primary teaching post was in a school on a large council estate in the south of Bristol where high levels of poverty and social deprivation, and their associated disadvantages, continue to be prevalent. I began as a keen and energetic young teacher, determined not to be ground down by the widespread view at the time, sadly also by some of my fellow teachers, that the children attending the school were beyond our help. I stayed for 14 happy years at the school, and while I cannot claim to have transformed lives, my life was changed by my experiences there. I quickly discovered that the key to motivating and inspiring young learners can only be achieved through committed relationships with them, and that teaching with compassion and creativity, and having high aspirations for all children, regardless of their starting point, can, and does, make a difference to their academic success and, possibly more importantly, to their confidence and resilience. By 1995 I was proud to be part of a team of aspirational teachers whose work was recognised by the National Commission on Education as succeeding 'against the odds' with children previously considered inevitably, and irrevocably, marred by their social background (Hamlyn, 1995).

As my classroom teaching became increasingly characterised by my ability to successfully engage troubled, and troubling, children, my next significant career move was to become a peripatetic Behaviour Support Teacher for the local authority. Being a behaviour specialist, at a time when new ways of thinking about children's social and emotional needs, and mental health, were emerging, enabled me to access some of the most innovative and exciting training of my career. Having already been influenced by the well-known frameworks of Maslow's hierarchy of human needs (Maslow, 1971) and Bronfenbrenner's (1979) ecological model, I was strongly drawn to those who advocated an holistic, inclusive, approach to behaviour. I became an enthusiastic follower of the work of Maines and Robinson (1998, 2004) and Rogers (1995, 2002) who promote non-blameful, positive strategies for children whose behaviour is challenging to adults. When the educational and social benefits of emotional literacy became evident (Goleman, 1996; Antidote, 2003; Weare, 2004), I enthusiastically studied and promoted it in schools and early years settings, as well as providing staff training in other prosocial activities such as peer mediation (Noaks and Noaks, 2009; Cremin, 2002) and peaceful conflict-resolution (Betsy, 2002; Hopkins, 2004). These further embedded my conviction that when children understand their own and others' feelings and behaviour they will become more compassionate and empathic citizens.

During my later career as a lecturer in education at Bath Spa University, and Programme Leader for the Primary and Early Years Initial Teacher Training programmes, I was privileged to access a vast range of academic research and resources at the click of a button, not previously available to me during my own undergraduate (and even postgraduate) days. This opened up a world of theory and discourse which, combined with discussions and debates with students and colleagues, enabled me to question and extensively challenge my own, as well as others', teaching philosophy, choices and methods to date. It also provided me with easy access to the most up-to-date developments and ideas from some of the greatest educational thinkers of our time. This privileged access (which continues to be far more extensive than can be found on popular internet search engines) enabled me to explore and expound the concept of Behaviour for Learning (Ellis and Tod, 2009, 2015) and Emotion Coaching (Gottman and DeClaire, 1997) in an increasingly rigorous and critical way. Whilst I found my views on compassionate approaches to challenging behaviour, and the importance of emotions in learning, were endorsed, I also discovered, and embraced concepts and ideas that are now embedded in my attitude to education and schools. For example, the principles for excellence in early years practice through proponents such as Rinaldi (*op. cit.*) and Nutbrown (*op. cit.*), the essential role of the key person for children's emotional well-being (Elfer *et al.*, 2012) and the imperative of reflective, and reflexive, practice (Paige-Smith and Craft, 2007). My own research and authorship also took me further into the realms of attachment theory (Holmes, 1993; Hughes, 2006) and the effects of trauma and resilience (Cairns, 2002; Bomber, 2007). Additionally, my work in initial teacher training that entailed visiting trainee teachers in different schools and early years settings gave me invaluable insights into diverse practices and teaching styles, and even more opportunities to extend my understanding of the efficacy of relationship-led, values-based education.

You will find the influences of all of the above apparent in this book, either explicitly referenced or implied through anecdotal evidence, and you will discover that imbued throughout is an overarching and persistent aspiration for social justice and equity in education.

It was also at Bath Spa University that my relationship with Nicki Henderson was forged. I met her on the day of my interview and her warm, friendly welcome immediately put me at ease. Her manner towards me had a significant impact in terms of my impression of the university and my motivation to succeed in the interview. I later discovered that Nicki's positive, open-hearted approach extends to everyone she meets, from small children to Cambridge dons, from anxious students to influential directors of education. Her warmth and humour is generous and unprejudiced. She also has an intelligent, principled approach to education and teaching, which will be expounded in this book. I learned, and continue to learn, from her that combining our heads and our hearts in all our encounters is the most productive, powerful, and enjoyable, way to work and teach.

Finally, I would like to share a personal experience that had a profound influence on my life and significantly shaped my values as an educator and advocate for children. For this example, I return again to my childhood.

My older brother Paul was unusual as a child; he behaved in strange and sometimes bizarre ways which were hard to understand and exasperated my parents and his teachers. Nowadays it would be recognised that he was displaying symptoms of autistic spectrum disorder (ASD) but this was the 1960s and at that time, autism was not a diagnosable condition. The language of special educational needs was not even in the education lexicon: the *Warnock Report*, which led to the first ever SEN legislation in the UK, did not come into being until 1978 (Warnock, 1978). So in that era, teachers felt free to describe Paul as 'defiant', 'anti-social', 'unteachable', 'an idiot' and far worse. Inside the classroom he was constantly being humiliated or punished for his behaviour and little attempt was made to help him access any learning. He also spent considerable amounts of time out of the classroom, either having been sent to stand outside in the corridor, or in the headteacher's office, or sent home on a temporary suspension (much to the embarrassment and frustration of my long-suffering parents). Children throughout our primary school, following the teachers' lead, were cruel to Paul and bullied him for being 'the weird kid'. Whilst I played happily with my friends, I often witnessed my brother wandering around the playground alone, in his own world, either systematically ignored, ridiculed, name-called or being beaten up by his peers, while teachers turned a blind eye. I instinctively knew that what was happening to Paul wasn't right, but I was his younger sister by four years, and as this was a time when children were rarely listened to by adults in authority, I was powerless to help him. Later, when I became an adult, and a teacher, myself, I was able to reflect on the connection between those early memories and my advocacy for love and compassion in schools. The injustice of Paul's treatment, the abusive and ignorant behaviour of his teachers towards him, the unchallenged cruelty of other children, and the lack of understanding or support for my parents has never left me. It is an emotional connection which has informed and motivated my work for nearly 40 years. And if this book achieves one thing, my hope is that it will move you to treat all children in school with the love and respect that my brother deserved and failed to receive.

Summary: making our values visible

Writing this book has afforded us the opportunity to reflect deeply together on our combined 70 years knowledge of working in schools, and to encapsulate what we have long felt in our individual hearts about our vision for education. Borne out of our long stimulating discussions, the list below clearly sets out the core values that underpin our own practice and permeate a relationship-based approach to teaching and learning. Honing these values was not easy and the seeming simplicity of each bullet point belies all the hard thinking, and consideration that lies behind them. However, the process of generation in itself is testament to the power of human connection and open-hearted collaboration, where individual knowledge and skill is recognised, ideas and output compassionately yet rigorously critiqued, and decisions made based on a shared common goal. We feel especially proud to be associated with these values. And whilst it is important for you to come freely to your own philosophical principles and understandings, we hope as you read further into the book that you will be reassured, and inspired, by the validity of those presented here:

- We advocate a new approach to education: one that emphasises relationships and connections, with the potential to improve children's life-chances, cognitive ability, motivation to learn, and positive mental health and well-being.

- In accordance with our feminist principles we reject any claims or assumptions that 'the close association between caring and mothering' (Shin, 2015: 497) means that relationship-based practices are more likely to be 'instinctive and innate' and thus favoured by us because we are women and mothers. We believe *all* practitioners should model and teach children how to show love, care, tolerance, respect, openness and honesty with each other.

- We recognise children as resilient, confident and self-assured. We place an emphasis on children as active, independent, risk-takers, capable of leadership, self-regulation, with the right to be involved in all decision-making that affects them.

- We recognise childhood as a stage in its own right and not merely as a preparation for adulthood. We also acknowledge that childhood is not always the 'care-free period' recalled by nostalgic adults looking back after time. Growing up is difficult, even in the best of circumstances.

- We believe that children deserve the love and support of sensitive, thoughtful adults who are ethically and culturally aware, and who can nurture them through their childhood, preserving their dignity and gaining their respect.

- Our purpose is to demonstrate a 'common humanity', whereby difference is acknowledged, dissimilarity celebrated, and individual achievements recognised, resulting in an equitable experience for all.

▓ We respect the social nature of children and that learning accordingly needs to be an active experience. One that is designed to provoke rich dialogue and sustained shared thinking between all participants through cooperation, negotiation, experimentation and discovery.

Ultimately it will be your own values and beliefs that will guide how you receive the messages we are giving about relationship-based pedagogy. Throughout the book we will therefore encourage you to consider what is important in your own thinking, to acknowledge where these priorities have come from and to question how they are shown in your practice.

The following section will help you to further understand and define what we mean by a relationship-based approach.

A relationship-based approach

Over the last decade, and exacerbated by the current Covid-19 pandemic (Andrew *et al.*, 2020; NFER, 2020), increasing attention and concern has been given to the state of children and young people's well-being and mental health and the subsequent impact on their immediate and long-term physical health, education and lives. According to Digital NHS (2020) the rates of mental disorders have increased with one in six (16.0 per cent) children aged 5 to 16 years being identified as having a probable mental disorder, increasing from one in nine (10.8 per cent) in 2017. Additionally, Public Health, England (2019) report that 10 per cent of young people aged 8–15 experience a low sense of well-being, with children and young people identifying a lack of loving and trusting relationships, feeling supported and having a sense of connection as key contributory factors.

If the true character of a society is revealed in how it treats its children, we should all be ashamed that in the 2018 OECD survey of 15-year-olds, the UK was ranked 29th for life satisfaction out of a total of 30 OECD countries. *The Good Childhood Report* (Children's Society, 2020), similarly concludes that, compared to 23 European countries, by the age of 15 our young people are the least satisfied with their lives and have the second highest levels of sadness.

Where are we going so wrong with our children and young people?

There is no doubt that schools have a serious and important role to play in nurturing and supporting children's positive mental health and emotional well-being. And yet there is also acknowledgement that not only are the ' "old frameworks for school" not equipped to engage with the current state of young people's lives and complexity' (McLaughlin and Gray, 2015: 6), but the overriding culture of testing and performativity could have significant implications for the children's well-being and mental health as well as schools as safe social and emotional spaces (Wyness and Lang, 2016). Marsh (2017: 400) challenges the 'short- sighted pursuit of targets and curriculum coverage' that manifests in an over-emphasis on individuality and decontextualised knowledge (Moss, 2017). Many schools, perhaps understandably, focus their resources and practices on the limited areas in which they will be publicly held accountable (Alexander and Potter, 2015).

Against this backdrop, we welcome and join a growing body of literature advocating a 'better model of education – a new approach emphasising relationships, connection, and meaning' (McLaughlin and Gray, *op. cit*: 6), where schools will be judged on their ability to embed the promotion of positive well-being and mental health throughout the learning culture and curriculum, as well as in staff training and continuing professional development.

Championing this view Kumar (2005: 38) recommends that 'rather than being guided by external bodies . . . schools needed to be guided by the quality of interaction between pupils, teachers, parents and local community'. Likewise, Boddy (*op. cit*: vi) argues that 'our education system can only be made fit for purpose for the new generation when teachers and parents work together to create schools of warm-heartedness'. He presents a compelling argument for an ethical approach to education and schooling, emphasising unity of the 'human family' and the ability to 'connect' warmly with each other.

Much of what we know about learning through relationships has its origins in the work of Lev Vygotsky (1896–1934), the Russian child psychologist who asserted that learning is relational (1978). He promoted the value of social interaction and the importance of the mutual construction of learning supported by sensitive and attentive adults (see also Chapter 3). Laevers (1998), similarly established a link between well-being, levels of involvement and deep-level learning centred around the notion that sensitive adult interaction would result in positive changes in a child's social, emotional and cognitive capacity, leading to better attitudes to learning, outcomes and life experiences.

Analysis of the available literature helps us to build up a critical understanding of the scope of relationship-based pedagogy. It is a complex, multi-faceted approach, encompassing the following characteristics:

- The word 'relationship' is used to signal the centrality of relationships in all aspects of teaching and learning, resulting in positive mental health and well-being as well as high levels of achievement and academic outcomes.

- All relationships in a school matter. This includes harmonious interaction and increased depth of interest and understanding between adults and children, between children and their peers and between the school and its community.

- In its richest form learning is a mutually constructed undertaking with value attributed to different approaches to problems and a readiness to plan, share and participate fairly and equitably.

- Responsibility and willingness to understand, adjust and change individual personal attitudes and behaviours are acknowledged, understood and worked on, in order to facilitate respect, and accommodate the needs of other members of the school family.

Whilst we hope you find this definition of a relationship-based approach to education helpful, it is not intended to be perfect or to be set in tablets of stone. It is designed to generate thought-provoking discussion and to support you in developing a deeper understanding and ownership of the critical issues.

How to use this book

There is no right or wrong way to use this book. It has been written to enable you to develop your understanding of relationship-based pedagogy. Whether you choose to read diligently from cover to cover or dip in randomly, the hope is it will provide a catalyst to open up new types of conversations and practices.

Chapter 2 identifies the underpinning characteristics and attributes that strengthen effective relationships and will encourage you to examine your own attitudes and behaviours. It will explore and justify the human characteristics of love, trust, respect and empathy and contest that these relationship-based qualities can be developed and are not merely 'intuitive' – the way teachers naturally are.

Chapter 3 explores the importance of securing a positive learning culture and supports you in developing both the physical and emotional environment to provide for this. It will draw on research that suggests that when a setting acts either as an extension to a home, or provides an alternative model to an adverse one, children are motivated to learn, feel optimistic and confident to take risks.

Chapter 4 highlights the inherent interconnectedness between teachers and children and its importance in a relationship-based approach. It will propose a guide for successful connectivity, with practical examples, and will explore the role of attachment and early trauma, and how you can provide protective factors by being attuned and empathic.

Chapter 5 examines behaviour through a relationship-based lens. It will enable you to model and teach positive learning behaviour for all children by providing practical classroom examples. It will demonstrate how you can promote prosocial behaviour within a loving context underpinned by the principles of love and commitment, limit-setting and learning and development.

Chapter 6 considers the possible interruptions, and ruptures in relationships, and the neurobiology occurring when this happens. It will provide clear, authentic techniques for helping rebuild connections and will introduce you to restorative practices, including the conflict resolution steps and peer mediation, to support relationship repair.

Chapter 7 focuses on the inevitable as well as the unpredictable changes in school life with a particular emphasis on the emotional impact this has on children's relationships. It will provide strategies to support children through a range of transitions from moving into a different learning context (e.g going into the hall for assembly) to moving to a new setting (e.g secondary school). Underpinned by change theory, you will be supported to ensure that the process of change is conducted in a loving way, providing safety and continuity for everyone.

Chapter 8 is dedicated to the 'legacy of love' and celebrates the powerful and positive influence that loving teachers can have on young children's lives. Using real scenarios and testaments from the perspective of the children themselves, the chapter will encourage you to understand the value of a pedagogy that ensures that all children, and indeed all members of the learning community, can develop in the context of relationships and the emotional environment surrounding them.

This book offers the following pedagogical features specifically designed to enhance your understanding of relational teaching:

> *'Chapter objectives'* outline the key areas to be discussed and what you can expect to achieve by reading the chapter.
>
> *'The lens of the authors'* offers a practical context to the issues discussed in the chapter, helping you to understand how theory and ideas are actually applied and the possible outcomes of these.
>
> *'Pictures of practice'* are intended to provide you with practical examples that demonstrate how other teachers have developed and resolved relationship-based aspects in their practice and provide you with an evidence-based model.

Each chapter will end with *'Prompts for reflection'* that encourage you to understand how your own relationship-based pedagogy can be adapted and changed. For many of you it will be the first time that you have been directly invited to focus on your pedagogy in this way. 'Prompts for reflection' will help you to become aware of your own relationship-based lens, to consider whether your view is shared by the children in your class, and to envision the power of an approach to your teaching centred on the quality of human interactions and connections.

Each chapter will offer practical suggestions for *'Shared language'* designed to promote rich, meaningful and respectful dialogue that is used consistently throughout the whole school. Moreover, we recognise that as a society we are constantly using language to evolve and transform our ideas and beliefs into concrete reality. In promoting relationship-based language we seek to move away from the existing dominant discourse and to 'create influence'; to change, and to promote a variant to the accepted cultural or social 'norm'. We hope that the relationship-based words and phrases introduced here become common parlance, giving teachers both the permission to advocate teaching as an act of love, as well as a shared language to describe and define it.

A *'Chapter summary'* at the end of each chapter will highlight key issues raised and confirm your developing understanding of a relationship-based approach to teaching.

Each chapter concludes with an annotated list of recommended *'Further reading'* including relevant books, articles and reports. This feature serves as a guide to independent study and provides a useful point for those of you who wish to deepen your knowledge of a particular area.

Prompts for reflection

- Think about the teachers that have influenced, inspired and had the greatest impact on you both as a learner and as a person. Who were they? What made them 'stand out'? Did a positive teacher–student relationship play a part in your view of them as a 'good' teacher?

- How much value do you place on reciprocal relationships? With the children? Other members of staff? Parents? Wider community? How is this value demonstrated?

- Consider the conflicts and tensions that exist within the current education system. Does what is valued and measured structurally and systematically (e.g. through centrally driven government policies, practices and procedures) align with your personal and professional values?

- Is there a place for challenging the status quo to drive change? If so, how can this be achieved in both a reasoned and professional manner?

Shared language

Children: We use the term 'children' (as opposed to 'kids') to describe young people of primary school age, including those in the nursery or early years class. We recognise all children as capable and competent with the capacity to make intelligent and informed decisions about matters that interest and affect them and promote their right to full and active participation in society.

Parent: The generic term 'parent' is used to describe the adult(s) who look after and care for the child at home. This might be their natural/biological parent, foster parent or carer from their immediate or extended family.

School: The generic term 'school' is used to indicate any setting or environment where children or young people are educated (no matter their age).

Teachers: Any adult in the school community who helps children to acquire knowledge, competence or virtue (e.g. teaching assistant, trainee teacher, early years practitioner, parent helper).

Teaching: Describes the sensitive intervention and facilitation between teachers and children that enables learning and curiosity to be extended or consolidated. This includes real-life problem-solving and opportunities for creative thinking and exploration as well as instruction, modelling, questioning, etc.

Chapter summary

In this chapter we have introduced you to our own thinking bias, the values that we find important and our related practices. We have examined the rationale for a relationship-based approach to education and presented a summary of the characteristics that define it. The chapters that follow will provide you with an opportunity to extend your understanding and to explore different insights, theories and practice.

Further reading

Hawkes, N. (2013) *From My Heart: Transforming Lives Through Values.* Carmarthen: Independent Thinking Press.

Underpinned by his own experience as a teacher and headteacher, Hawkes writes about his vision for a 'value-based' approach to education. The book supports the reader to understand the underpinning philosophy of the approach and uses anecdotes to suggest how these are applied in school practice. The frequent invitations to 'pause' will encourage you to question your own values and where they may have come from.

Thornton, L. and Brunton, P. (2015) *Understanding the Reggio Approach* (3rd Edn). London: David Fulton Publishers.

If you want to find out more about the renowned approach to early years education promoted in Reggio Emilia, this book provides accessible analysis of the key themes. It highlights the ideas that practitioners should consider when reviewing and reflecting on their practice.

References

Alexander, T. and Potter, T. (Eds) (2015) *Education for Change: Transforming the Way We Teach Our Children.* London: RoutledgeFalmer.

Andrew, A., Cattan, S., Costa-Dias, M., Farquharson, C., Kraftman, L., Krutikova, S., Phimister, A. and Sevilla, A. (2020) *Learning During the Lockdown: Real-Time Data on Children's Experiences During Home Learning.* IFS Briefing Note BN288. Available at: www.ifs.org.uk /uploads/BN288-Learning-during-the-lockdown-1.pdf [Accessed 20.5.2020].

Antidote (2003) *The Emotional Literacy Handbook.* London: Fulton Publishers.

Betsy, E. (2002) *You Can't Come to My Birthday Party! Conflict Resolution with Young Children.* Ypsilanti, MI: High/Scope Educational Research Foundation.

Boddy, D. (2017) *Mind Their Hearts: Creating Schools and Homes of Warm-Heartedness.* Woodbridge: John Catt Educational Ltd.

Bomber, L. (2007) *Inside I'm Hurting: Practical Strategies for Supporting Children with Attachment Difficulties in Schools.* London: Worth Publishing Ltd.

Bronfenbrenner, U. (1979) *The Ecology of Human Development: Experiments by Nature and Design.* Cambridge, MA: Harvard University Press.

Cairns, K. (2002) *Attachment, Trauma and Resilience: Therapeutic Caring for Children.* London: British Association for Adoption and Fostering.

Children's Society (2020) *The Good Childhood Report.* Available at: www.childrenssociety.org.uk/sites/default/files/2020-11/Good-Childhood-Report-2020.pdf [Accessed 22.11.2020].

Cremin, H. (2002) Pupils Resolving Disputes: Successful Peer Mediation Schemes Share Their Secrets. *Support for Learning,* **17** (3), pp. 138–143.

Digital NHS UK (2020) *Mental Health of Children and Young People in England.* Available at: https://files.digital.nhs.uk/CB/C41981/mhcyp_2020_rep.pdf [Accessed 22.11.2020].

Elfer, P., Goldschmeid, E. and Selleck, D. (2012) *Key Persons in the Early Years: Building Relationships for Quality Provision in Early Years Settings and Primary Schools* (2nd Edn). Abingdon: Routledge.

Ellis, S. and Tod, J. (2009) *Behaviour for Learning: Proactive Approaches to Behaviour Management.* Abingdon: Routledge.

Ellis, S. and Tod, J. (2015) *Promoting Behaviour for Learning in the Classroom: Effective Strategies, Personal Style and Professionalism.* Abingdon: Routledge.

Fabian, H. (2002) *Children Starting School: A Guide to Successful Transitions and Transfers for Teachers and Assistants.* London: David Fulton.

Goleman, D. (1996) *Emotional Intelligence: Why It Can Matter More Than IQ.* London: Bloomsbury Publishing.

Gottman, D. and DeClaire, J. (1997) *The Heart of Parenting: How to Raise an Emotionally Intelligent Child.* London: Bloomsbury Publishing.

Hamlyn, P. (1995) *Success Against the Odds: Effective Schools in Disadvantaged Areas.* Abingdon: Taylor and Francis.

Hattie, J. (2012) *Visible Learning: Maximising Impact on Learners.* Abingdon: Routledge.

Hawkes, N. (2013) *From My Heart: Transforming Lives Through Values.* Carmarthen: Independent Thinking Press.

Henderson, N. (2019) *An Exploration of the Views of a Group of Practitioners About Relational Teaching and Underpinning Characteristics.* Dissertation submitted in part fulfilment of the regulations for the MA in Early Childhood Studies, Bath Spa University, Bath.

Holmes, J. (1993) *John Bowlby and Attachment Theory.* London: Routledge.

Hopkins, B. (2004) *Just Schools: A Whole-School Approach to Restorative Justice.* London: Jessica Kingsley Publishers.

Howe, A. and Richards, V. (Eds) (2011) *Bridging the Transition from Primary to Secondary School.* London: Routledge.

Hughes, D. (2006) *Building the Bonds of Attachment: Awakening Love in Deeply Troubled Children.* Lanham, MD: Jason Aronson Publishing.

Jelley, F. and Sylva, K. (2017) *Engaging Parents Effectively: Evaluation of the PEN Home Learning Project.* Sutton Trust. Available at: www.suttontrust.com/wp-content/uploads/2017/11/PEN-Report.pdf [Accessed 12.10.2018].

Jones, P. and Welch, S. (2010) *Rethinking Children's Rights: Attitudes in Contemporary Society.* London: Continuum.

Kumar, S. (2005) Human Scale Education. In T. Alexander and T. Potter (Eds) *Education for a Change: Transforming the Way We Teach Our Children*. London: RoutledgeFalmer.

Laevers, F. (1998) *The Leuven Involvement Scale for Young Children: LIS-YC: Manual*. Leuven: Centre for Experiential Education.

Loe, R. (2015) *Relationships for Learning: Making the Implicit Explicit*. Available at: https://relationalschools.org/2015/08/21/relationships-for-learning-making-the-implicit-explicit/ [Accessed 2.11.2018].

Loe, R. (Ed) (2017) *The Relational Teacher* (2nd Edn). London: Relational Schools.

Maines, B. and Robinson, G. (1998) *Punishment: The Milder the Better* (2nd Edn). Bristol: Lucky Duck Books.

Maines, B. and Robinson, G. (2004) *Self-Esteem at the Centre: Practical Strategies for Managing Behaviour and Growing Emotional Literacy*. London: Paul Chapman Publishing.

Malaguzzi, L. (1998) History, Ideas and Philosophy. In C. Edwards, L. Gandini and G. Forman (Eds) *The Hundred Languages of Children: The Reggio Emilia Approach*. Greenwich: Ablex.

Marsh, H. (2017) Relationships for Learning an Overview. In R. Loe (Ed) *The Relational Teacher* (2nd Edn). London: Relational Schools.

Maslow, A. (1971) *The Farther Reaches of Human Nature*. New York: Viking Press.

McLaughlin, C. and Gray, J. (2015) Adolescent Well-Being and the Relational School. In C. McLaughlin (Ed) *The Connected School: A Design for Well-Being – Supporting Children and Young People in Schools to Flourish, Thrive and Achieve*. London: Pearson.

Moss, P. (2017) Power and Resistance in Early Childhood Education: From Dominant Discourse to Democratic Experimentalism. *Journal of Pedagogy*, **4** (1), pp. 11–32.

NFER. Nuffield Foundation (2020) *Impact of Covid-19 on Mainstream Schools, England*. Available at: www.nuffieldfoundation.org/project/impact-of-covid-19-mainstream-schools-england [Accessed 22.1.2021].

Noaks, J. and Noaks, L. (2009) School-Based Peer Mediation as a Strategy for Social Inclusion. *Pastoral Care in Education*, **27** (1), pp. 53–61.

Nutbrown, C. (1999) *Threads of Learning* (2nd Edn). London: Paul Chapman Publishing.

Paige-Smith, A. and Craft, A. (Eds) (2007) *Developing Reflective Practice in the Early Years*. Maidenhead: Open University Press.

Public Health England (2019) *Mental Health and Well-Being Tool Kit: Children and Young People*. Available at: www.gov.uk/government/publications/better-mental-health- jsna-toolkit/5-children-and-young-people [Accessed 22.11.2020].

Rinaldi, C. (2006) *In Dialogue with Reggio Emilia: Listening, Researching and Learning*. Abingdon: Routledge.

Rogers, B. (1995) *Behaviour Management: A Whole School Approach*. Melbourne: Scholastic.

Rogers, B. (2002) *Classroom Behaviour: A Practical Guide to Effective Teaching, Behaviour Management and Colleague Support*. London: Sage Publishing.

Shin, M. (2015) Enacting Caring Pedagogy in the Infant Classroom. *Early Child Development and Care*, **185** (3), pp. 496–508.

Sylva, K., Melhuish, E., Sammons, P., Siraj-Blatchford, I. and Taggart, B. (2004) *Effective Pre-School Education.* London: DfE.

Thomas, G. (2017) *How to Do Your Research Project: A Guide for Students.* London: Sage.

Vygotsky, L. S. (1978) *Mind in Society: The Development of Higher Psychological Processes.* Cambridge, MA: Harvard University Press.

Warnock, M. (1978) *Special Educational Needs: Report of the Committee of Enquiry into the Education of Handicapped Children and Young People.* London: HMSO.

Weare, K. (2004) *Developing the Emotionally Literate School.* London: Paul Chapman Publishing.

Wyness, M. and Lang, P. (2016) The Social and Emotional Dimensions of Schooling: A Case Study in Challenging the 'Barriers' to Learning. *British Educational Research Journal,* **42** (6).

2 Teachers are humans too

Chapter objectives

- To explore the connection between your internal motivations (values, beliefs and philosophies) and external influences (cultural, historical, professional) and how these are played out in your practice.

- To provide opportunities to reflect on your developing teacher identity, drawing on recognised psycho-social theory.

- To understand how reflexive competencies can help guide your continuing professional development and support you to be resilient to address change and challenge.

- To present the relational qualities of love, trust, respect and empathy as fundamental to teaching, learning and to the development of human culture

- To give you the confidence to use the term 'love' to describe the genuine depth of the connection you have with your children.

The lens of the authors

During our careers we have focussed on supporting teacher trainees and experienced teachers to improve their practice. This experience shows us that whilst the need for effective assessment, planning and expertise of subject knowledge is important, the most powerful and transformational developmental conversations have centred on the necessity and impact of building positive pupil relationships in order to secure high levels of engagement and learning. Our detailed analysis of thousands of teacher, tutor and school-based mentor lesson observations likewise provides evidence that the most successful teachers demonstrate deep emotional connections with their learners, characterised by a judicious balance of consistency, trust, respect, empathy and love.

Whilst *The Teachers Standards* (DfE, 2012: 12) recognise that teachers need to 'maintain good relationships with pupils', our subsequent research (Henderson,

DOI: 10.4324/9781003120537-2

2019) reveals these particular human characteristics or personal qualities are too easily dismissed as 'inherent', and that specific guidance on developing them is needed. We advocate an approach where the skills and attributes involved in establishing respectful, trusting and constructive relationships with children are systematically and intellectually facilitated as core requirements.

This chapter will support you with this key aspect of your practice. It will help you to know more about yourself, your teacher identity and philosophy in order that you can enhance your relationship-based pedagogy underpinned, and reassured, by sound practical experience and educational theory. Be prepared to remove your rose-coloured spectacles and have some soul-searching conversations with yourself in front of a full-length mirror!

Our approach throughout this chapter is underpinned by the following key principles:

> *Teaching is more than an academic pursuit:* It requires your personal and emotional investment and the human behaviours that you employ are as important (if not more so) to children's experiences as any other aspect of your teaching practice.
>
> *In order to support positive, mutually respectful relationships, you need to have established an honest relationship with yourself:* Your identity as a teacher is underpinned by your confidence in who you are, how your relationship-based qualities are played out in practice and the serious consideration you give to understanding their influence and impact.
>
> *Teachers are human too:* Just as the best way to teach a child is to see them as a whole, complex and empathic human being; children need to be able to relate to you too. It is your human qualities that will affect children's motivation and engagement with their learning whilst also supporting them to find an affirming place in society. Your ability to show your human side will ultimately be how, or indeed whether, you are cherished and remembered.

Introduction

You will already have been called upon, perhaps in a supporting statement or letter of application, to articulate the dispositions and attitudes that brought you into the teaching profession. You may have highlighted your love of learning, your ability to engage with young children or your prowess in a particular subject. You might also have reflected on the qualities you have admired in your own teachers: their consistency, humour, or compassion shown at a particular time of need. You could be cognisant of the kind of teacher you are, aspire to be and moreover know the demands and responsibilities that this will bring. This chapter will help you to unpick the many conscious and unconscious factors that will already, and continue, to have influenced your understandings and motivations.

Who are you? (Values and beliefs)

The first chapter has revealed our conviction that our upbringing, the significant adults in our early childhood, and our subsequent life experiences, have influenced who we are and how we interact with others. We believe it is crucial to your own professional, and indeed personal, development that your own values and attitudes are brought fully into your conscious awareness since it is these that will ultimately determine the kind of teaching and learning context you offer the children.

Picture of practice – becoming aware of your values

Alisha has a Year 2 class and is in her second year of teaching. She was brought up in a family that, she now recognises, were sticklers for good manners. As a child, Alisha very quickly learned the importance of saying 'please' and 'thank you' and was often held up as a good example by her friends' parents, when she was invited over to visit. In time, these embedded family values began to guide how Alisha unwittingly judged others and this was particularly brought to the fore when she first joined her current school. Alisha found herself making inappropriate value judgements about those children in her class who were not used to the same social and ethical codes. She also acknowledged she was taken aback by the children's parents who were prone to infiltrating their everyday language with swear words. Alisha admitted to her headteacher that she was actually afraid of some of them and recognised that this was creating a barrier in her ability to build relationships with both the parents and the children. With support from her headteacher, Alisha was able to resolve the tension between her own particular value base and her classroom manner and practice. She learnt the importance of modelling specific praise and when it was most appropriate to champion her 'manners cause' (e.g. during snack time) or let it rest (e.g. when a child was distressed after a challenging play-time). Alisha also came to accept where she had less influence, such as the amount of swearing at the school gate and focused her attention instead on the warmth and positivity in her own communication. Over time, Alisha found that once her own attitude had changed, the level of respect shown to her by both the children and their parents was raised. Alisha believed that this was largely due to the positive relationships between them.

Research suggests that Alisha's experience is not uncommon, and that the expectations of philosophy, language and character, customary to some teachers, have the potential to prohibit them from genuinely connecting with certain groups of children and their families (Lareau, 2011). Pollard (2018) reports that similar issues that have been raised in relation to gender and race. In this example, however, Alisha demonstrates that she is able to reflect on her personal values and beliefs, to recognise where they have come from (the 'voices from [her] childhood' (Hawkes, 2013: 14), and crucially to make changes to her thinking and practice.

In doing so Alisha demonstrates what Pollard (*op. cit*: x1x) refers to as an 'interesting combination of moral commitment and open-mindedness'. For not only does she show that she is able to *reflect* on her practice, but moreover that she can make improvements to it by questioning the very fabric of her cultural foundations. Alisha's ability to be *reflexive* is what ultimately leads to the significant improvements in the quality and depth of her teaching relationships. Whilst reflecting on practice is commonly held up as an essential part of professional development and practice (Arthur and Cremin, 2014; Cunningham, 2008; Pollard, 2014), it is reflexivity that focuses directly on our ability to know and understand ourselves. Indeed, as we will see later, it is the reflexive teacher who is able to navigate the many challenges and changes to policy and context, whilst still reconciling their beliefs and values. In order to develop your relationship-based pedagogy it is critical for you to demonstrate reflexivity in your own practice and to explore how your own beliefs, lived out, for example, in how you act and what you say, guide and impact your emotional response or instinctive reaction to others.

There will be many examples where the influence of others will have had a profound and positive impact on your character and values development. These role models will no doubt have shaped the many beliefs that have brought you into the teaching profession in the first place: the celebration of dissimilarity modelled by an inspirational English teacher; the resolve to give to those less fortunate instilled by your grandmother; the importance of ambition championed by a compassionate football coach. Being aware of your values can help you to assess whether these behaviours and beliefs are consistent with what you actually do, and whether, as Pollard (*op. cit*: xvii) asks, your value system or philosophy is compatible with your actual classroom practice. A trusted colleague in school can help you to identify this, as can the children in your class who will instinctively pick up on your values as soon as you speak to them! Chapter 4 will support you in developing these ideas further.

Of course, as teachers we have a legal responsibility, based on *The Teachers Standards* (DfE, 2012: 14) 'to maintain high standards of ethics and behaviour, and to ensure that personal beliefs are not expressed in ways, which exploit pupils' vulnerability or might lead them to break the law'. Whilst we understand that it's highly unlikely that anyone comes into the profession to deliberately harm or undermine children, it is an acknowledged part of our human development that we all have prejudices and biases. Whether or not we choose to act upon these determines the effect they can have on our ability to form mutually respectful relationships. Our motivation here is to help ensure that your established beliefs are not *inadvertently* creating barriers to your relationships with children and their parents who, as Hawkins (2016: 35) reminds us, 'will always see more than you think you reveal'. It is crucial therefore that your self-awareness extends to recognising the influence you have on those you teach. Just as key role models in your life will have affected your values and interests, you also have the potential to shape and persuade the children in your care. The principle of the colloquial adage, 'children do what children see' derives from the social learning theory proposed by the Canadian psychologist Albert Bandura. Bandura (1977) explains how new behaviour can be learnt by observing others and how a teacher's actions, attitudes and emotional reactions can therefore be mirrored and replicated by the children. Anybody who has the privileged opportunity to observe their children 'playing teachers' will know this to be true. Children have a remarkable capacity to notice and mimic not just what you say, but moreover the tone in which you say it! Knowing this means that you can use your influence, and your developed awareness of your emotional response or triggers to increase your level of connection and rapport, especially with children who require careful and very tailored efforts. Chapters 4 and 5 elucidate these concepts further.

Who are you? (Human characteristics)

Since it is the quality of your relationships that enable children to flourish as learners and human beings, it is important to explore the specific qualities or traits that support and facilitate this. It is worth saying at the outset that it is perhaps too commonly accepted that the teachers who place a greater weighting on the relationship-based aspects of their practice share certain characteristics or personality traits that are somehow bestowed on them at birth as a gift, and the way some teacher's 'naturally are' (Henderson, *op. cit*: 63). We are anxious to dispel this myth that relationship-based pedagogy is for the preserve of the few, those that are intrinsically pre-disposed that way, or those that actively choose to place this aspect at the centre of their practice. The human characteristics discussed here involve learned behaviours that can be displayed and communicated in dynamic ways, just as with any teaching skills they can and need to be systematically developed and reflected upon.

Although much of the theoretical literature implies that relationships between teachers and children are important, the particular human characteristics or qualities that support this bond are rarely discussed. To that end The Relational Schools Foundation (available at: https://relationalschools.org) developed their own *Relational Proximity Framework* (Loe, 2017: 115): 'a tool to measure the distance or connection between two people or organisations and determine how well each party engages with the thinking, emotions and behaviours of the other'. The 'Experiences in Relationships' section of the Framework is probably most closely associated with the human characteristics we seek to explore here and are identified as being 'connectedness, belonging, mutual understanding, mutual respect and shared identity' (*ibid*: 115).

The humanistic psychologist, Carl Rogers (1902–87) offers some further insights into the conditions for secure relationships. He identifies three essential qualities – *acceptance*: respecting and being tolerant to the differing beliefs of others; *congruence:* being honest, genuine and authentic; *empathy:* understanding and relating to the feelings of others. Having all three elements in place would, according to Rogers (1959), result in *unconditional positive regard:* a relationship founded on understanding and giving. This theory is reflected in the work of Fielding (2006) who advocates a relational approach referred to as 'human flourishing' where respect and commitment to every child as holistic human beings are central.

In his classification of teacher types, Hargreaves (1972: 80) identifies 'Entertainers', as opposed to 'Lion Tamers', who, he suggests, want to be connected to their pupils and understand their challenges and concerns. Entertainers are trustworthy, available to the children, deliver on their promises, remember significant events, and take opportunities to talk about events in their own lives as well as that of their pupils. Entertainers want to be remembered for their human connection as well as their application of subject and pedagogical knowledge. Whilst we might debate whether the term 'Entertainers' does justice to a teacher who is seriously committed to building emotional connections with their children, the qualities expressed here do align with those most often recognised as important by the children themselves. *The Children Act Now* (2001, cited in Jones and Welch, 2010: 172) lists these as being: reliability – keeping promises, practical help, care and support, time to listen and respond and seeing children's lives in the round – not just their problems. Marsh (2012: 162) similarly found young people related best to the teachers who were 'friendly, flexible, engaging, as well as the ones who notice, seek interactions and care'.

Our own priority afforded to the relationship-based 'human characteristics' has been heavily influenced by the Reggio Emilia approach to learning, reflective of those identified here, and evidenced by adults who are sensitive and empathic to the part their own behaviours play in securing positive and authentic relationships (Rinaldi, 2006). In Reggio Emilia professional development encourages educators to constantly evaluate their own role and the subtleties of the shared relational experience. Describing this philosophy as a 'pedagogy of relationships' the educators of Reggio Emilia maintain that it is only when time is taken to build loving, respectful and trusting relationships with the children and families that they can become confident and successful in their own roles. This view, mirrored in our own knowledge, experience and values, and echoed in the theory analysed earlier, leads us to believe that, in order to satisfy their relational needs, children need to be supported by adults who, above all others, appreciate and display the human characteristics of respect, honesty, empathy and love. To that end further exploration of each of these will be given later in this chapter.

What is your teacher identity?

So far this chapter has focussed on your personal values and beliefs and we have suggested that your understanding and application of these internal characteristics can steer and determine the relationship-based element of your practice. It is important now to acknowledge that the development of your teacher self or identity is also shaped and controlled by external elements such as government legislation, education policy, the current reporting regime, as well as your own teaching context: type of school, relationship with colleagues, access to professional research/authoritative opinion, etc. These external influences have the potential to affirm your view of the type of teacher you want to be, and also have the power to bring these convictions into question. Part of the development of your teacher identity means that you will be constantly reflecting, re-examining and reconciling your idealism and practice as you are faced with new initiatives, understandings and knowledge. Recognising the importance of a relationship-based approach to teaching and learning may well be an example of such dissonance. You are interested (even committed) to the approach but haven't yet seen it modelled in the environment in which you teach or perhaps are 'frustrated with the preoccupation with other things, that are less important' (Henderson, 2019: 69). Moss (2017) recognises the same tension commenting that a relationship-based approach may appear to be directly opposed to the current dominant neoliberalist discourse characterised by a culture of performativity and a language of production. Wortham and Jackson (2012: 1) similarly suggest that, 'to envision education as a set of processes intended to enhance relationships is a radical departure from most mainstream educational research and practice'.

However, throughout history there are numerous examples where the existential boundaries of educational policy and practice have altered in response to debates and contestations arising from both individual and collective levels. As Hargreaves (2003: 24) reasons: 'There is no value in reviving a Julie Andrews approach, "these are a few of my favourite things" . . . teachers must build a new professionalism where they learn to teach in ways they were not taught, and [develop] a capacity for change and risk.'

Whilst change and challenge are not easy, we urge you to draw comfort and strength from the growing body of authoritative opinion which is opposed to the current paradigm manifested in pressures on time, the demands of the curriculum, and the prioritisation of assessment to areas of accountability. Instead, school leaders are encouraged to take risks, to stand up for what they believe and to take courage derived from a strong sense of moral purpose (Alexander and Potter, 2015; Buck, 2016; Radcliffe, 2012). At the same time, pressure is being placed upon Ofsted to hold schools accountable for their ability to promote children's well-being, positive mental health and adopt a relationship-based culture to the school and curriculum. In 2017, speaking at the 2017 *Festival of Education*, Amanda Spielman (HM Chief Inspector) acknowledged herself that 'our inspection framework doesn't yet fully capture the substance of education' and some commentators see the additions to the Ofsted Inspection Framework (Ofsted, 2019) as a step towards resolving this gap. Certainly the requirement for schools to demonstrate a 'positive culture' and an increased emphasis on the 'appreciation of human development' (*ibid*: 10–11) could be seen as a welcome shift towards meeting the current complexity of children's lives. For many critics, however, the adaptations have not gone far enough. Promoting this view, Kidd (2009: 33) calls for an approach that focuses on 'measuring what is valued: happiness, love, collaboration, confidence, caring attitudes and critical and constructive thinking'.

As the momentum for radical developments gains impetus and the real impact of the Covid-19 pandemic is felt (Andrew *et al.*, 2020; NFER, 2020; Spielman, 2020) this will undoubtedly be a transformative time for education. Your capacity to critique and question policy and curricula will place you in a good position to be part of the relationship-based revolution!

The aspects discussed in the following sections will help empower you to navigate the inevitable shifts in policy and culture.

Self-efficacy

How confident you are in your ability to succeed as a teacher and how far you live up to your convictions and expectations will ultimately be determined by your self-efficacy. Bandura (1997) identified that personal efficacy is derived from four principal sources of information: performance accomplishments (repeated success leading to a 'mastery' of skills), vicarious experience (observing and learning from the success of others), verbal persuasion (validation and encouragement from others) and physiological states (awareness of the impact of anxiety and stress). Recognised strategies to develop self-efficacy include being open-minded to feedback from others; undertaking observations of as many other teachers as possible; pursuing action-based research and continuous professional development; taking an interest in authoritative opinion; and, perhaps hardest of all, finding pragmatic ways to relax your mind.

Research tells us that teachers with higher levels of self-efficacy demonstrate motivation and resilience and are therefore more likely to experience occupational success (Vieluf *et al.*, 2013), cope with change and implement innovations (Hawkins, 2016), and consequently remain within the teaching profession (Chesnut and Burley, 2015). There is also well-documented evidence that teachers' self-efficacy is an important protection factor against exhaustion, stress or burn out (Weber and Greiner, 2019).

Image of the child

Throughout your teaching career you will need to become proficient in implementing a number of different strategies and approaches to meet your school or national agendas. Our research and extensive experience have shown that if you hold true to your image of the child and use this as your moral guide or compass it will help you to sustain your motivation as you navigate your way through new, and possibly troubled, waters. Hawkins (*op. cit*: 24) replicates many of our own conversations when she urges us not to 'lose sight of the child; they are central to what you do; they are why you get up in the morning'. It was this very same sentiment that led us to display a sign on the office door reminding us that we were working 'for the benefit of the children everywhere!' You might find it equally helpful to keep a picture of a particular child in mind or find an inspirational quotation. The following, for example, exemplifies a very clear allegiance to an image of a child who deserves a relationship-based approach to teaching and learning:

> [We acknowledge] a child who has a recognised right to be respected as a [human] subject of individual, legal, civil and social rights . . . a child who has an enormous need to love and be loved and a responsibility for practitioners to satisfy this need.
>
> (Valentine, 2004: 4)

Reflexivity

As we have explored earlier in the chapter, it is your ability to be reflexive that will help determine how open-minded you are to understanding the impact of your teacher presence and communication style, and how deeply you are prepared to look into the 'messages' that you are unwittingly sending out in relation to others. In the same way your ability to be reflexive will help you to question, reason and rationalise how you respond to the process of change. Strategies to support the development of reflexivity include routinely asking questions such as:

- Why am I thinking this way?

- What assumptions am I making?

- Am I holding any preconceived ideas about the situation? Are these presenting as prejudices or biases?

- Have I responded in this way before? Is it an appropriate response now?

- Are the potential barriers real or perceived?

With regular and disciplined practice of this type of questioning your ability to analyse and understand your own thought processes, assumptions and prejudices will, in time, become a 'habit of mind'. In that way you can learn to become a confident, empowered agent with the ability to play a more proactive and fundamental part in re-culturing the professional community.

Human characteristics

Research shows that a dynamic interrelationship between the human qualities of trust, empathy, respect and love lie at the root of relationship-based pedagogy. The following section will therefore expand on each of these elements.

Trust

One of the first activities that we used to ask the PGCE trainees to undertake involved passing around the tutor group a 'blown' egg: one that has had the insides removed but where the shell remains intact. We did this to demonstrate, not the fragility of children, although of course at varying times they can be vulnerable, but more to show how much faith their parents were putting into our hands as they relied upon us to keep their children physically and emotionally safe. As teachers, it is our responsibility to prove to the parents, and moreover the children, that this level of trust is warranted.

A relationship-based approach demands that you plan and provide for the development of trust just as you would do for any other essential component of your teaching. Trust building starts from the very first day that you meet the children and first impressions last! Howes and Ritchie (2002: 5–6) agree that it is only 'once children can trust the teacher they can use [them] to organize and structure their learning', and that children without trust will 'spend their time in school resisting, trying to control or avoiding the teacher'. This principle is based on the application of the British psychoanalyst, John Bowlby's (1907–1990) evolutionary attachment theory to relationships (1969). Bowlby's research concluded that all children come into the world biologically pre-programmed to form attachments with others and that successful attachments between infant and primary caregiver (usually a mother) will serve as a template for what they expect and trust in their future relationships. This concept of 'attachment' is explored in much greater detail in Chapter 4. However, it is important to acknowledge here that the children's capacity to accept you as trustworthy will depend to some extent on their previous relationship history. Part of your responsibility will be to understand this and to be aware that with some children you will need to work even harder to demonstrate that you can be relied upon to follow up on your promises, fulfil their expectations and stay true to your word. That said, for the minority of children who have suffered severe interruptions in their attachment to their primary caregiver, you may also need to seek additional and professional support. For that reason you need to be as cognisant of the children's relational development as you are of any other aspect of their personal, social and emotional development.

In order to secure trusting relationships, the children will need to know that they can get help from you when they need it (this could range from helping with the laces on a new pair of shoes to a revelation about online bullying); that you can provide comfort and emotional security (in the way that the child likes this to be given); that the classroom is organised to provide for their needs (e.g. individual learning aids or resources); that you can preserve and protect their dignity (for example by validating their ideas and contributions with sensitivity); that the pattern and rhythm of the day is predictably structured (and that any changes are anticipated or treated as rehearsed 'surprises'); and that the learning outcomes are thoughtfully and responsibly matched to the children's level of development (they are relevant to their age/stage and interests). Above all you will need to ensure that your response to any of these situations is consistent and reliable. Children will build their understanding and expectations of the nature of their relationship with you based on how you have reacted in the past (Howes and Ritchie, *op. cit.*). In other words they will only continue to ask you for help if they see that you respond to their request willingly and consistently. Equally children will only learn the value of a desired behaviour if they see it being explicitly modelled to them. The more you demonstrate your trust in the children, the more they will emulate and follow your example.

Picture of practice – building trust

Angus has 30 children in the Year 5 class. One of the children, Emma, shows in her behaviour that she finds it difficult to wait for Angus's attention and often calls out and disrupts the other children's learning as well as her own. Recognising the importance of gaining Emma's trust, Angus begins to use as many impromptu opportunities to make connections with Emma: engaging her in conversation at playtime or in the lunch hall for example. Angus discovers that they have a shared passion for cats and they both bring in photos of their own to show the other. At the same time, Angus sets out clear and agreed strategies to help Emma understand that whilst their attention is with the other children she is still being 'held in mind'. These strategies include agreeing when Emma will be working with Angus (sometimes at the start of the lesson); showing a thumbs up from across the classroom as a sign that Angus is thinking of her, or leaving an egg-timer on her table indicating when Angus will return. Over time, as Angus and Emma build a more trusting relationship, Emma is able to become a more successful member of the class and at the same time the learning context for the other children is preserved.

Picture of practice – showing trust

Sam has planned a Halloween-themed learning episode for the Nursery Class designed to help develop the children's fine motor skills. The activity is laid out on a tabletop and is resourced with a variety of pumpkins, hammers and nails. The children elect to come back to the activity again and again and show high levels of enjoyment and engagement as they attempt to hammer the nails into the pumpkins. Sam has already taught the children to handle the equipment correctly and has, through demonstration, shown them techniques that are the most effective and safe. The language used has been clear and unambiguous and correct application has been enthusiastically noticed and rewarded. This level of trust is not unusual in the nursery and the children enjoy free access to materials (including scissors), pouring their own water at snack time and helping themselves from the snack buffet when they are hungry. The children know that the grown-ups trust them to use the apparatus appropriately and they in turn, live up to this expectation.

Closely associated with the theme of trust is the value that children attribute to the importance of knowing that teachers are also real people, human beings with interests and lives of their own. This desire is mirrored in our own research (Henderson, *op. cit*: 70) with 100 per cent of respondents agreeing to the question 'How important is to your practice that the children know you have a life outside of school – that they see you as a "human" as well as a teacher?'. One respondent qualified their agreement by saying: 'Children need to be able to relate to you. Being human allows them to see things such as you are a mother, father and a friend. This can enable them to have a role model in every aspect of their lives' (Henderson, *ibid*: 71; questionnaire response).

All the research participants recognised the importance of finding a 'likeness', or 'common ground', or 'shared enthusiasms' with the children in order to establish deeper relationships with them (*ibid*: 71). This resonates with the longitudinal study undertaken by Nias (1989) who interviewed teachers for over a decade to elicit their feelings about being a teacher. Several of her interviewees described the necessity of teachers revealing their vulnerability. Our own research also evidences a teacher's willingness to show their fallibility and the importance of demonstrating this to the children in the pursuit of a trusting relationship. One participant explained, 'you have to show them that you are real and authentic, only human, and not perfect. You have to be honest and genuine and part of that is saying sorry. Like when you've forgotten to bring in something you said you would' (Henderson, *op. cit*: 71; semi-structured interview).

Empathy

Your ability to be empathic will also be essential in developing your connection with the children, especially in times of increased tension or crisis. It will help you to better understand the reasoning behind a child's behaviour and support you to resolve conflict, to pre-empt triggers and hopefully prevent similar episodes in the future. Being empathic shows the children that you are aware of their feelings, that you have noticed that they're experiencing something significant and that you want to be proactive in helping them. In other words, empathy is about finding a way to relate to a child and to be able to say, 'I want to understand how this feels to you, and show you how you can get past these feelings'. In this way empathy is understood not only as an internal emotional state but moreover a particular way of communicating that can be modelled and demonstrated.

This view fits with the work of Cassidy *et al.* (2016) who assert that it is not enough for teachers to just model caring, compassionate behaviour; children have to experience authentic empathy from their teacher in order to truly understand what a mutually responsive relationship feels like. In her research on learning relationships in schools, Cooper (2010: 86) identifies four different ways in which teachers demonstrate empathy: '*fundamental*', '*profound*', '*functional*' and '*feigned*', and you may find it useful to consider which of these types you recognise in your own practice.

Fundamental empathy is evident when you are building relationships with children but do not yet know them well. You are demonstrating this type of empathy when you are paying attention, listening carefully, showing signs of interest and using positive verbal and non-verbal communication, typically lots of eye contact, smiles and nods. You also tend to reflect the child's own style of language before developing new language and moderate your tone of voice to mirror the child's: e.g. talking quietly if the child seems embarrassed or shy, or responding jovially with individuals who are lively.

Profound empathy is evident when you know children well, can interpret and understand their feelings, and read their mood. You are demonstrating this type of empathy when you are giving personal levels of care, concern, time and sole attention to individual children. You tend to treat each child as a unique individual and 'treasure their differences' (Cooper, *ibid*: 87), knowing how to approach them when they are distressed, e.g. whether close physical contact or a particular tone of voice will soothe or agitate them further. It requires you to be self-aware and sometimes to draw on your own childhood experiences and fallibilities to connect with children, even sharing your own feelings with them. Central to profound empathy is the ability to seek affinity with those children that you may find difficult to like, finding some point of contact and developing a relationship from that point, rather than pushing your own agenda.

Functional, or *relative*, empathy is evident in whole class situations and is an adapted form of empathy for managing large groups. You are demonstrating this type of empathy when you have a mental representation of the whole group and treat the class as one entity, to communicate a unifying message. Although children benefit most from individual empathic interactions, there are times when you can feel a predominant mood in the room and it is appropriate to acknowledge it, e.g. when you notice a feeling of eagerness and energy, with some children becoming wound up, and you say 'I can tell you are all excited about tomorrow's trip' or when you sense a feeling of apprehension and nervousness in the room, and say 'I know you are all feeling anxious about today's test'. That said, it is also important to acknowledge that not all the children will be feeling the same, and some individuals may experience emotional dissonance when you use a 'one size fits all' expression; so functional empathy is only partially successful in creating effective connections, although it can play a role in creating a sense of unity and belonging in your classroom.

Feigned empathy is evident when you display superficial signs of empathy but it is unsupported by the way you behave. This can occur when you recognise what a child is feeling and contrive to convey concern or understanding, for example by your facial expression, but are not really experiencing an empathic response internally. Unless you are a consummate actor, it is hard to sustain this approach and other aspects of your behaviour, such as tone of voice, body language or your actions will reveal your lack of authenticity; children are usually quite intuitive at sensing this. Feigned, or fake, empathy teaches children not to trust you, or their own emotions, and is a barrier to creating reliable, sustainable connections. So we recommend you give attention to whether you are employing it as a strategy and cease its practice.

We would also add to this list '*invisible* empathy' which occurs when you genuinely have an internal empathic response but it is not evident from the way you communicate. You may not be aware that your facial expression, tone of voice or body language are not congruent with what you are feeling inside, and using video feedback or asking to be observed by a colleague or mentor may bring this to light. You can then develop your communication skills to mirror your internal world more effectively.

Respect

Respectful relationships lie at the very heart of the approach to early childhood education in Reggio Emilia. This extends to relationships between the children, parents, educators, the environment and with society beyond. Bruner (2004: 27) identifies this aspect of practice as, 'a rare form of courtesy, a precious form of reciprocal respect'. Certainly the value placed on mutual respect is shared and underpinned by a historical sense of community as well as an image of children as competent, active learners, and protagonists of their own learning. In practice this means that the children's ideas and opinions are actively sought, heard and respected as fundamental 'rights' (Rinaldi, *op. cit.*). The children are consequently known for their confidence and high levels of self-esteem as well as their ability to hypothesise, reason, listen, negotiate and their positive interaction with all aspects of the learning community.

Respected as an international beacon of excellence, the influence of this approach is felt in many aspects of the UK education system today. Moreover, the legacy of the *United Nations International Convention on the Rights of the Child* (UN General Assembly, 1989), with its focus on respecting children's social-cultural, as well as civil rights, has inspired a number of initiatives such as youth parliaments, school forums and Unicef's (2021) Rights Respecting Schools award in order to satisfy the promotion of children's rights and responsibilities as a whole-school priority.

As the Reggio Emilia experience shows us, however, embedding a wider and more fundamental respectful dynamic to education policy and practice necessitates a re-evaluation of traditional assumptions about children. As Loreman (2009: 3) suggests: 'Any attempt to better respect childhood means valuing children's time; enjoyment of childhood; relationships with others; contributions to family and society; individuality and diversity; abilities and capacities.' As teachers we are in a unique position to advocate and influence this agenda.

Table 2.1 Respectful practices.

Promoting a 'culture of participation' (Jones and Welch, *op. cit*: 180)	Preserving the 'dignity of the child' (Loreman, *op. cit*: 88)
For example: ■ Children are given opportunities to take decisions for themselves (e.g. choice of activities, resources, grouping, how they will document their understanding) ■ Children's ideas and contributions are routinely valued and respected ■ Opinions from all the children, irrespective of their age/ability, about matters that genuinely concern them, are sought and their ideas are taken seriously, and acted upon (e.g. through circle times and school forums) ■ All members of the school community model and practice active listening and are encouraged to acknowledge each other's points of view, recognising that there may be disagreement ■ Learning environments provide for children's capacities and capabilities with accessible resources and multiple opportunities for risk-taking ■ Children are in the best position to make decisions about their personal needs such as when they want to go to the toilet, have a drink, or rest and recover	For example: ■ The school ethos and culture of understanding and tolerance is modelled and expected ■ The school is actively inclusive and welcoming for all children and communities with dissimilarities being recognised and respected by all ■ Children's right to privacy is respected; confidences are only shared when there is a safe-guarding concern ■ Children are consulted before their ideas, learning and achievements are publicly displayed and shared with others ■ All conversations about children and their families are undertaken respectfully ■ Group names and classroom positioning reflect a positive image of all the children ■ The use, tone and volume of language from all members of the school community is consistently respectful ■ High expectations for conduct are sought by an understanding of the individual child, their history and the reasons behind their behaviour ■ Time is taken to explain the rationale behind a learning activity, which is designed to have an authentic purpose

A relationship-based approach to teaching and learning supports the principles and practices discussed in Table 2.1 in order to build, develop and preserve the children's respect.

Love

It is an interesting observation that whilst we can all talk confidently and *ad infinitum* about our 'love' of a particular piece of music, variety of food, favourite book and even an item of clothing, when it comes to describing the deep and emotional connection we have with our children many of us ultimately default to phrases such as 'care' or 'kindness'. This is borne out in our own research with one respondent concluding: 'I don't think we use the expression love very often in teaching. [Pause] Oh, I don't know how I feel about that. [Pause] I don't know' (Henderson, *op. cit*: 63; semi-structured interview).

A similar tension is revealed in the research by Kidd (*op. cit*.), Page (2018) and Recchia *et al.* (2018) who also found that, whilst educators were highly committed to getting to know and understand children, they described them in terms of their 'development' or 'learning' when asked to reflect on their relationship-based practice. And yet, as Maslow's (1970) theory of human motivation bears testament, love, along with belonging and self-esteem, is identified as an essential psychological need that must be provided for in order for a person to thrive and indeed survive. Fredrickson (2012: 17) argues that the other physiological needs, also identified by Maslow, are more easily met and recognises that what is more often longed for is love, which she describes as the 'most essential emotional experience for thriving and health'. Fredrickson challenges us to extend our definition and understanding, beyond a romanticised or other contextually inappropriate form of love, and to consider that:

> love is the upwelling of three interwoven events. First, a sharing of positive emotions between you and another; second, a synchrony between your and the other person's biochemistry and behaviours; and third, a motive to invest in each other's well-being that brings mutual care.
>
> (*ibid*: 17)

Olson (2014: 86) similarly intellectualises a definition of love by stressing that 'the love we have for our students is based on innumerable daily brief instances of positivity resonance with them, times when our brain and neurochemistry has been ebbing and flowing in a synchronized dance and our social engagement system, the ventral vagus nerve, has been activated'.

These descriptions help to justify the legitimacy of the concept of love within professional discourse and moreover the acceptance of it as a serious and essential feature of teaching practice. This acknowledgement is long overdue. It is time, as Shin (2015) suggests, that we raise the debate about loving practices away from the 'natural alliance' with a predominantly female early years workforce who are 'innately mothering', to a serious pedagogical approach that requires recognition, training and attention in policy making. Only in this way will the very real concerns, about 'false accusations' and how others may view the '"appropriateness" of their actions' (Page, *op. cit*: 140) be addressed and allayed. We can only counteract the prevailing negative social connotations associated with love and relationships in the context of schools with confidence and conviction if we stand united in our own belief that, 'our education system can only be made fit for purpose for the new generation when teachers and parents work together to create schools of warm-heartedness. . . [with] an abundance of love' (Boddy, 2017: 144). Our aim throughout this book is to unapologetically promote this understanding.

Picture of practice: teaching as an act of love

Michael is in Year 6 and although he loves playing football with his friends at playtime there is very little else at school that he feels connected to. His teachers are becoming more and more concerned about Michael's ability to engage with his learning. He is increasingly removing himself from the class or employing tactics that result in him being separated from his peers. In order to understand and help regulate his behaviour, Michael has recently been working with Karen, a part time member of staff, who is a trained artist with experience in nurture interventions. Karen welcomes the opportunity to take a small group of children, including Michael, to a local sculpture garden. During the visit Michael reveals that his grandfather enjoyed sculpturing and had once had one of his sculptures displayed in an exhibition in London. Several days later Michael brings into school a newspaper report about his grandfather's sculpture and takes great pride in sharing it with both Karen and the headteacher. Michael is delighted to subsequently be given his own piece of sculpture stone and enjoys using the equipment safely and responsibly. During the coming weeks Michael spends time working with Karen and also in his mainstream class. The class teacher notices that Michael is becoming more settled in class and is reducing the number of anger outbursts and challenging behaviour. Towards the end of term, Michael is chosen by his peers to be their 'star of the week' in the customary celebration assembly. Michael chooses not to sit on the designated chair at the front of the hall but instead listens whilst his teacher celebrates his positive learning behaviour and the pride that he is now taking in his work. Michael asks the headteacher if he can see her after assembly. When Michael later comes to her office he is clutching a parcel, wrapped in yellow tissue paper, and immediately offers it to the head. She is overwhelmed to discover a beautifully sculptured eagle (the school emblem) hidden amongst the paper and a clear assertion from Michael that he would like her to keep it 'always'. The headteacher sees the absolute joy on Michael's face and knows that this is the result of the investment that he, his peers and the whole staff team have put into securing mutual and positive emotions. The headteacher understands that this network of interwoven relationships and connections is testament to the impact of love as a powerful mechanism for change.

Prompts for reflection

■ Reflect on our own beliefs and values and consider where they have come from. Do any of them have the potential to undermine or alienate groups of children in your class? School?

■ How do you show your values in practice? Does a friend/colleague recognise these in your actions too? Is there a disconnect between what you say you believe and what you actually do? Why might this be?

■ What do your children want and expect from the relationship with you? How do you know?

■ How could the questions in the reflexive section of this chapter help you to feel confident to use the term love to describe the deep emotional connection between you and your children?

■ How do you convey to the children that they are understood, respected, loved?

■ How do you know that the children are feeling these emotions?

Shared language

Mutual trust: A sense of understanding that nothing will be said or done to compromise the safety, reputation or dignity of the other and that 'mistakes' or 'breakdowns' are acknowledged and reconciled.
Reciprocal respect: An appreciation of each person as a feeling human with their own valuable heritage, competences, skills and different points of view.
Love: Describes the dynamic bond that develops between teachers and pupils as they connect through shared experiences, emotions, purpose and understanding.

Chapter summary

This chapter demonstrates that a relationship-based approach to teaching demands a strong understanding of who you are (your values, beliefs and prevailing countenance), a clear sense of 'teacher identity' (how you see yourself acting and operating in the role) and moreover a developing 'self-efficacy': your confidence in your ability to preserve and reconcile how the reality of your practice matches up to your expectations. The chapter suggests that teaching makes exacting demands upon your emotional and character development and highlights the human qualities of empathy, trust, respect and love as part of your professional development, offering strategies to support the application in a classroom context.

Further reading

Hawkins, S. (2016) *Outstanding Primary Teaching and Learning. A Journey Through Your Early Teaching Career*. London: Open University Press.

This book offers theoretical knowledge and practical advice as it guides you through an aspirational and developmental journey towards becoming an 'outstanding' teacher. The reflective activities, prompts and checklists offer opportunities for you to gain insightful understandings of your core beliefs and motivations.

Grimmer, T. (2021) *Developing a Loving Pedagogy in the Early Years: How Love Fits with Professional Practice*. Abingdon: Routledge.

The underlying principle of this book fits well with our own in that it seeks to champion the concept of love as an appropriate and fundamental pedagogy in education. Focusing on early childhood settings, this book explores how educators can support their children by holding them in mind, valuing them and promoting their best interests. The case studies and questions serve as inspiration for practice as well as reflection.

Rinaldi, C. (2006) *In Dialogue with Reggio Emilia: Contextualising, Interpreting and Evaluating Early Childhood Education (Contesting Early Childhood)*. Abingdon: Routledge.

This book offers a reflective account from Carlina Rinaldi, the former director of the municipal early childhood centres in Reggio Emilia. It will help you to understand the strength of an approach that is underpinned by an image of a child as capable and competent and where educators value, respect and prioritise the relational element of their practice.

References

Aldgate, J. and Statham, J. (2001) *The Children Act Now – Messages from Research: Studies in Evaluating The Children Act 1989*. London: Department of Health Stationery Office.

Alexander, T. and Potter, T. (Eds) (2015) *Education for Change: Transforming the Way We Teach Our Children*. London: RoutledgeFalmer.

Andrew, A., Cattan, S., Costa-Dias, M., Farquharson, C., Kraftman, L., Krutikova, S., Phimister, A. and Sevilla, A. (2020) *Learning During the Lockdown: Real-Time Data on Children's Experiences During Home Learning*. IFS Briefing Note BN288.

Available at: www.ifs.org.uk /uploads/BN288-Learning-during-the-lockdown-1.pdf [Accessed 20.5.2020].

Arthur, J. and Cremin, T. (2014) *Learning to Teach in the Primary School* (3rd Edn). London: Routledge.

Bandura, A. (1977) *Social Learning Theory*. Eaglewood Cliffs, NJ: Prentice Hall.

Bandura, A. (1997) *Self-Efficacy: The Exercise of Control*. New York: W.H. Freeman.

Boddy, D. (2017) *Mind Their Hearts: Creating Schools and Homes of Warm-Heartedness*. Woodbridge: John Catt Educational Ltd.

Bowlby, J. (1969) *Attachment and Loss: Vol. 1. Attachment*. New York: Basic Books.

Bruner, J. (2004) Reggio a City of Courtesy, Curiosity and Imagination. *Children in Europe*, **6**, p. 27.

Buck, A. (2016) *Leadership Matters*. Woodbridge: John Catt Educational Ltd.

Cassidy, J., Gross, J., Mikulincer, M., Shaver, P. and Stern, J. (2016) A Lifespan Perspective on Attachment and Care for Others: Empathy, Altruism, and Prosocial Behavior. In J. Cassidy and P. Shaver (Eds) *Handbook of Attachment Theory, Research and Clinical Applications* (3rd Edn). London: Guilford Press.

Chesnut, S. R. and Burley, H. (2015) Self-Efficacy as a Predictor of Commitment to the Teaching Profession: A Meta-Analysis. *Educational Research Review*, **15**, pp. 1–16.

Cooper, B. (2010) In Search of Profound Empathy in Learning Relationships: Understanding the Mathematics of Moral Learning Environments. *Journal of Moral Education*, **39** (1), pp. 79–99.

Cunningham, B. (Ed) (2008) *Exploring Professionalism*. London: Institute of Education.

DfE (2012) *Teacher Standards*. Gov.UK. Available at: https://assets.publishing.service.gov.uk/government/uploads/system/uploads/attachment_data/file/665520/Teachers__Standards.pdf [Accessed 20.11.2020].

Fielding, M. (2006) Leadership, Radical Student Engagement and the Necessity of Person-Centred Education. *International Journal of Leadership in Education*, **9** (4), pp. 299–313.

Fredrickson, B. (2012) *Love 2.0: How Our Supreme Emotion Affects Everything We Feel, Think, Do, and Become*. New York: Hudson Street Press.

Hargreaves, A. (2003) *Teaching in the Knowledge Society: Education in the Age of Insecurity*. New York: Teacher College Press.

Hargreaves, D. H. (1972) *Interpersonal Relationships and Education*. London: Routledge.

Hawkes, N. (2013) *From My Heart: Transforming Lives Through Values*. Carmarthen: Independent Thinking Press.

Hawkins, S. (2016) *Outstanding Primary Teaching and Learning: A Journey Through Your Early Teaching Career*. London: Open University Press.

Henderson, N. (2019) *An Exploration of the Views of a Group of Practitioners About Relational Teaching and Underpinning Characteristics*. Dissertation submitted in part fulfilment of the regulations for the MA in Early Childhood Studies, Bath Spa University, Bath.

Howes, C. and Ritchie, S. (2002) *A Matter of Trust: Connecting Teachers and Learners in the Early Childhood Classroom*. New York: Teachers College Press.

Jones, P. and Welch, S. (2010) *Rethinking Children's Rights: Attitudes in Contemporary Society*. London: Continuum.

Kidd, D. (2009) *Assessment as an Act of Love*. Available at: www.library.teachingtimes. com/articles/assessment-as-an-act-of-love [Accessed 15.5.2018].

Lareau, A. (2011) *Unequal Childhoods: Class, Race and Family Life* (2nd Edn). Berkeley: University of California Press.

Loe, R. (Ed) (2017) *The Relational Teacher* (2nd Edn). London: Relational Schools.

Loreman, T. (2009) *Respecting Childhood*. London: Continuum.

Marsh, H. (2012) Relationships for Learning: Using Pupil Voice to Define Teacher – Pupil Relationships That Enhance Pupil Engagement. *Management in Education*, **26** (3), pp. 161–163.

Maslow, A. H. (1970) *Motivation and Personality*. New York: Harper and Row.

Moss, P. (2017) Power and Resistance in Early Childhood Education: From Dominant Discourse to Democratic Experimentalism. *Journal of Pedagogy*, **4** (1), pp. 11–32.

Nias, J. (1989) *Primary Teachers Talking: A Study of Teaching as Work*. London: Routledge.

Nuffield Foundation (NFER) (2020) *Impact of Covid-19 on Mainstream Schools, England*. Available at: www.nuffieldfoundation.org/project/impact-of-covid-19-mainstream-schools-england [Accessed 22.1.2021].

Ofsted (2019) *Education Inspection Framework*. Available at: https://assets.publishing. service.gov.uk/government/uploads/system/uploads/attachment_data/file/801429/ Education_inspection_framework.pdf [Accessed 22.1.2021].

Olson, K. (2014) *The Invisible Classroom: Relationships, Neuroscience and Mindfulness in School*. New York: Norton and Company Inc.

Page, J. (2018) Characterising the Principles of Professional Love in Early Childhood. *International Journal of Early Years Education*, **26** (2), pp. 125–141.

Pollard, A. (2014) *Readings for Reflective Teaching in Schools*. London: Bloomsbury.

Pollard, A. (2018) *Reflective Teaching in Schools*. London: Bloomsbury.

Radcliffe, S. (2012) *Leadership Plain and Simple* (2nd Edn). Harlow: Pearson Education Ltd.

Recchia, S., Shin, M. and Snaider, C. (2018) Where Is the Love? Developing Loving Relationships as an Essential Component of Professional Infant Care. *International Journal of Early Years Education*, **26** (2). Available at: www.tandfonline.com/doi/abs/1 0.1080/09669760.2018.1461614?scroll=top&needAccess=true&journalCode=ciey20 [Accessed 12.11.2018].

Rinaldi, C. (2006) *In Dialogue with Reggio Emilia: Contextualising, Interpreting and Evaluating Early Childhood Education (Contesting Early Childhood)*. Abingdon: Routledge.

Rogers, C. (1959) A Theory of Therapy, Personality and Interpersonal Relationships in the Client-centred Framework. In S. Koch (Ed) *Psychology: A Study of Science. Formulations of the Person and the Social Context*. New York: McGraw-Hill.

Shin, M. (2015) Enacting Caring Pedagogy in the Infant Classroom. *Early Child Development and Care*, **185** (3), pp. 496–508.

Spielman, A. (2017) *Speech at the Festival of Education*. Available at: www.gov.uk/ government/speeches/amanda-spielmans-speech-at-the-festival-of-education [Accessed 19.8.2017].

Spielman, A. (2020) *Speech at the Launch of the Ofsted's Annual Report, 2019/20.* Available at: www.gov.uk/government/speeches/amanda-spielman-launches-ofsteds-annual-report-201920 [Accessed 22.1.2021].

UN General Assembly (1989) *Convention on the Rights of the Child.* United Nations, Treaty Series, vol. 1577, p. 3. Available at: https://www.refworld.org/docid/3ae6b38f0.html [Accessed 08.9.2021]

UNICEF (2021) *Rights Respecting Schools Award.* Available at: www.unicef.org.uk/rights-respecting-schools/rrsa-programme-update/ [Accessed 30.1.2021].

Valentine, M. (2004) *The Reggio Emilia Approach to Early Years Education* (5th Edn). Scotland: Learning and Teaching.

Vieluf, S., Kunter, M. and van de Vijver, F. J. R. (2013) Teacher Self-Efficacy in Cross-National Perspective. *Teaching and Teacher Education*, **35**, pp. 92–103.

Weber, K. E. and Greiner, F. (2019) Development of Pre-Service Teachers' Self-Efficacy Beliefs and Attitudes Towards Inclusive Education Through First Teaching Experiences. *Journal of Research in Special Educational Needs*, **19**, pp. 73–84.

Wortham, S. and Jackson, K. (2012) Relational Education: Applying Gergen's Work to Educational Research and Practice. *Psychological Studies*, **57** (2), pp. 164–171.

School
A community to live, love and learn

The lens of the authors

In our respective roles we have had the privilege of visiting a number of really excellent schools. They have stood out to us because of their ability to show that they are doing something really special *with* and *for* the children. On entering such a school, the positive emotional chemistry is immediate and palpable. As a visitor you are anticipated, smiled at, shown where to wait, where the toilets are and offered a warm welcome that instantly helps you to relax and feel 'at home'. Waiting in the reception area you can see that the value attributed to human interaction and common courtesy is not just reserved for visitors: it permeates the many interactions you see with parents and children and is further reflected in the celebration of learning and achievements lovingly displayed on the walls. These schools are alive with the sound of children's voices as they engage in negotiation with adults who actively listen and challenge their reasoning. The overriding ethos is one of purposeful interest, where curiosity is launched, and where careful attention is being paid to developing the children's hearts and characters as well as their heads and minds.

 DOI: 10.4324/9781003120537-3

This chapter celebrates the essence of the 'community' culture captured here; aptly described by Noddings (1991: 161) as being, 'places in which teachers and students live together, talk to each other, reason together, take delight in each other's company'. The chapter will support you in realising a similar ambition for your school and classroom environment. Reflecting on the complexity of current thinking on learning environments, we explore child-centred and constructivist theories, organisational and aesthetic features of the learning space and other factors contributing to the school's overall physical and emotional climate.

Our approach throughout this chapter is underpinned by the following key principles:

> '*We need to envision the purpose of education as a means of personal and collective growth*' (Alexander and Potter, 2005: 197): We believe the purpose of education is to enable children to develop as responsible human beings who are loving, caring, kind and compassionate.
>
> '*We need new learning relationships and new [communities] of learning to support them*' (Buckley, 2005: 178): Only when schools realise their potential to foster and support the development of democratic practices (resilience, responsibility, tolerance, negotiation, critical thinking) will the children of today be enabled to understand and ethically direct the changes to our economy, technology and society in the future.
>
> '*We all belong to the same human family*' (Boddy, 2017: 121): We are all naturally interdependent. The African proverb 'It takes a village to raise a child' utilises this understanding and recognises that an entire community of people must interact with children for them to learn and grow in a safe, healthy and loving way.
>
> '*We should not be afraid of making schools that are too beautiful*' (Vecchi, 2002: 12): The care and attention put into resourcing the environment is regarded as both an expectation and an entitlement. Children have a right to an irresistible, warm, welcoming, and well organised environment (both indoors and outdoors) that provides for a wealth of sensory experiences to stimulate curiosity, offer choice and provide comfort, reflecting the interests and achievements of both the children and their community.

The purpose and role of schools

It might seem a rather bold objective, in the midst of a book about relationship-based pedagogy, to be calling into question the fundamental role of education. However, in the same way that your teacher identity (explored in Chapter 2) is shaped by external influences, so too are the pedagogical preferences of schools subject to the changing nature of government policy and wider societal expectations and values. Education in a very real sense paints a symbolic picture of the esteem in which children are held.

In the UK we have historically selected to develop schools as the central place for our children and young people to acquire the skills that society deem important for them. Created in the nineteenth century during the Industrial Revolution, it is commonly recognised that our school system was set up largely to fulfil the requirements of an industrial world. The subsequent focus on the production of technical skills and instruction has ultimately resulted in an education system driven by knowledge acquisition, outcomes, targets, tests and league tables (Bethune, 2018). And even though the world that children are growing up in now, let alone in the future, is very different from the nineteenth century one, in many ways the classrooms of today are still reflective of an outdated model that often places the teacher at the front of the classroom 'delivering' knowledge to the children who sit as passive recipients. This view fits with the understandings of a Year 1 child who recently described her school experience as being: 'first we watch while the teacher does her own work on the white board and then we go away to do ours!' Given the increasing capacity and convolution of children's lives we believe the priority of education has to be about so much more than this.

We therefore promote a different possibility for the purpose of education, one that is fit *for* the children of today and anticipates *for* the children of the future. This principle is championed by Dahlberg and Moss (2005: 179) who explore a centralised political view of education that gives direction for future change, free of the constraints of party bias and focussed on 'new modes of human possibility'. McGettrick (2005: 35) similarly describes education in terms of the benefits it can bring to society in developing children's 'gifts and talents' whilst exposing them to the feelings of 'love, beauty, compassion, goodness and other positive human emotions and feelings'.

Believing in the enormous capabilities and capacities of children demands a concept of education that recognises children's rights and responsibilities as righteous and democratic citizens. Schools in effect become 'loci of ethical practice' (Dahlberg and Moss, *op. cit*: 65) or a 'laboratory for social transformation' (UNESCO, 2012). As Dahlberg *et al.* (2007: 76) suggest 'when the human encounter is the basis for pedagogy, as well as for ethical relationships, then to facilitate and accomplish these encounters becomes the "true" role of [schools]'. In a similar way Kumar (2005: 38) promotes a 'return to human scale of schools' in which the school is valued for its sense of intimacy, community and relational potential'. For a relationship-based approach to teaching and learning this emphasis is significant. If, as McGettrick (*op. cit.*) argues, education is 'the conversation from generation to generation', we believe that an approach that fosters cooperation, community, debate and discussion would be a fitting and worthy mandate to pass on.

This practice chimes with the description of the excellent schools we highlighted at the beginning of the chapter, where schools are viewed first and foremost as communities of social and democratic development and where the physical and emotional environment both reflect and facilitate this priority. Simply stated, the purpose of schools is to establish intelligent, social environments that are expressly designed to influence the moral development of children in a 'locus of participation and dialogue' (Dahlberg *et al.*, *op. cit*: 74).

A social climate of sharing, participation and communication

Much of what we already know about the importance of the social context of schools derives from the sagacious developmental theorists, namely Dewey, Bandura, Vygotsky and Bruner who collectively highlight the importance of communication, and interaction in the construction of knowledge and understanding, resulting in an increased appreciation for an environment that supports and enables social reciprocity.

Table 3.1 offers an insight into the key understandings of the aforementioned theorists and offers strategies that will support you in developing a learning environment in which social participation can flourish.

Table 3.1 Summary of theories.

Theorist	Theory	Implications for the learning environment
John Dewey (1859–1952)	'Progressive Education' (1938)	▪ Importance of active, hands-on learning and discovery ▪ Awareness of biological needs and desires and how these can be met through the school day ▪ Opportunities for democracy and active participation from the children
Jerome Bruner (1915–2016)	'Sociocultural Theory' (1977) ▪ Learning happens naturally through interaction with others and the environment. ▪ 'Cultural transmission' occurs between humans	▪ Importance of group collaboration and interaction ▪ Flexible open spaces to enable learning through discovery, exploration and investigation ▪ Organisation and independent access of resources and 'concrete objects' ▪ Ethos that encourages active dialogue and listening between teacher and children ▪ Importance of modelling and strategies to support language acquisition (questions, sentence frames, etc.)

(Continued)

Table 3.1 (Continued)

Theorist	Theory	Implications for the learning environment
Lev Vygotsky (1896–1934)	'Social Constructivist Theory' (1978) ▪ Cognitive development is enhanced with the guidance and support of a more knowledgeable other enabling the individual to learn within their 'Zone of Proximal Development' ▪ Culture and the language of the culture are significant in learning	▪ Emphasis on collaboration and space for children to move around in to engage in active and playful learning ▪ Opportunities for children to explore a range of learning relationships ▪ Learning episodes begin with a provocation, hypothesis or a 'big question' so that children are able to engage in problem-solving under adult guidance or in collaboration with more capable peers ▪ The ethos supports positive emotional development with a recognition of trusting relationships with and between the children
Albert Bandura (1925–)	'Social Learning Theory' (1977) ▪ Social interaction plays a fundamental role in the development of cognition ▪ Learning happens through demonstration and instruction, followed by attempts on the part of the 'apprentice' to emulate the 'master', followed by a good deal of practice	▪ Opportunities in the learning environment for children to come back to projects to rehearse and refine their understanding ▪ Space needed to keep on-going learning without it being tidied away ▪ Displays and resources offer prompts and learning cues to extend the children's learning ▪ Social interaction is valued and facilitated through a network of different relationships ▪ Different social areas should be provided to allow different forms of interaction ▪ Learning spaces enable creative spaces for 'play', conversation and relaxation

The implication of these principles, generated as a result of contemporary thinking about the social nature of how children learn, are simple: the learning environment should encourage 'doing' and 'playing' and facilitate episodes of 'sustained shared thinking and talk' between all of its members (Siraj *et al.*, 2015). We would like to emphasise the 'shared' here. It is common knowledge that as teachers we do too much of the talking. If this view resonates with your own practice, think about (and action!) how your classroom organisation, and how the overall ethos (i.e. the children's willingness to participate and take risks) encourage children to confidently justify, rationalise and deepen their lines of dialogue and participation (Alexander, 2020).

Picture of practice – promoting children's talk

A group of children are investigating the properties of shapes; they are on the carpet area and have access to a wide range of 2D and 3D bricks. The class teacher (Phil) is positioned on the carpet with the children and plays alongside them. Phil spends time listening to the children and also 'talks out loud' about what he has noticed. Phil encourages the children to talk about what they see and uses a range of open-ended questions to facilitate this (e.g. Why do you think that? How do you know? Can you be sure? Is there anything else to consider? Is there another way? What do you think? Do you agree with that?). Phil uses a mini-plenary part way through the session to encourage the children in the group to tell the other children in the class what they have noticed. The other children are encouraged to ask questions using a range of strategies that are clearly embedded into their everyday practice: e.g. the children are given an opportunity to think before answering a question; time is given for them to formulate and rehearse their question with a partner, and children use a number of familiar sentence stems to frame their question. The classroom ethos is such that the children readily exchange questions and answers; incorrect answers are welcomed, acknowledged and used to unpick and further develop the children's understanding.

We welcome this pedagogical approach, based on social learning through interrogating and investigating learning questions. This is exemplified in the use of open-ended resources, authentic problems to solve, responsive feedback (Hattie, 2011) and playful contexts to explore, where teachers and children learn together in a negotiated, shared learning experience. We recommend that when considering the placement, organisation and nature of the resources in your own classroom it will be essential to have this understanding at the forefront of your mind. Remember, as we explored in Chapter 2, the classroom environment will reflect your values, ideology and belief in how children learn and your views about their capabilities; the children will be very astute at tuning into these subliminal messages. Paying attention to the social and emotional dimensions of your classroom environment will go a long way to enabling children to see themselves as socially capable citizens and successful achievers.

Socially capable citizens

As the kind of co-constructed and relationship-based learning we are advocating here relies heavily on an exchange of rich and extended dialogue, it is important to acknowledge the significance of language as a 'socio-cultural tool' (Bruner, 1977; Vygotsky, 1978). We understand that the way teachers use, model and value language has the capacity to extend and enhance children's knowledge and give them 'intellectual power' (Nutbrown, 1996: 36). At the same time it is also worth considering that language acquisition can equally serve to undermine and alienate certain groups of children to whom the vocabulary, structure and meaning may be unfamiliar and difficult to understand. This means that in order to ensure that *all* children are benefiting from an approach that places interaction and dialogue at the heart of its social processes, we need to understand the assumptions, habits and taken-for-granted aspects of our teaching practices: the '*habitus*' (Bourdieu, 1978) which are embedded in our cultural identity, and are transferred in our day-to-day interactions and expectations. In practice this means valuing the home culture of all of the children to such an extent that they feel confident to try out, experiment with and ultimately employ, language patterns and practices that are reflective of their development as socially capable citizens. This understanding can have important implications for a school's approach to challenging the barriers to learning, particularly in areas of a low socio-economic demographic.

It is worth stating, however, and in line with the argument presented by Payler and Georgson (2017), that we do not wish to present a view that some groups of children require a deficit model of education based purely on 'compensation'; more that in our commitment to become relationship focussed teachers we need to be cognisant of how we are connecting with, planning for and supporting *all* learners in an appropriate and equitable manner. As Payler and Georgson (*ibid*: 195) conclude, teachers 'have to perform a delicate balancing act, combining an understanding of the social and cultural capital that each child brings from their home background with an awareness of the knowledge, dispositions and attitudes that are more likely to make it easier for children to succeed in our society'.

Whilst addressing inequalities and promoting social mobility may certainly be part of your motivation (or indeed moral imperative) you will need to consciously show in your practices that the families, experiences and the cultural dissimilarities of all the children are important and that your approach is respectful and equitable. To that end, Moll *et al.* (2001, cited in Waters and Maynard, 2017: 81) use the constructive expression 'funds of knowledge' to describe and add worth to the aspects that children bring with them from home. In practice this means ensuring that your school and classroom environments are both reflective and respectful of the children's backgrounds and that you strive to build reciprocal relationships with their families by being empathic, contextually relevant, and understanding. Research tells us the closer and the more productive these relationships are the more the children will benefit.

This understanding is reflected in Urie Bronfenbrenner's (1917–2005) *Ecological Systems Theory* (1977) which recognises that an individual's development is affected by everything in their surrounding environment. Dividing the environment into five different levels, Bronfenbrenner concludes that only when all the different elements of the ecological systems are working together in a positive way does the individual develop to their full potential and capacity (Guy-Evans, 2020). Linking this to an educational context means working tirelessly to ensure that the school ethos reflects the value attributed to good communication and reciprocal relationships between a child, their peers, parents and school, embracing a philosophy of partnership where information exchange flows willingly and where power and responsibility are shared. This is particularly important for those children who have additional needs and have many dealings with a wide variety of professionals.

The synergy between the environmental features and this fundamental principle demands that, in terms of the class and school environments, spaces are designed *with* and *for* all members of the school community to be heard and seen, meet together, meet with others, and fully participate in the life of the school in an innovative model of genuine partnership.

Community participation

Increasing parental participation in education has become a priority for many schools, who understand that it enhances 'cultural capital' (Bourdieu, *op. cit.*), promotes educational achievement and has positive effects on children's mental health and well-being. Moreover it is increasingly recognised that when this philosophy extends to include relationships between the school and the wider community the short- and long-term benefits can be even greater.

Picture of practice – community participation

This primary school recognises that so much of what their children learn and understand about their lives takes place before the school day starts and after it ends. They equally want to redress the common adage that children leave their reality at the school gate and pick it up again on the way home. That is why community engagement and involvement is such an important aspect of the school's philosophy.

The school already has very well established contact with the local business sector who variously sponsor sports equipment, ingredients for cooking, visit as 'role models' and have representation on the governing body. The children are seen and known in the community and often use local events or features as starting points for their learning. Their projects are displayed in the local supermarket, shop windows and community arts café. Links with the local pre-school providers (including child minders), secondary school and other primary schools in the area are valued with many opportunities for visits, exchanges of information, resources, expertise and joint community projects. The school welcomes volunteers in many shapes and forms including, but not limited to, enrichment opportunities before and after school, such as mentoring, yoga clubs, and football teams. The caretaker runs a very popular origami club at lunchtime! Local church or religious and voluntary charity organisations regularly contribute to the school's assemblies. The weekly celebration assembly sees the attendance of local residents from 0–90! Opportunities for professional learning, sporting and leisure activities, are held on the school site and/or supported through the school. The children at the school have recently been involved with the local council in designing a new playground area. The children's ideas have been taken seriously and several have been acted upon. The school is working hard to ensure that there are more opportunities where the children can become more actively involved in community decisions and where their full rights of participation are acknowledged.

This school exemplifies the view of community involvement as an active and shared responsibility; one in which there is a collective aspiration to raise civic-minded children who will contribute positively to society. A key element of the emerging practice here is the emphasis on the concepts of children's rights and the value attributed to their capacity to make informed decisions about their spaces and futures. Jones and Welch (2010) recognise this dynamic as an important aspect of a rights-informed approach and suggest that all organisations and services need to reconsider the nature and capacity of their relationships with children, in order to promote a more inclusive community and healthy democracy.

Familial comfort

The concept of school providing a 'home away from home' is an important consideration for a relationship-based approach that offers an intimate and familial feel. Noddings (*op. cit.*) compares teachers to 'good parents [who] should be concerned first and foremost with the kind of people their charges are becoming'. Loe (2017: 135) points to a similar correlation when he states, 'If schools perform better when they look like homes, then peers look out for each other as siblings might, and great teachers understand how to build relationships like parents'.

We understand of course that an 'idealistic' view of a home doesn't necessarily replicate the chaotic and stressful home life of many of the children we teach, and indeed the homes of the teachers! We argue, however, that the very fact that schools can offer an alternative model to a challenging one (i.e. an environment that is purposefully welcoming and safe) promotes an even greater incentive for schools to be *homely*. Research also confirms that when children feel a secure attachment to school and when it functions as an extension of home, or an alternative to an adverse one, children are happier, healthier and achieve better academic outcomes (Loe, *ibid.*).

Central to the development of an intimate school environment is the recognition that as human beings we are happiest when we operate in groups akin to family communities or 'tribes'. As Cozolino (2012: 245) states, 'Tribal teachers become loving and protective parents to their pupils, who in turn become caring and supportive siblings to one another'. Similarly in his exploration of 'tribal classrooms', Bethune (*op. cit*: 12) acknowledges our tribal roots, likens our social instincts to those of a 'big family' and highlights the familial qualities of love, kindness, cooperation and cohesion. He states that 'if we can create this atmosphere in our classrooms, children can begin to flourish'.

Picture of practice – the school family

A new headteacher has recently been appointed in a large primary school. The school has had three headteachers in the last five years, three changes of name and three uniform designs. The morale of the staff is low; parents' trust and loyalty is even lower and the measured outcomes for children through the floor. In an attempt to create a unified and happier environment and to promote a sense of collective pride and belonging, the headteacher begins to refer to the school as a 'family', using the term in the newsletter, the welcome poster in the entrance hall and whenever the school is gathered together. In assemblies the headteacher talks about the qualities that support a family connection and uses a visual wool web to illustrate how members of the school community (including the staff) are bonded through their common interests and shared experiences. At first the children ridicule the use of the term, openly declaring 'we're not a family'. The staff, equally, but perhaps less openly, dismiss the use of the expression as trite and unnecessary. Over time, and with a clear school improvement plan in operation, the headteacher begins to hear the children and staff use the expression 'family' in their day-to-day utterances about the school. Parents are heard welcoming new members of staff to 'the family' and displays around the school begin to reflect the familial qualities valued and discussed in regular circle times and class assemblies. Moreover, the ethos of the school begins to take on the *feel* of a family with children expressing a sense of belonging and showing a greater propensity to take risks, play and explore. Several years later when it was time for the headteacher to leave the school, one of the children declared 'but you can't leave us, you're head of our family!' The head teacher is confident that this child, and their peers, is now equipped with the necessary skills to understand and manage a change in this relational dynamic.

In this example the headteacher unapologetically uses the concept of a family unit to promote a shared vision for the school. It is an effective strategy that both unites the members of the community as well as provides them with an aspirational and clear direction for future change. In their mantra the head teacher associates the idea of 'family' with rootedness in developing a sense of belonging, the quality and nature of contact and interdependence between its members, as well as recognising the importance of generating the social and moral boundaries as a shared endeavour. In many ways this approach is reminiscent of the Eastern view of a family commonly understood as being associated with 'those that travel along and beside you'. A school family is equally defined and dependent on its multi-generational community, each recognised and valued because of their varying roles and responsibilities. Underpinning the success of this familial dimension is the appreciation, respect and love for the other family members. Olson (2014: 32) similarly advocates a school culture that allows, 'us to feel seen as human beings . . . and feel safe enough to risk vulnerable exchanges'. The Education Inspection Framework (Ofsted, 2019: 10) likewise calls for inspectors to evaluate the extent to which 'relationships among learners and staff reflect a positive and respectful culture'. In our opinion this judgement encompasses the way children relate to each other, 'as siblings might' (Loe, *op. cit*: 135), as well as the interactions between staff, children and parents which give scope for all individuals to have their identity, personality, interests and capabilities realised. This means for example that staff members are recommended for further professional development or training, parents are enabled to utilise their strengths and experiences with opportunities for skill development, and children are given regular access to positive role models that raise or affirm their understanding of who and how they might be.

Picture of practice – eating and playing together

In order to foster and develop closer interaction between children of all ages across the school, changes are made to its organisation. Traditionally playtimes have been time-tabled so that the KS1 and KS2 children have used the outside space separately. This was born out of the concern, raised by staff, that the older children were dominating areas of the playground, with the possibility that the younger children would be hurt or feel undermined. In order to counteract this negative view the playground is arranged into 'zones' with the children, and all grown-ups, including teachers, teaching assistants (TAs) and lunchtime staff, being carefully and systematically introduced to the possible resources, expectations, and, where appropriate, intended purposes of each zone. Areas that have previously been 'off limits' to the children (wild areas, climbing frames, out-door learning areas and some indoor spaces) are 'opened' up so that opportunities for purposeful play are extended. Play 'leaders' and 'buddies' are elected by the children and given additional duties in each zone.

At the same time lunchtimes are set up to facilitate 'family' groupings on each table. Older children are given responsibility for helping younger children to manage their food, and initiate conversation. All children are trusted to pour their own drinks, use glass beakers and china plates. The old plastic trays are dispatched to the recycle bin. The dining room (school hall!) takes on a new homely feel with flowers on each table and music playing gently in the background. Members of the senior leadership team join the children to eat their lunch, and many of the other grown-ups, including students and TAs, similarly choose to spend this valuable time with the children, chatting as their social partners. Children are noticed and praised when they, for example, try new foods, manage their cutlery successfully, set the tables, help to clear away and apply respectful conventions. Certificates and 'shout outs' are, with the children's agreement, presented in weekly whole-school celebration assemblies to acknowledge and promote these expectations.

Inspired by the practice in Reggio Emilia, these examples illustrate the importance placed on using all opportunities to promote 'self-sufficiency, social interaction and friendship' (Thornton and Brunton, 2005: 39). However, it is worth noting that such changes do not happen quickly or overnight. Children will need to be explicitly taught these skills and in turn the staff will need to believe that the children can be trusted to be autonomous and take responsibility. This positive view of the children's capabilities needs to permeate and embody every aspect of the school's ethos. Equally, discussions about the opportunities for children to further benefit from structured interaction with children from other classes and age groups, as well as with their 'best friends' (see Morris, 2017), need to be held so that a principled and consistent whole-school approach can be agreed.

As well as demonstrating the familial implications of the school environment, these examples also highlight the value attributed to the aesthetic appeal of the school. Vecchi (2008: 67) describes this attention as the 'search for beauty' and argues that children have 'a right to grow in places that are well maintained and pleasant'. In the same vein Strickland (2002) in a *TED Talk* highlights the attention given to the environment as being an essential part of the success of his vocational schools built in the toughest neighbourhood in Pittsburgh. He says the effort, for example, afforded to the installation of fountains and the choice of artwork, isn't merely about 'window dressing' but the fact that 'Everywhere your eye turns, there's something beautiful looking back at you, that's deliberate. That's intentional. In my view, it is this kind of world that can redeem the soul.'

Our assertion is that children deserve an environment that demonstrates the worth attributed to them and that the choices made about the quality and type of the resources and materials need to be reflective of the high regard in which they are held. In other words, the nature of the school 'home' needs to mirror the same love and care that you are showing the children. Many of these decisions will not demand financial implications. For example, the way the children's learning is displayed, the placement, organisation and quality of the resources, the use of natural materials and collections, the attention given to the use of colour, light and space. In the same way that shop windows or food counters tempt and entice customers, resources in the classroom should be presented in such a way to intrigue, captivate and inspire children, awakening all of their sensorial perceptions. We have long known the value of providing for multisensory encounters that motivate learning through exploration and stimulate cognitive development. In addition, we recognise the importance of providing sensory experiences as a means of familial comfort. The power, for example of 'the good smelling kitchen' (Strozzi and Vecchi, 2002: 23) recognised in the schools in Reggio Emilia, mirrors the same seductive influence of freshly brewed coffee or home-baked bread when viewing a potential new home! When organising your learning space we suggest that you consider how you are providing for both comfort as well as stimulation through each of the senses. We recommend that you involve the children and the parents in this process too as they are likely to have different perspectives. The patterns and issues that emerge from an exercise like this can have exciting and illuminating influence on your future practice and provision.

An important aspect of any familial environment is the opportunity for all of its members to access areas where they are able to rest, repair and to recover. Appreciating children's innate needs and desires, Vecchi (*op. cit*: 67) calls for the inclusion of spaces that provide 'a sort of shelter to which the children go to "cool out" for a while when there is a saturation of relations: a sort of battery recharge that enables them to renew their energies'. In recognition of this principle, we believe it is crucial to ensure there is a designated space in your classroom that provides for this kind of comfort, an 'island of intimacy' (Jackson and Forbes, 2015: 33). We also recommend a space that takes the form of a 'cosy nest' encased in an opaque material and furnished with cushions and resources that enable children to de-escalate and recuperate. In addition, many teachers provide breakout tables or learning stations that are equally designed to offer children the space, time and opportunity to acknowledge, accept their feelings, calm their bodily sensations until they are sufficiently relaxed and able to rejoin the other children. An increasing number of schools are also recognising the need to provide alternative, therapeutic provision to enable children to explore their feelings, identity and relationships. The development of school gardens, forest schools, the adoption or regular visits from therapy animals, and increased opportunities for physical and creative expression are increasingly welcomed for their ability to provide comfort, distraction and stimulation.

In addition, the benefits of a specific space dedicated for nurture groups are increasingly recognised. Developed over 40 years ago, the concept of a nurture group traditionally involves the employment of two specifically trained members of staff who support individuals and groups of children (identified through a Boxall Profile) who require particular support with their confidence, self-esteem and in behaving positively (visit https://nurtureuk.org for more details). Research suggests that this kind of nurture provision enables children to become better at managing their emotions (Cooper and Whitebread, 2007) and at empathising with others (Sanders, 2007). As a result they are able to form more positive relationships with peers and teachers and in turn improve their chances of learning and achieving.

Picture of practice – Bubble Room

Visitors to the Bubble Room often remark on its homely feel and liken it to walking into someone's kitchen or living room, with one even declaring that they were looking around for the stairs to the bedroom! Standing at the door you can see why. The 'lounge' has a large comfortable settee, adorned with cushions and demarked with a soft textured rug. The lighting in this area is low. The adjacent floor area resembles a multi-sensory work site with resources chosen for their ability to calm and distract and are beautifully displayed in wicker baskets. The craft table is currently set up to enable the children to investigate the properties and expressive potential of clay and wire. There are projects that the children will obviously return to. The colour on the walls is subtle and the few displays, although full of positive images, are clearly designed not to over-stimulate. The kitchen area is dominated by a large pine table with chairs that are as varied in design as the children that are about to sit down on them! The smell of toast is both welcoming and soothing. The overall ethos is one of purpose and serenity. Conversation flows easily and naturally as the children and adults prepare the breakfast. The routine is familiar and predictable. The physical and emotional comfort and affection provided by the Bubble Room means these children are usually, in time, able to rejoin their mainstream classes, feeling both protected and in some sense of control. In a similar vein, across the day, week, term and year, the Bubble Room is home to a number of individuals or groups of children who benefit from a provision that is specifically designed to give them opportunities to understand and manage their emotions, reflect on their behaviours and develop positive relationships: for breakfast, during play-time, a defined programme of study and intervention, over lunchtime, or at moments of immediate crisis and need.

Many of the evidence-based components recognised in a nurture group provision, such as the one previously described, have been shown to benefit not just the identified groups and individuals for whom it was intended, but moreover the whole school population, helping to create a nurturing ethos where *all* children feel safe, heard and valued (Binnie and Allen, 2008). Indeed, we also believe that many of the practices and benefits associated with nurture provision resonate closely with a relationship-based approach to teaching and learning and, as such, can be successfully and consistently embedded across a familial school:

- Nurturing and supportive environment: The overall look and feel of the school is one of welcome, warmth and beauty with opportunities for all members of the family to enjoy connection, rest and rejuvenation.

- Calm and purposeful ethos: The school and classrooms are tidy and organised, helping children to focus and support their self-regulation.

- Recognising biological needs and desires: Children are actively encouraged and enabled to stay hydrated, to eat a healthy and balanced diet and to exercise regularly. Food is routinely shared at 'breakfast' or 'snack time' with much opportunity for social learning and active listening.

▓ Respect for personal rhythms: Time is organised according to children's own sense of time, their personal rhythms, different levels of concentration and energy and what they need for the projects they are working on.

▓ Regular routines: Structures and patterns of the day are familiar and anticipated with clear warnings given to the children of changes to routine; support and preparation for transitions and other changes will help the children to develop internal structure, and assist in the development of strong relationships (see Chapter 7).

We equally believe that these same principles can be applied to the attention and thought given to areas of the school that are designed for staff and parental use.

For some schools the emotional and physical environmental needs discussed here are recognised, reflected and already part of the everyday practice and ethos. For others, however, there will be a need for radical and transformative change, a willingness to be open to new ideas and a propensity to act. This development will demand courageous leadership and a commitment to the application of the fundamental values and ethics that underpin a relationship-based approach to education. Changing a school culture is not easy and even if you are the head-teacher you will need to gain the support and enthusiasm of other team members to initiate and influence the development of the practices explored here. For others of you who feel that you perhaps have less status and authority it is important to recognise that you also have the opportunity to influence future understandings and expectations. It was, after all, the vision of one individual, Loris Malaguzzi (1920–1994) who took responsibility for developing a new discourse that inspired the now world-famous pedagogical work in Reggio Emilia and that recognised the fundamental interconnection and value of the aesthetic, emotional and physical dimensions of a learning community in equal measure.

Prompts for reflection

▓ What is the purpose of your school?

▓ How are visitors, parents and children welcomed to the school?

▓ What 'clues' do the reception and entrance areas reveal about the values attributed to democracy, and the identity, equality and interdependency of all members of the school community?

▓ What 'messages' does the physical environment of the school/classroom give out about what is important for children?

▓ In what ways does your classroom/school enable the children to be comforted?

■ How does the school enable the children to take part in running the school as a community?

■ How does the school reflect what is happening and important for the community? How does the community reflect what is happening and is important for the school?

■ Which spaces in the school provide opportunities for connection and rich dialogue between the children, parents and staff? Are there any that need to be changed or adapted?

■ How is each of your senses stimulated in your classroom, or as you walk through the school?

Shared language

(School) Family: The meaningful bond that unites a group of individuals through their shared experiences and understanding, providing a sense of belonging and comfort.

(School or classroom) Ethos: The overall feel of the learning space, incorporating multiple dimensions of organisational, social, emotional and linguistic elements that enable groups and individuals to feel valued and respected, whilst supporting their positive well-being and mental health.

(School or classroom) Culture: The values, languages, communication and behavioural codes shared and understood by a learning group. This should both positively reflect and represent the cultural makeup of the surrounding community

Chapter summary

This chapter has highlighted the essential role of schools in providing opportunities for social communication and participation between all members of the school community and recognised the synergy between this aspiration and the emotional and physical environment. It has highlighted the importance of the familial and comforting ethos of the school and the practical resource implications in realising this.

Further reading

Bethune, A. (2018) *Wellbeing in the Primary Curriculum: A Practical Guide to Teaching Happiness.* London: Bloomsbury Publishing Plc.

This book offers practical ideas and activities for teachers to use in order to help preserve children's (and their own) positive mental health and well-being. Underpinned by evidence and research from the science of positive psychology, it is designed to support teachers to develop a classroom culture of kindness and happiness.

We recommend that you visit social media image galleries such as pinterest.com for lots of inspiration for your classroom and school environments. Equally it will be useful to look at displays in shops, hospitality outlets, museums, etc. to see how items and artefacts are laid out to appreciate the emotional awakening of all the senses.

References

Alexander, R. (2020) *A Dialogic Teaching Companion*. Abingdon: Routledge.

Alexander, T. and Potter, J. (Eds) (2005) *Education for a Change: Transforming the Way We Teach Our Children*. Abingdon: RoutledgeFalmer.

Bandura, A. (1977) *Social Learning Theory*. Eaglewood Cliffs, NJ: Prentice Hall.

Bethune, A. (2018) *Wellbeing in the Primary Curriculum: A Practical Guide to Teaching Happiness*. London: Bloomsbury Publishing.

Binnie, L. M. and Allen, K. (2008). Whole School Support for Vulnerable Children: The Evaluation of a Part-Time Nurture Group. *Emotional and Behavioural Difficulties*, **13** (3), pp. 201–216.

Boddy, D. (2017) *Mind Their Hearts: Creating Schools and Homes of Warm-Heartedness*. Woodbridge: John Catt Educational Ltd.

Bourdieu, P. (1978) The Forms of Capital. In J. Karabel and A. H. Halsey (Eds) *Power and Ideology in Education*. Oxford: Oxford University Press.

Bronfenbrenner, U. (1977) Toward an Experimental Ecology of Human Development. *American Psychologist*, **32** (7), pp. 513–531.

Bruner, J. S. (1977) *The Process of Education*. London: Harvard University Press.

Buckley, J. (2005) Young People at the Centre of School Change. In T. Alexander and J. Potter (Eds) *Education for a Change: Transforming the Way We Teach Our Children*. Abingdon: RoutledgeFalmer.

Cooper, P. and Whitebread, D. (2007) The Effectiveness of Nurture Groups on Student Progress: Evidence from a National Research Study. *Emotional and Behavioural Difficulties*, **12** (3), pp. 171–190.

Cozolino, L. (2012) *Attachment-Based Teaching: Creating a Tribal Classroom*. New York: W.W. Norton and Company.

Dahlberg, G. and Moss, P. (2005) *Ethics and Politics in Early Childhood Education*. London: RoutledgeFalmer.

Dahlberg, G., Moss, P. and Pence, A. (2007) *Beyond Quality in Early Childhood Education and Care* (2nd Edn). London: Routledge.

Dewey, J. (1938) *Experience and Education*. New York: Palgrave Macmillan.

Guy-Evans, O. (2020) Bronfenbrenner's Ecological Systems Theory. *Simply Psychology*. Available at: www.simplypsychology.org/Bronfenbrenner.html [Accessed 24.2.2021].

Hattie, J. (2011) *Visible Learning for Teachers: Maximizing Impact on Learning*. Abingdon: Routledge.

Jackson, S. and Forbes, R. (2015) *People Under Three: Play Work and Learning in a Childcare Setting* (3rd Edn). London: Routledge.

Jones, P. and Welch, S. (2010) *Rethinking Children's Rights: Attitudes in Contemporary Society*. London: Continuum.

Kumar, S. (2005) Human Scale Education. In T. Alexander and J. Potter (Eds) *Education for a Change: Transforming the Way We Teach Our Children*. Abingdon: RoutledgeFalmer.

Loe, R. (Ed) (2017) *The Relational Teacher* (2nd Edn). London: Relational Schools.

McGettrick, B. (2005) What Is Education For? In T. Alexander and J. Potter (Eds) *Education for a Change: Transforming the Way We Teach Our Children*. Abingdon: RoutledgeFalmer.

Moll, I., Amanti, C., Neff, D. and Gonzalez, N. (2001) Funds of Knowledge for Teaching: Using a Qualitative Approach to Connect Homes and Classrooms. *Theory in Practice*, **XXX1** (2), pp. 132–141.

Morris, K. (2017) Attachments and Relationships. In J. Moyles, J. Georgeson and J. Payler (Eds) *Beginning Teaching Beginning Learning in Early Years and Primary Education* (5th Edn). London: Open University Press.

Noddings, N. (1991) Stories in Dialogue: Caring and Interpersonal Relationships. In C. Witherell and N. Noddings (Eds) *Stories Lives Tell: Narrative and Dialogue in Education*. New York: Teachers' College Press.

Nutbrown, C. (Ed) (1996) *Respectful Educators – Capable Learners*. London: Paul Chapman Publishing Ltd.

Ofsted (2019) *The Education Inspection Framework*. No. 190015. Available at: www.gov.uk/government/organisations/ofsted. [Accessed 19.2.2021].

Olson, K. (2014) *The Invisible Classroom: Relationships, Neuroscience and Mindfulness in School*. New York: Norton and Company Inc.

Payler, J. and Georgson, J. (2017) Social Class and Culture: Bridging Divides Through Learner Agency. In J. Moyles, J. Georgeson and J. Payler (Eds) *Beginning Teaching Beginning Learning in Early Years and Primary Education* (5th Edn). London: Open University Press.

Sanders, T. (2007) Helping Children Thrive at School: The Effectiveness of Nurture Groups. *Educational Psychology in Practice*, **23** (1), pp. 45–61.

Siraj, I., Kingston, D. and Melhuish, E. C. (Eds) (2015) *Assessing Quality in Early Childhood Education and Care: Sustained Shared Thinking and Emotional Well-Being (SSTEW) Scale for 2–5-Year-Olds Provision*. London: Trentham Books.

Strickland, B. (2002) Rebuilding a Neighbourhood with Beauty, Dignity, Hope. *Tedtalks*. Available at: www.ted.com/talks/bill_strickland_rebuilding_a_neighborhood_with_beauty_dignity_hope/transcript?language=en [Accessed 19.2.2021].

Strozzi, P. and Vecchi, V. (Eds) (2002) *Advisories*. Reggio Emilia: Reggio Children.

Thornton, L. and Brunton, P. (2005) *Understanding the Reggio Approach*. London: David Fulton Publishers.

UNESCO Institute for Statistics [606] (2012) *A Place to Learn: Lessons from Research on Learning Environments*. Available at: https://unesdoc.unesco.org/ark:/48223/pf0000215468 [Accessed 19.2.2021].

Vecchi, V. (2002) Grace and Care as Education. In *Atelier 3 Furnishings for Young Children* (English Edn). Regio Emilia: ISAAF/Reggio Children.

Vecchi, V. (2008) What Kind of a Space for Living Well in School? Metaproject for an Environment for Young Children. Reggio Children & Domus Academy Research Centre. *Exhibitionist*, Spring. Available at: https://static1.squarespace.com/static/58fa260a725e25c4f30020f3/t/594981c546c3c49f77c8cfa4/1497989628803/EXH_spg08_What_Kind_of_Space_for_Living_Well_in_School_Vecchi.pdf [Accessed 20.2.2021].

Vygotsky, L. S. (1978). *Mind in Society: The Development of Higher Psychological Processes*. London: Harvard University Press.

Waters, J. and Maynard, T. (2017) Organizing the Environment: Inside and Outside the Classroom. In J. Moyles, J. Georgeson and J. Payler (Eds) *Beginning Teaching Beginning Learning in Early Years and Primary Education* (5th Edn). London: Open University Press.

The ties that bind

Creating strong connections in your classroom

Let no one be deceived, the important things that happen in schools result from the interaction of personalities.

(Waller, 1932: 1)

Chapter objectives

■ To present the social constructivist roots of relationship-based teaching and reinforce the significance of effective communication in your practice.

■ To consider authenticity, affirmation and affect (the 'Triple As') as a foundation for successful interactions and connections.

■ To recognise the impact of different attachment styles, and early trauma, on brain development and the importance of attunement and empathy.

■ To signpost recent pedagogies that use relationship-based practices.

The lens of the authors

We are both skilled communicators and throughout our careers have deliberately developed our social and communication competencies because we believe that children deserve to feel connected, through clear, unambiguous, positive interactions with their teachers. Consequently, we have endeavoured to find ways to connect with all our learners, to the best of our ability. Our observations of an enormous range of both experienced and trainee teachers has shown us that connectivity is key to great teaching and learning, and only happens when conscious, considerate communication is occurring in the classroom. Also, we have found interacting with children to be one of the most enjoyable aspects of teaching, particularly when we have made a connection with children who seem reluctant or unable to relax into a relationship with us. Our competence and confidence as communicators has grown as a result of years of observation, practice and training

DOI: 10.4324/9781003120537-4

in how to use verbal and non-verbal language effectively and, perhaps more importantly, how to read and understand the cues that children give us. This chapter condenses our combined knowledge and experience of powerful and sensitively responsive communication with children and will support you in developing your own skills of interaction and connection.

Our approach is underpinned by the following key principles:

> *All children deserve an authentic relationship with their teacher:* Being true to yourself is fundamental to relationship-based teaching, and how you communicate with children reflects your reliability and trustworthiness.
> *Feeling good about ourselves comes from positive interactions with others:* Children can develop high self-esteem when your exchanges with them are encouraging, affirming and recognise their talents and interests.
> *Communication that engages our feelings stays with us longer:* When there is an emotional element to your interactions, you and the children can experience a deep connection that has a lasting impact.
> *Teachers can be key attachment figures for children:* Children can become securely attached to you, as part of their multiple attachments, when your responses to them are consistently sensitive, attuned and empathic.

It is possible to connect with every child. Although some children may be harder to reach than others, it is possible for you to connect with each child in your class if you are patient, persistent and willing to drop your own agenda and find out what matters to them.

Introduction

Whether you are engaging in solving a maths problem or taking the register, talking aloud to the whole class, or using silent, non-verbal gestures, the very act of engagement fires neurons in the brain, creates emotional connections, and forms relationships between you and your learners. If these relationships were visible you would see a complex and intricate web of connections; connections which are created and sustained through conscious and nonconscious interactions (Olson, 2014). Moreover, the nature of these interactions has a profound impact on children's cognitive, emotional and social development; communication that is grounded in relationship-based values, can make a powerful difference to the effectiveness of your teaching.

Nelmes (2019: 55) describes the classrooms where teachers create an ethos of care as ones where learning situations generate powerful feelings of connection and intimacy and, whilst he acknowledges that this level of emotional vulnerability can be daunting for some teachers, he exhorts us to recall our own childhoods and remember the teachers at school who cared about us, and how our relationships with them made a significant difference to our motivation to learn. Nelmes also identifies teacher 'presence' as a key component, saying: 'You have to be there – in the classroom – able, ready and willing to connect. You cannot just wait. You have to act, to bring the pupil to you. You must let nothing divert you.' The implication of this is clear: if you want children to commit to positive learning experiences with you, you have to commit to them whole-heartedly and communicate in a way that supports strong connections between you.

Social constructivist theory

As we have already mentioned in Chapters 1 and 2, the theoretical roots of relationship-based pedagogy arguably lie in the fertile soil of social constructivism. Expounded by Dewey (1859–1952), attributed to Vygotsky (1896–1934) and further developed by Bruner (1915–2016) and others, social constructivism describes learning as a social process in collaboration with a guiding adult, or more capable peers, as partners on a learning journey (Vygotsky, 1978). This emphasis on collaborative social interaction for interpreting and integrating knowledge, can provide us with a blueprint for the connectedness between learners that we are seeking in a relationship-based approach. Opportunely, Vygotsky's concept of the zone of proximal development (ZPD) and Bruner's theory of scaffolding (Wood *et al.*, 1976) continue to be key components of teacher training programmes, and provide a valuable starting point for considering connectivity in the classroom.

In early years education, social constructivist methodology has evolved further, with pedagogies that have relational connections at the heart of learning leading the way. Familiar examples include the use of 'provocations' (often child-led), to engage with children on areas of mutual fascination or concern, and where adults are 'listening closely to children's suggestions and questions, probing their thinking, and encouraging children to respond to each other's ideas' (Gandini *et al.*, 1998: 37). Moreover, a longitudinal study of the effectiveness of early years provision from 1997 to 2004 demonstrated that the use of 'sustained shared thinking', where meaning is elicited and co-constructed between adults and children, has a powerful impact on young children's social and emotional development as well as their cognition (Siraj-Blatchford, 2009: 1). This is also evident in primary classrooms where dialogic teaching methods are prominent, and where adult–child and child–child interactions are prioritised over didactic teaching styles (Alexander, 2020). Language is an integral tool in this process and it is with this in mind that this chapter will explore how to use language in its broadest sense, verbally and non-verbally, to communicate in a way that fuels positive connections and drives out disconnection.

Creating positive connections – the Triple As

When your teaching is grounded in relationship-based values, your interactions with children are distinguished by being consistently *authentic*, *affirming* and *affecting* which we refer to here as the 'Triple As'.

Being *authentic* in your interactions with children is a key component in successfully engaging with them and gaining their respect, especially with those children who are cautious about trusting you (Bialystok, 2016).

Using *affirming* language, both verbal and non-verbal, in your communications with children supports their sense of self-worth and self-efficacy, resulting in them having higher aspirations for learning as well as displaying more prosocial behaviour (Denton, 2015).

Third, connecting with children that is *affecting* means acknowledging the underlying emotions present in any learning process, and in doing this you strengthen children's emotional resilience and capacity for compassion and empathy (Cassidy *et al.*, 2016).

Being authentic

Much of the literature about being authentic in learning situations focuses on sincerity and being true to yourself. Definitions include: 'being sincere, candid, or honest' (Kreber and Klampfleitner, 2013: 479), 'a genuine presentation of self' (Cranton, 2001: 54) and 'to be the "most me" I could be' (Bialystok, *op. cit*: 316). Cranton and Carusetta (2004) identify four elements to teacher authenticity: being genuine in your communications, speaking honestly without intent to deceive or manipulate; being congruent in your words and deeds, this means 'walking the talk' by modelling what you are saying and demonstrating that you believe it and live it; encouraging authenticity in others through modelling authentic interactions with them and expecting the same in return; and living a critically reflective life by questioning your motivations, avoiding repetitive, or thoughtless, interactions and being willing to take risks in order to be true to yourself. The first of these characteristics refers to speaking honestly, and we agree that children have the right to be told the truth, and not be deceived or misinformed, whatever their age or level of understanding. The exception to this is when the truth would put a child at risk, and you have a responsibility to sensitively balance honesty with safety. This can be challenging when you have developed a positive relationship with a child and are trying hard not to lose their trust.

Picture of practice: withholding the truth to keep Jamie safe

Alex has worked hard to build a trusting relationship with Jamie who moved into their class from another school in January with a history of several moves and disrupted relationships. Jamie lives with mum and two half siblings and is estranged from dad who is about to be released from prison. Alex has made a positive connection with Jamie through their interest in science and, knowing that Jamie has repeatedly been let down by adults in the past, has so far tried to be consistently authentic and honest. Alex has limited information but has been told confidentially that when Jamie's dad comes out of prison no contact will be allowed between them. For safeguarding reasons, Jamie has not been told this yet and Alex does not have permission to disclose it. One morning Jamie arrives in school looking very animated and excitedly rushes up to Alex with important news – announcing that dad is back and is going to pick them up at home time. Alex is immediately concerned and wants to be truthful with Jamie and gently say that this can't happen, but knows that this level of honesty is not possible. Instead Alex chooses to focus on Jamie's feelings and says: 'How excited you are! I saw you this excited last week as well, when we were testing balloons in science, and you were literally jumping with excitement because yours went so high, do you remember?' Although this is clearly a deflection technique, it does recognise Jamie's feelings in the moment and preserves a connection between them. Jamie seems a little frustrated by this response but does not react negatively and is willing to be distracted by talking about science experiments for a while before getting on with the first morning task. Alex immediately sends a message to the school office to alert the headteacher (who is the designated safeguarding officer) to Jamie's announcement and to clarify what the arrangements are for home time. Alex also intends to follow up with Jamie's mum and support worker as soon as possible to confirm when and how the truth can be shared, and help support Jamie through any feelings of disappointment or anger about not being able to see dad.

It is not uncommon for teachers to have confidential information that they have to keep from children, and in this situation Alex holds knowledge that it would be unsafe to share with Jamie. The immediacy with which Alex has to respond to Jamie is not unusual either. The choice between being completely open and honest, as Alex would like to be, and withholding the truth from children is often not ours to make, and safeguarding decisions can sometimes have consequences that will challenge you. By choosing to redirect the conversation, Alex retains an authentic connection by recognising Jamie's feelings without triggering painful, nonconscious emotional memories. With dilemmas like these, it is still possible for you to be true to your values and genuine in your interactions with children, even when you are avoiding telling them the whole truth. What matters is that your intentions are sincere and your motivation is to prioritise the child's emotional, and sometimes physical, safety. Being confident that you have behaved with integrity is a prerequisite for authenticity.

Avoiding communicating with intent to manipulate children is another common dilemma. It can sometimes be tempting to use your understanding of how emotions affect learning, and your knowledge of children's internal motivations, to manipulate them into being compliant, to deliberately act in ways that may make you feel more in control. For example, acting affectionately towards a child when you do not genuinely feel that way in order to get them to do what you want, or pretending to be angry about a particular behaviour when you do not actually have a problem with it in order to regain authority. When you use coercive methods like these you may experience a brief sense of satisfaction, but the response will be compliance rather than cooperation and, as we will discuss when we address congruence shortly, children are astute and, even when they respond in the way you are hoping for, internally they will be experiencing dissonance and confusion. You will be restricting the potential for genuine connectivity between you and limiting the opportunity to help them understand themselves or learn how to develop authentic relationships with others.

Being consistently congruent in your language and behaviour, so that you say what you do and do what you say, is a clear demonstration of your authenticity, although it is not uncommon for teachers to either struggle with this or overlook it as unimportant. Shouting loudly at children to 'be quiet!' is a classic teacher-hypocrisy, as is telling a child you are 'disappointed' with them when you are clearly angry. Similarly, you may have cultivated a different voice for teaching than your natural one, believing that it gives you more authority; but children can be very astute at recognising when you are being disingenuous or insincere and not your true self. The fact that they may rarely challenge you about it is not necessarily because they do not notice it, but because it is so familiar to them that they are inured to it. We suggest that as most children learn the unspoken 'rules of engagement' between teachers and children quite early in their school career, they become complicit in preserving the *status quo*. Rather than perpetuate this, we invite you to explicitly notice when your words or actions are contradictory and encourage the children to notice it too.

Being authentic is about communicating in a way that espouses your values (Kreber *et al.*, 2007) and when you model this with children, you are not only integrating your beliefs with your actions but are also helping children to learn how to be true to themselves. Bialystok (*op. cit*: 317) comments: 'a teacher who has wrestled with her own identity and strives to be "true to herself" may be in a stronger position to help students "find" and accept their own identities'. If this is coupled with an explicit expectation on your part that children communicate with you, and each other, in an equally authentic way, this will deepen the respect and trust between everyone in your class.

The final aspect of authenticity cited by Cranton and Carusetta (*op. cit.*) concerns being critically reflective and questioning your motivations. Having already discussed this in detail in Chapter 2, we refer you back to the importance of reflexivity when developing your teacher identity. However, when reflecting on your practice, we encourage you to also consider whether you are providing authentic experiences for children in the tasks you set them. We believe that as far as possible adult directed activities should have relevance in the real world and be fit for purpose. For example, if you ask children to write letters, then let them be to a real person or organisation, and actually post them; if you ask them to measure the classroom, then let it be because you are rearranging the furniture and want to see what will fit where, and then actually use the measurements to rearrange the room. In this way you are providing meaningful learning experiences that bring an authenticity to your teaching that matches your authentic teacher persona.

Being affirming

When you intentionally provide positive, affirming experiences for children, neural pathways fire in their brains which, with repetition, will strengthen over time and contribute to their developing a positive and optimistic outlook (Olson, *op. cit.*). The founder of Positive Psychology, Martin Seligman, advocates teachers' deliberate use of positive language in classrooms, both verbal and non-verbal, to improve children's self-esteem as well as educational outcomes (2002, 2011). This is supported by research which shows that some strategies using an affirming approach do indeed result in increased engagement and success, particularly from children who find it difficult to connect with their teachers or to follow school expectations (Ciarrochi *et al.*, 2016).

If being affirming is to make a difference to your relationship with children, and theirs with each other, valuing individuality and uniqueness is a key component. However, making statements that are specific to a particular child based on their appearance, natural attributes, or possessions can diminish, or even damage, the connections you are trying to create.

Although, for example, complimenting a child on their new haircut, recognising a child's height as an asset, or saying you like the new backpack a child has just brought to school may seem appropriate conversation-openers, and are often seen as a way to create rapport, especially with children that are hard to connect with, these type of comments can also create confusion and division. Children have very little control over their appearance or their possessions, and absolutely none over their physical features, so singling these out as advantages or showing how glad you are that they have them, implies that you value something they usually had no part in creating and which they have no power to change. Also, onlookers may react negatively to hearing you make comments about attributes which they can never attain, and it can bring an unwanted divisive element to your classroom.

That said, due to the nature of socialisation and the prevalence of commenting on personal appearance or acquisitions in our society, children often invite you to notice these aspects of themselves and you will want to respond. In such situations, a suitable response would be to notice the feature without giving a value judgement, and using description rather than approval. For example, 'I've got a new haircut' could be greeted with 'I can see your eyes better now that your fringe is shorter!'; 'I'm so tall my dad says I would be a great basketball player' with 'yes, most basketball players are quite tall'; and 'do you like my new backpack?' with 'What a lot of pockets! You can probably fit everything you need for school in there!' When spoken with attention, energy and enthusiasm, you can still create a connection and avoid causing potential harm.

Conveying a positive belief in children's abilities fosters connectivity more powerfully than valuing personal attributes, and by affirming the strengths and interests of each child in your class, as well as sharing your own skills and fascinations with them, you can really enhance the network of relationships in the room. Olson (*op. cit*: 142) refers to 'strengths-spotting' as noticing and acknowledging particular skills or expertise that children have which they have acquired or developed either in school or, perhaps more importantly, outside of the school curriculum. Showing that you value abilities such as skateboarding, dancing, computer gaming, or doing magic tricks, as much as maths or science, can provide an important boost to some children as well as give you an entry into their world, and often a place to start when you are struggling to form a relationship with them. Similarly, sharing your own skill at, for example, juggling or interest in tap dancing will give children an entry into your life, a way to help them know more about you and provide an additional opportunity for them to make an authentic connection with you. Discovering and encouraging children's interests and fascinations, and sharing your own, is a vital way of building your relationship with them as well as modelling how to develop connections with others, even when the interest is not a shared one. For example, a child who is disengaged with learning and has limited friendship skills, yet a fascination with, and extensive knowledge of, tropical fish might respond well to your using fish-related icons and pictures, stories, poetry and even maths problems with fish in them, in everyday lessons. They could also be invited to talk about their interest to the class, and answer children's questions. In showing you value their interest and expertise, you are giving them recognition and respect and although it might not instantly win them friends, you are demonstrating that they are a valued member of the class and you are modelling how to build rapport with others.

Dweck (2017) argues that acknowledging children's skills and interests also needs to be underpinned by helping them to develop a positive way of thinking in order for them to be more fully engaged and experience success in their learning. In coining the term 'growth mindset' she advocates encouraging children to understand that acquiring knowledge and skills occurs through effort and persistence rather than the talents you are born with, or a 'fixed mindset' (Robins, 2012: 54). Many of the strategies taken up by a growth mindset approach include becoming aware of the words and phrases you habitually use in the classroom and intentionally increasing your use of positive, or affirming, language. For example, when a child gets a maths problem wrong, rather than pointing out that the answer is incorrect, before helping them, you might say: 'you haven't got it right *yet*'. Some schools have taken this further and eliminated the words 'wrong' and 'fail' completely, replacing them with alternatives such as 'almost there', 'not quite' and 'not yet'. Whilst these classroom methods have been criticised for giving children a false sense of reality, and unlike the 'real world', there is compelling evidence that strategies like these can significantly increase engagement and motivation (Denworth, 2019).

Other verbal language changes that you can make to provide affirmation for children include changing the emphasis of a comment from a negative to a positive one and replacing 'but' with 'and'. For example, when a child becomes frustrated during a plenary session because you did not choose them to answer your question, and they kick the child in front of them, rather than saying: 'I know you wanted to be chosen but it's not ok to behave like that', you could say: 'I know you wanted to be chosen and I need you to keep your feet to yourself'; or when you tell the class that they cannot after all have their much loved swimming gala because the pool is closed, rather than saying: 'I know you were looking forward to the swimming gala but I'm afraid it's been cancelled', you could say: 'sadly we've had to cancel the swimming gala and I know many of you will be disappointed'. This small and seemingly simple change can have a profound effect, not only on how children react, but also to your own brain chemistry.

Being affecting

Communication that is affecting purposefully engages the emotions of the receiver and generates feelings within them; in short, its aim is to *affect* them, as Moran and John-Steiner (2003: 82) state: 'Collaboration is not just an intellectual endeavour; rather, it is like an affair of the mind in which emotions can transform the participants'. To understand the rationale for communicating with children in this way, we need to delve into the world of neurobiology and appreciate how brains and bodies respond to emotional contact.

Porge's Polyvagal Theory (2011) has shown that our autonomic nervous system (ANS), a control system that manages our perception of safety and triggers alarms when we feel unsafe, provides us with an inbuilt survival mechanism. It begins in the brain stem and connects to our large organs (lungs, heart, bowels, etc.), operating constantly and nonconsciously. When our brains perceive us to be safe, our ANS is in a parasympathetic vagal state which we experience in our body as feeling reasonably relaxed with a regular breathing rhythm and a moderate heartbeat, and our mind is calm but alert and ready to engage; this is the optimal state for learning. However, when our brains perceive danger, our ANS instantaneously moves into a sympathetic vagal state which we experience in our body as feeling extreme tension, with tight muscles, rapid breathing, a racing heartbeat, and our mind is either empty and blank or frantically scrambling to marshal our thoughts; we are in fight/flight/freeze mode and are completely closed to learning (Olson, *op. cit.*). For children to feel safe and be fully engaged in your classroom, you need to help them maximise their parasympathetic vagal state and support them to recover quickly when they are triggered into a sympathetic vagal state. When we balance our vagal states well, we have what is known as good 'vagal tone' and research tells us that to help children achieve this, you need to communicate in a way that creates emotional connections (Porges, 2011; Van der Kolk, 2014). This means not only noticing and acknowledging how you think children are feeling when they are distressed (which we look at in more detail in Chapters 5 and 6), but also by making the language of emotions commonplace in your classroom. For example, when affirming a particular skill or interest a child has, as described in the previous section, include how you feel about it: for example, 'I'm *intrigued* by your fascination with fish. . .', 'I'm *excited* to see you're so enthusiastic about cycling', 'I'm *surprised* you know so many tricks!' Also, when you comment on how children interact with each other, use feelings words to describe what you see: for example, 'I'm so *pleased* you two are cooperating so well now', 'I'm *delighted* that your group are working so hard', 'I feel so *proud* of all of you for solving the problem without my help'.

Interestingly good vagal tone can also be developed through deep or extended breathing as it has been shown to alter brain wave patterns; so singing, humming, whistling, playing a wind instrument or practising breath work through yoga or mindfulness lessons, are all worthwhile practices for you to try for yourself and to use with children.

Being in a parasympathetic vagal state is the brain's default position, so when you use affecting language that children are familiar with, it will be like stroking the fur of a cat or dog in the natural direction it grows (head to tail) and will provide comfort, reassurance and a sense of well-being. However, for children who are unused to affection or have nonconscious negative emotional memories, your language may have the opposite effect and will be more like stroking fur against the natural direction, prompting uneasiness and discomfort. When this happens, instead of feeling a warm connection with you, children may find your words 'disconfirming' and may feel confused or threatened (Olson, *op. cit*: 5). This could trigger their neural pathways into a sympathetic vagal state and they may withdraw and disengage from you, or divert you with an aggressive or abusive response. Rather than being cautious in using emotional language, research shows that by increasing and repeating interactions that include emotions, children's brains become more receptive and open, and over time are more likely to react parasympathetically than not (Olson, *op. cit.*). You can contribute to this progress by not shying away from using affecting language, and being persistent even when children have a negative reaction, and preparing for the behaviour that might result (see Chapter 5 on different response styles to challenging behaviour).

Moreover, to create strong emotional connections with children, your non-verbal communication is even more important than the words you use. We communicate non-verbally through our eyes, facial expression, posture, gestures, mannerisms and movements. It is now widely agreed that each of these aspects are perceived and interpreted, often nonconsciously and even peripherally, by onlookers. Even the smallest change, a glance, a slight hand movement, or tilt of your head, can make a big difference to how children's brains respond and whether they have a parasympathetic or sympathetic vagal reaction (Olson, *op. cit.*). Consequently, being proficient at using body language is essential for communicating affectively. The guiding principles in this are: attention, warmth and openness. Use frequent eye contact that is a soft gaze rather than a stare, and in a whole-class situation, focus on each child for at least ten seconds before moving to another child (this is the optimum time for a child to feel noticed, although it may feel longer than you, or they, are used to); use an open relaxed posture whether sitting or standing, and avoid crossed legs or arms; be spatially aware and position yourself near enough to children so that they can see and hear you easily, but not so close that they feel uncomfortable; use facial expressions that are congruent with the context: animated to demonstrate enthusiasm and interest, calm and attentive to demonstrate when you are listening; use positive hand and head gestures such as thumbs up, silent clapping or nodding to show acknowledgement and recognition; and smile often with genuine warmth and affection. It is also important that when you are speaking, your body language matches your tone of voice so that the message you are trying to convey is clear and unambiguous; for example, using a concerned look when correcting a child and a frown or 'thinking face' when puzzling over a question. Much of this may seem self-evident and you may already be confident about the way you express yourself non-verbally to children; however, we recommend you ask an observer to watch you teach, or video yourself teaching, and from the feedback/playback critique your body language, and in particular how it is received by different children, in order to develop and improve your skills.

A significant way you can increase affective communication in your classroom is to emphasise emotions through activities that teach and promote emotional literacy.

Picture of practice: using circle time to create emotional connections

Jan regularly uses circle time with Year 4 as an opportunity to get to know the children better, to explore their views and ideas, and to give them greater confidence, articulacy and autonomy. It is a time for reflection, building a sense of belonging and developing social and emotional skills. On this occasion Jan initiates an activity to help illustrate how we can all be connected through feelings. After an initial warm up game, Jan brings out a large ball of string and explains that the main part of the session is to acknowledge how other people's actions make us feel, and how they affect us all. Jan gains eye contact with a child across the circle and says 'Chris, when you helped Jordan this morning, I felt glad' and, holding onto the end of it, throws the ball of string to Chris which he catches, and the string between them now forms a visible connection. Jan instructs Chris to choose someone else in the circle, say something they did and how it made them feel and holding onto the string, throw the rest of the ball to them. Chris hesitates at first and then says 'to Kyle, you made me happy when you played football with me' and throws the ball of string to Kyle which he catches. This continues until eventually, there is a criss-crossed web of string across the circle, connecting all the children. Jan then asks them to put the string down on the floor so they can see how they are all connected to each other and then invites them to talk in pairs about what they thought about the activity. This is followed by a round with a talking object (a soft toy chosen by the children) when every child has the opportunity to share their thoughts with the whole group. Comments include: 'it was hard to think what feeling I had', 'I couldn't think of anything at first until I remembered when I played with Terry at playtime', 'I thought no one was going to choose me and I didn't want to be left out', 'the string looks all a tangly mess now but it isn't really', 'I like it that we were all joined together at the end'. Jan listens closely and gives her full attention to each child's comments but does not show approval or disapproval, adding her thoughts only when it is her turn when she says 'I notice everyone said something that made them glad or happy and I don't think we always feel that way towards each other'. The talking object is then placed in the centre of the circle and individuals can pick it up if they have something more to add or want to contribute another question. This leads to a fuller discussion in which some children refer to Jan's comment, with one saying 'if someone said something bad, we would've all felt bad because we were joined with the string'.

In this circle time activity, Jan knew that the children already had a fairly extensive feelings vocabulary due to the emotional literacy work they had already done, and that they could refer to the Emotions Board displayed in the classroom which identifies different feelings, illustrated with the children's very expressive pictures and photographs, if they were stuck on what feeling to name. Embedding emotional literacy in your classroom, over and above regular Personal, Social, Health and Economic (PSHE) lessons, is crucial for a circle time activity like this one to be successful. That said, it is exactly activities like these which will help grow healthy emotional connections between children, and we encourage you to include them in your practice. Jan trusted that the children felt safe enough to express their feelings honestly, and was aware that there were one or two children with scores to settle, but was prepared to gently re-direct any child who said anything harmful to another, and remind them of the 'no put-down rule' in circle time. Establishing this rule is useful in any classroom, whether you are using circle time or not, and requires you to invest some time, preferably at the beginning of the year, exploring what a 'put down' is, how it can be expressed and what it looks like, verbally and non-verbally, and what it feels like to be on the receiving end of it. This also needs to include how misunderstandings occur through misinterpreting what someone says or does, and how to express your feelings safely without hurting others (more on this in Chapter 6 when we look at the causes of broken relationships and how to repair them).

Jan was surprised at how consistently positive the children were to each other and suspecting that there was some reluctance to admit feelings such as anger, frustration, or sadness directly towards another child in front of the whole class, was gratified that following her comment about this, a child added 'if someone said something bad, we would've all felt bad'. The children may also have been choosing to express only 'positive' feelings because they believed it was what Jan wanted to hear, and it could have been another example of 'please the teacher' which, as we have mentioned previously, can result in a culture of compliance rather than cooperation and lead to dishonesty and confusion. By allowing this to be discussed, as Jan did, you open the possibility of changing that culture and encouraging greater authenticity between everyone in the class.

The issue of any child not being chosen to receive the ball of string and feeling left out was another potential concern, and Jan was prepared to tackle this if it occurred by reminding them that in circle time 'everyone is of value, and valued' and 'no one is ever left out'. In our considerable experience of leading many circle times, we have found that once this principle is established, children will monitor it themselves and fiercely protect the right of every child to be included! It does, however, mean that there may be some long pauses as some children need more time than others to think of what to say, as well as who to say it to, and including every child in a class of 30, or more, children can be very time consuming. Modelling patience, and helping all children to be able to wait for others to have their turn, can be very challenging; so we recommend that it is carefully timetabled at a time of day, time in the week, and time in the term, when the children are most able to manage it. It is also helpful to warn children in advance what the task will be so they can prepare for it and you can help the ones who might struggle to think of their contribution. Additionally, although we suggest that circle time be a regular weekly event, you could alternate long ones like this one with those that have shorter activities and are less demanding.

Attachment and trauma, attunement and empathy

Attachment theory tells us that when children experience connections in their early life that are mostly loving and attentive, with people who are attuned to their needs, they grow to know what love is and believe themselves to be worth loving. At the same time, their brains respond by developing neural pathways for understanding the world socially, emotionally and cognitively, which continues into their school life: 'if a child can develop and maintain a positive attachment to school, and gain an enthusiasm for learning, they will do so much better in their lives' (The Child Safety Commissioner, 2007: iv). Through repeated experiences from appropriately responsive attachment figures, children create a mental representation (an 'internal working model') of humans as capable, trustworthy and well-meaning and come to know the world as a generally safe and caring place to explore. Moreover, through the familiarity of attuned, empathic responses from their caregivers, children develop their own capacity and competency to make positive, reciprocal, connections with others (Cassidy *et al.*, 2016).

The theory of evolutionary attachment was originally conceived by John Bowlby (1907–1990) who observed that most humans seem to have a natural capacity for empathy, compassion and care, and that the nature of infant/maternal interactions can help to explain its presence or absence (1969, 1988). This theory was supported empirically by Ainsworth *et al.* (1978) and subsequently confirmed through numerous studies, more recently using brain imaging techniques, which have further extended our knowledge of attachment and its importance in brain development (Gerhardt, 2004; Conkbayir, 2017). We now know that babies will attach to whatever figure supplies their needs, regardless of gender, biological relationship, or age (or even if they are human). We also know that children can form multiple attachments and that they will continue to seek out and create them, not just during infancy but throughout childhood and adolescence, and even into adulthood. Consequently, when a young child moves from a home environment to an educational setting their brain continues to refine, adapt and develop neural networks as a result of new encounters and attachment relationships. So as a teacher, you are influencing new wiring in the brain as well as potentially changing any pathways associated with insecure attachment which may have developed during infancy: 'entering school gives a child another chance to develop some deep, long-lasting relationship-based circuitry' (Olson, *op. cit*: 54). The majority of children are securely attached to their main caregiver(s) and are consequently open to forming a positive relationship with you in school. However, children who have experienced early care-giving that was insufficiently responsive or loving, become mentally traumatised and are likely to have an insecure attachment style. There are three types of insecure attachment you may encounter: avoidant, ambivalent, and disorganised (Ainsworth *et al.*, 1978; Main and Solomon, 1990), each with associated behaviours that can impact negatively on children's relationships with you, and create barriers to learning (Morris, 2017). Additionally, when a young child witnesses or experiences violence, a major incident or sudden change in their lives which they have not been helped to understand or process, it will have an impact on their brain chemistry and their feelings of safety, and it is likely to be harder for them to form positive connections with you or others. It is also worth noting that even securely attached children may have short periods of insecurity, which can make a difference in how they relate to you. We expand on this further in Chapter 7 when we discuss the impact of separation anxiety.

We will not go into detail here about different attachment styles, or the effects of early trauma, as there is a plethora of accessible research and literature available to teachers about the causes and consequences of insecure attachment and trauma, as well as organisations providing guidance and training on how to support children in school; for example, Attachment Aware Schools (available at: www.mentallyhealthyschools.org.uk/resources/attachment-aware-schools/), Kate Cairns Associates (available at: https://kca.training/) and Trauma Informed Schools UK (available at: www.traumainformedschools.co.uk/).

We encourage you to extend your knowledge and understanding of this crucial aspect of children's development, even if you do not currently have a child in your class with a diagnosed attachment disorder, or who has experienced trauma, in order to enhance your effectiveness in making and sustaining strong connections with all children. Although we recognise that some children will need extensive additional support to experience anything like a secure attachment with you, we believe that every child in your care deserves the opportunity for you to become a key attachment figure in their lives. With that in mind, we will consider how you can optimise the conditions to achieve secure connections with children through the recognised attachment attributes of attunement and empathy.

Being 'attuned' is autological in that it literally means to 'tune in' to another person, and this is evident in caregiver/infant relationships when the caregiver knows a baby well enough to differentiate whether they are hungry, tired or bored, and responds accordingly to meet those needs. With school-aged children, your attunement is evident when you know individuals well enough, and are sufficiently alert to identify subtle changes in their expressions and behaviour, and respond to this in an appropriately sensitive and compassionate way (see Chapter 5 for examples of responding compassionately). Attunement is also apparent when you accurately gauge the mood of your whole class and shift the emphasis of your teaching to meet their needs; for example, when there has been a serious incident in the playground and the children come in visibly upset but also energised and stimulated by it and you choose a quieter, more reflective activity rather than the highly active one you had planned. Perry (2000: 20), who describes attunement as the core of good teaching, believes that the skills and capacity to be sensitive to someone else can be taught. He refers to being attuned as 'reading the rhythms of the child' and encourages teachers to be attentive and receptive to all the cues which children provide, especially through non-verbal signals, such as eye movements, facial gestures or tone of voice. By using all your senses and observational skills you can increase your ability to recognise the signals of children's internal worlds as well as notice the mood of the room (Pianta *et al.*, 2008). To help you develop better attunement we suggest the following practices:

- Learn how to still your mind: practising techniques such as breath work, meditation or mindfulness can help you get into a calm state for short moments throughout the school day and sensitise you to what is happening around you

- Talk less and listen more: reducing teacher-talk and using active listening skills can have a profound effect on children's engagement and can also enhance your ability to notice the nuances in how children are communicating

- Give yourself time to pause: regularly stopping to just watch, listen and absorb what is happening in the classroom can help you notice the less obvious signals children are displaying

- Leave the classroom: as long as the children are safe, removing yourself from the room for a couple of minutes, taking a breath, and re-entering the space can help you see the children with fresh eyes

- Move around the classroom more: changing where you position yourself in the room enables you to literally see children from different perspectives, and you may pick up cues from children's behaviour that you might otherwise miss

Although strategies such as these may take effort and practice on your part, it is crucial in enabling you to mobilise secure attachments and help build children's brains: 'teacher-student attunement is not a "nice addition" to the learning experience, but a core requirement' (Cozolino, 2013: 18).

Empathy is a core relational quality which we have already discussed in Chapter 2, and which we will briefly revisit here as a reminder of its importance in creating strong connections with children. It is often considered to be the ability to metaphorically put yourself into someone else's shoes and fully understand what they are experiencing, to take their perspective in that moment, and suspend your own judgement. Additionally, unlike sympathy, empathy is also characterised by having an affective as well as cognitive aspect: that is, being able to resonate with the emotions that the other person is feeling, 'holding the child's experience in mind *and* heart' (Stern *et al.*, 2015: 4). Moreover, empathy is not only felt as an internal emotional state but is also associated with a particular way of communicating, meaning its expression is demonstrable. It is observable in adult/infant relationships when a caregiver intuitively mirrors a baby's expressions of emotion: for example, smiling back and making happy sounds in response to a baby's smile, or using a concerned expression and making soothing sounds to comfort a crying baby. With school-aged children, your empathy is evident when you give your full attention to children, listen to them carefully and show that you are not only interested in what they are saying and doing, but also that you understand and care how they are feeling about it.

Dr Margot Sutherland, Co-Director of Trauma-Informed Schools UK, states that schools can provide protective factors to ameliorate the toxic stress created by early trauma and insecure attachment, and proposes that schools create a mentally healthy culture for all children. She goes on to recommend that children feeling listened to, understood and having their feelings validated, be high on teachers' agendas (Sutherland, 2019). We believe that you can successfully achieve this in your class through skilful attunement and empathy, and that all children, not just those with damaging pasts, deserve to have high quality connections with you.

Recent pedagogies that support connectivity

In this final section on creating positive connections, we will signpost examples of classroom practices that have connection at their core. They each use and promote cooperation and collaboration in learning situations and could be considered the precursors to relationship-based pedagogy. The three popular pedagogies we have chosen, Philosophy for Children (SAPERE, 2020), Critical Skills (Wilkinson *et al.*, 2006) and Building Learning Power (Claxton, 2002) embrace the principles of social constructivism and are enhanced with new knowledge from neuroscience and a greater understanding of meta-cognition (how we know what we know). Although none of their literature identifies them as such, they are all noteworthy in their use of relationship-based practices and can be applied in any classroom situation.

Philosophy for Children (or P4C) is a whole-school approach designed to enhance children's thinking and communication skills which, in addition to Vygotsky's theories, draws on the tradition of Socratic dialogue (Siddiqui *et al.*, 2017). This process of creating a 'community of enquiry' teaches children to listen carefully to each other, to explore differences of opinion respectfully, and to value the ideas of others, all of which are skills that are integral to a relationship-based approach. For more information, go to: www.sapere.org.uk/about-us.aspx.

The Critical Skills Programme (CSP) is another whole-school approach based on cooperative learning, with practical classroom application; it aims to create a collaborative learning community by: 'developing a classroom ethos in which self-esteem, motivation and engagement are maximised and stress is minimised' (Weatherley *et al.*, 2003: 4). Again, it follows Vygotskian principles and focuses on process rather than product, and on prioritising language as the main communicative tool. For more information on how to implement CSP, read Weatherley *et al.* (2003) *Transforming Teaching and Learning.*

Building Learning Power (BLP) became a highly popular approach in UK schools during the early 2000s and continues to form the basis of teaching strategies in many primary classrooms. It emerged from Guy Claxton's explorations into the nature of learning and a belief that positive dispositions towards learning can be developed if the right conditions are in place (Claxton, 2001, 2002). This approach makes social connections explicit and provides practical ideas on how to support positive relationships in the classroom. For further information, go to: www.buildinglearningpower.com/

Connecting during COVID: a note about home learning during the Covid-19 pandemic

At the time of writing we are in the throes of the Covid-19 pandemic with extended periods of school closures and online home-learning. Early research shows that there are wide disparities in engagement in online home-learning, with disadvantaged groups such as children with additional learning or social and emotional needs, and/or those living in poverty disproportionately affected. It confirms that good access to digital technology is crucial but also emphasises the importance of high-quality pedagogy, stating: 'the quality of teaching is more important than the method of delivery'. It goes on to highlight the importance of peer interaction during remote learning and the value of collaborative approaches (Education Endowment Foundation, 2020). These findings support our assertion that a relationship-based pedagogy is needed more than ever. The guiding principles of being authentic, affirming and affecting still apply, and in fact, require even greater attention and commitment from you, as you create new ways of maintaining children's engagement and positive relationships.

Prompts for reflection

▪ Revisit your knowledge of social constructivist theory. How can this help to inform your understanding of relationship-based communication?

▪ Using Cranton and Carusetta's (2004) four elements of authenticity, examine what motivates you to be authentic in your interactions with children.

▪ Consider your use of affirming language in the classroom and audit how you acknowledge children's strengths and interests.

▪ What can you do differently to promote greater use of emotional connections in your classroom and throughout your school?

▪ How might you use attunement and empathy to connect with children who you may find difficult to engage with?

▪ Reflect on your non-verbal communication: how are you demonstrating attention, warmth and openness?

Shared language

Being authentic: This describes being true to yourself and genuine in your communications. We subscribe to Cranton and Carusetta's (2004) identifying characteristics of being honest without intent to deceive or manipulate; being congruent in your words and deeds; encouraging authenticity in others; and being critically reflective by questioning your motives and the authenticity of your interactions.

Being affirming: This describes using positive language that deliberately acknowledges attributes that support self-esteem and mental health and well-being, and encourage engagement in learning. We advocate recognising strengths and interests rather than physical attributes or possessions, and valuing individuality and uniqueness.

Being affecting: Communicating affectively means using verbal and non-verbal language to give an emotional element to your everyday interactions. In this way you will engage the receiver's brain circuitry and create connections that are deep and lasting.

Attunement: A recognised method of encouraging secure attachment, 'attunement' literally means to 'tune in' to another person. By using all your senses and observational skills you can recognise what others are communicating to you, and how they are signalling their internal worlds which will enable you to respond sensitively and appropriately.

Empathy: Essential for creating strong connections; being empathic describes your recognition of another's emotional state which you demonstrate through congruent body language as well as compatible sounds and words.

Chapter summary

In this chapter we began by considering social-constructivism as a supporting theory for how we communicate in a relationship-based pedagogy, and have ended by signposting examples of practice that illustrate this. We have proposed the 'Triple As' as a guide to successful connectivity: being authentic, and true to yourself in all your interactions; being affirming, through positive language and by acknowledging children's strengths and interests; and being affective in recognising emotions and using the vocabulary of feelings when you are communicating. We have also explored the role of attachment and early trauma, how this impacts on brain development and children's ability to form relationships, and how you can provide protective factors through attunement and empathy. Additionally, we have offered some brief thoughts on how to connect effectively during the Covid-19 pandemic via digital technology.

Further reading

Olson, K. (2014) *The Invisible Classroom: Relationships, Neuroscience and Mindfulness in School.* New York: Norton and Company Inc.

This book provides detailed descriptions of how neurobiological processes are at work when we interact with children, and suggests strategies that support positive engagement and learning, even with the most seemingly distant, disengaged students. Olson writes in an inspiring and accessible style with authentic examples to illustrate his messages throughout. Themes such as nurturing students' strengths and practising mindfulness are particularly compelling.

Denton, P. (2015) *The Power of Words: Teacher Language That Helps Children Learn* (2nd Edn). Turners Falls, MA: Center for Responsive Schools Inc.

Paula Denton is an expert in communication skills and in this book she addresses how to use language, both verbal and non-verbal, to build a positive learning community and empower students. Her down-to-earth style and practical exercises will enable you to improve your skills and be more confident in your interactions with children and adults.

Van der Kolk, B. (2015) *The Body Keeps the Score: Mind, Brain and Body in the Transformation of Trauma.* London: Penguin.

Although not written for teachers, this fascinating and popular polemic provides a comprehensive account of the impact of trauma and offers innovative treatments for re-wiring the brain and body. If you are interested in trauma-informed practice and how to have better connections with children who are affected by trauma, this is an essential read.

References

Ainsworth, M., Blehar, M., Waters, E. and Wall, S. (1978) *Patterns of Attachment: A Psychological Study of the Strange Situation*. Hillsdale, NJ: Erlbaum Associates Inc.

Alexander, R. (2020) *A Dialogic Teaching Companion*. Abingdon: Routledge.

Bialystok, L. (2016) Should Teachers Be Authentic? *Ethics and Education*, **10** (3), pp. 313–326.

Bowlby, J. (1969) *Attachment and Loss: Vol. 1. Attachment*. New York: Basic Books.

Bowlby, J. (1988) *A Secure Base: Parent – Child Attachment and healthy Human Development*. London: Routledge.

Cassidy, J., Gross, J., Mikulincer, M., Shaver, P. and Stern, J. (2016) A Lifespan Perspective on Attachment and Care for Others: Empathy, Altruism, and Prosocial Behavior. In J. Cassidy and P. Shaver (Eds) *Handbook of Attachment Theory, Research and Clinical Applications* (3rd Edn). London: Guilford Press.

The Child Safety Commissioner (2007) *Calmer Classrooms: A Guide to Working with Traumatised Children*. Melbourne: Child Safety Commissioner.

Ciarrochi, J., Atkins, P., Hayes, L., Sahdra, B. and Parker, P. (2016) Contextual Positive Psychology: Policy Recommendations for Implementing Positive Psychology into Schools. *Frontier Psychology*. Available at: www.frontiersin.org/articles/10.3389/fpsyg.2016.01561/full [Accessed 25.1.2021].

Claxton, G. (2001) *Wise Up: Learning to Live the Learning Life* (Reprint Edn). Stafford: Network Educational Press Ltd.

Claxton, G. (2002) *Building Learning Power: Helping Young People Become Better Learners* (Reprint Edn). Bristol: TLO Ltd.

Conkbayir, M. (2017) *Early Childhood and Neuroscience: Theory, Research and Implications for Practice*. London: Bloomsbury.

Cozolino, L. (2013) *The Social Neuroscience of Education: Optimising Attachment and Learning in the Classroom*. New York: W.W. Norton and Company.

Cranton, P. (2001) *Becoming an Authentic Teacher in Higher Education*. Malabar, FL: Krieger.

Cranton, P. and Ellen Carusetta, E. (2004) Perspectives on Authenticity in Teaching. *Adult Education Quarterly*, **55** (1), pp. 5–22.

Denton, P. (2015) *The Power of Words: Teacher Language That Helps Children Learn* (2nd Edn). Turners Falls, MA: Center for Responsive Schools Inc.

Denworth, L. (2019) Debate Arises Over Teaching Growth Mindsets to Motivate Students. *Scientific American*. Available at: www.scientificamerican.com/article/debate-arises-over-teaching-growth-mindsets-to-motivate-students/ [Accessed 27.1.2021].

Dweck, C. (2017) *Mindset: Changing the Way You Think to Fulfil Your Potential* (Revised Edn). New York: Robinson.

Education Endowment Foundation (EEF) (2020) *Covid-19 Resources: Supporting Schools and Parents to Make the Most of Home Learning*. Available at: https://educationendowmentfoundation.org.uk/public/files/Publications/Covid-19_Resources/Remote_learning_evidence_review/Rapid_Evidence_Assessment_summary.pdf [Accessed 25.1.2021].

Gandini, L., Edwards, C. and Forman, G. (Eds) (1998) *The Hundred Languages of Children: The Reggio Emilia Approach – Advanced Reflections* (2nd Edn). London: Ablex Publishing Inc.

Gerhardt, S. (2004) *Why Love Matters: How Affection Shapes a Baby's Brain.* Hove: Routledge.

Kreber, C. and Klampfleitner, M. (2013) Lecturers' and Students' Conceptions of Authenticity in Teaching and Actual Teacher Actions and Attributes Students Perceive as Helpful. *Higher Education*, **66** (4), pp. 463–487.

Kreber, C., Klampfleitner, M., McCune, V., Bayne, S. and Knottenbelt, M. (2007) What Do You Mean by Authentic? A Comparative Review of the Literature on Conceptions of Authenticity in Teaching. *Adult Education Quarterly*, **58** (1), pp. 22–43.

Main, M. and Solomon, J. (1990) Procedures for Identifying Infants as Disorganised-Disorientated During the Ainsworth Strange Situation. In M. Greenberg, D. Cicchetti and E. M. Cummings (Eds) *Attachment in the Preschool Years: Theory, Research and Intervention.* Chicago, IL: University of Chicago Press.

Moran, S. and John-Steiner, V. (2003) Creativity in the Making: Vygotsky's Contemporary Contribution to the Dialectic of Development and Creativity. In R. K. Sawyer, V. John-Steiner, S. Moran, R. J. Sternberg, D. H. Feldman, J. Nakamura and M. Csikszentmihalyi (Eds) *Creativity and Development.* New York: Oxford University Press.

Morris, K. (2017) Attachment and Relationships. In J. Moyles, J. Georgeson and J. Payler (Eds) *Beginning Teaching Beginning Learning in Early Years and Primary Education* (5th Edn). London: Open University Press.

Nelmes, P. (2019) *Troubled Hearts, Troubled Minds: Making Sense of the Emotional Dimension of Learning.* Carmarthen: Crown House Publishing.

Olson, K. (2014) *The Invisible Classroom: Relationships, Neuroscience and Mindfulness in School.* New York: Norton and Company Inc.

Perry, B. (2000) Attunement: Reading the Rhythms of the Child. *Early Childhood Today*, **15** (2), pp. 20–21.

Pianta, R. C., Belsky, J., Vandergrift, N., Houts, R. M. and Morrison, F. J. (2008) Classroom Effects on Children's Achievement Trajectories in Elementary School. *American Educational Research Journal*, **45** (2), pp. 365–397.

Porges, S. W. (2011) *The Polyvagal Theory: Neurophysiological Foundations of Emotions, Attachment, Communication and Self-Regulation.* New York: Norton and Co.

Robins, G. (2012) *Praise, Motivation and the Child.* Abingdon: Routledge.

Seligman, M. (2002) *Authentic Happiness: Using the New Positive Psychology to Realize Your Potential for Lasting Fulfilment.* New York: Free Press.

Seligman, M. (2011) *Flourish: A Visionary New Understanding of Happiness and Well-Being.* New York: Simon and Schuster.

Siddiqui, N., Gorard, S. and See, B. H. (2017) *Non-Cognitive Impacts of Philosophy for Children.* Project Report. Durham: School of Education, Durham University Press.

Siraj-Blatchford, I. (2009) *Conceptualising Progression in the Pedagogy of Play and Sustained Shared Thinking in Early Childhood Education: A Vygotskian Perspective.* University of Wollongong, Faculty of Social Sciences – Papers 1224. Available at: https://ro.uow.edu.au/sspapers/1224 [Accessed 29.1.2021].

Society for the Advancement of Philosophical Enquiry and Reflection in Education (SAPERE) (2020) *What Is P4C?* Available at: www.sapere.org.uk/about-us.aspx [Accessed 7.12.2020].

Stern, J., Borelli, J. and Smiley, P. (2015) Assessing Parental Empathy: A Role for Empathy in Child Attachment. *Attachment and Human Development*, **17** (1), pp. 1–22.

Sutherland, M. D. (2019) The Key Components for a Mentally Healthy School. *Independent Education Today*. Available at: https://ie-today.co.uk/dashboard2/health-and-well-being/the-key-components-for-a-mentally-healthy-school/ [Accessed 30.1.2021].

Van der Kolk, B. A. (2014) *The Body Keeps the Score: Brain, Mind, and Body in the Healing of Trauma*. New York: Viking Press.

Vygotsky, L. (1978). *Mind and Society: The Development of Higher Psychological Processes*. Cambridge, MA: Harvard University Press.

Waller, W. (1932) *The Sociology of Teaching*. New York: Russell and Russell.

Weatherley, C., Bonney, B., Kerr, J. and Morrison, J. (2003) *Transforming Teaching and Learning: Developing 'Critical Skills' or Living and Working in the 21st Century*. Stafford: Network Educational Press.

Wilkinson, J. E., Martin, M., McPhee, A., McQueen, I., McConnell, F. and Baron, S. (2006) Implementing Critical Skills in UK Schools. *Journal of Education for Teaching*, **32** (4), pp. 423–434.

Wood, D. J., Bruner, J. S. and Ross, G. (1976) The Role of Tutoring in Problem Solving. *Journal of Child Psychiatry and Psychology*, **17** (2), pp. 89–100.

5 A relationship-based approach to behaviour

Chapter objectives

■ To offer a framework which promotes positive learning behaviour.

■ To provide tools to meet the behavioural needs of children within a loving context.

■ To present strategies that strengthen children's relational resilience and self-efficacy without being dependent on extrinsic rewards.

■ To reinforce the power of social and emotional competencies and emotional literacy in a school context.

The lens of the authors

During both our careers we have spent a considerable amount of time teaching and supporting children whose behaviour is challenging to adults. Influenced by our belief in holistic and inclusive teaching, our experience has shown us that a relationship-based approach to learning behaviour, using non-blameful, positive strategies, is the most humane, as well as the most successful, way of engaging children who are troubled, and troubling. We are also advocates of explicitly teaching social and emotional skills in the belief that when children understand their own and others' feelings and behaviour, they become more compassionate and empathic citizens. However, you will not find any behaviour management tips or quick fixes here; there are plenty of other books and blogs and websites around for that. This chapter is about behaviour for life, not for the short-term (or the faint-hearted!)

Our approach throughout this chapter is underpinned by the following key principles:

> *All behaviour is communication:* It is an outward, observable expression of our internal state and the way in which we demonstrate how we are feeling, (sometimes without using words); it is not 'good' or 'bad', it is just messaging.

DOI: 10.4324/9781003120537-5

Everyone is trying to get their needs met: There are basic human needs which have to be satisfied in order for us to thrive: physically, cognitively and emotionally. Children are often dependent on adults to supply those needs and may not be able to self-regulate when they are not met, resulting in challenging behaviour.

If you want someone's behaviour to change, you need to understand your own first: Self-awareness and self-regulation are prerequisites for helping others when you find their behaviour challenging or difficult. You need to be able to tune into your own feelings, and regulate your response, if you are to be successful in supporting someone else to behave differently.

Introduction

In this chapter we have taken as our reference point your role as being '*in loco parentis*'. Literally translated this means 'in the place of parents', and this duty of care is a legal responsibility that requires you to behave as a 'reasonable parent' would in order to keep children safe and well while they are with you (Elliott, 2019). We believe that your role as a surrogate parent is never more relevant than when you are promoting positive learning behaviour in your classroom, or responding to children when their behaviour concerns or challenges you. Consequently, throughout this chapter we deliberately include parenting advice from leading professionals in child development and psychology, along with academic research and guidance from educational experts on behaviour in school. With this in mind, we have taken the work of Hoghughi and Speight (1998) intended for parents, and combined it with the *Behaviour for Learning Conceptual Framework* (Ellis and Tod, 2009) designed for teachers, to provide you with a structure of behavioural expectations and encouragement which exemplifies our belief in children deserving a loving relationship with compassionate adults guiding them to behave well in school.

There are three key components to the framework (see Figure 5.1): 1. Love and Commitment 2. Limit-setting and 3. Learning and Development. Each part is of equal importance and when you combine all three you will provide a safe haven where positive learning behaviour can flourish.

1. Love and commitment

We are aware that it may seem a bold claim to say that when teachers demonstrate love and commitment towards children the result is more positive learning behaviour in their classrooms. However, we draw on the work of leading authors whose writing may not include such emotive words as 'love' but who nevertheless provide evidence of exactly that. Bill Rogers' numerous books on successful behaviour management are imbued with a respectful, caring, empathic approach (2004,

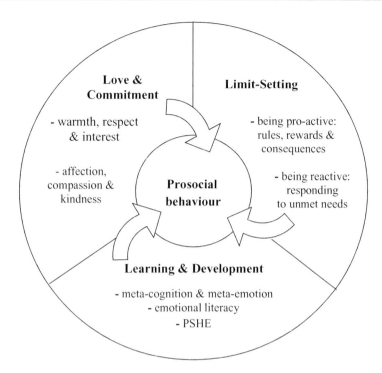

Figure 5.1 Framework to show the three key components for promoting prosocial behaviour.

Source: Adapted from Hoghughi and Speight (1998) and Ellis and Tod (2009).

2007, 2012, 2015), while Porter (2014) provides evidence that children become increasingly cooperative and decreasingly anti-social when adults provide emotional warmth and are consistently sensitive and responsive to their needs. Dix (2017: 3) explicitly refers to 'visible consistency, visible kindness' and 'deliberate botheredness' (*ibid*: 37) being key to positive behaviour in school, and Reyes *et al.* (2012: 709) demonstrate that when teachers are 'emotionally invested' and 'caring, supportive and emotionally available' children's levels of engagement and social unity are significantly higher. They describe these teachers as ones who regularly express warmth, respect and interest in their students and who are *affectionate, compassionate* and *kind.*

Being *affectionate* relates to making connections with children that are *affecting*, as we mention in Chapter 4: it requires you to connect emotionally with your learners, to allow yourself to be affected by them, and to respond with warmth and sensitivity to whatever behaviour they are displaying. Being aware of your own emotional response is key to this, and if you explicitly recognise feelings generated by children's behaviour, you can engage neural pathways in the brain that support positive emotional connections and increase receptivity (Porges, 2011; Van der Kolk, 2014). Verbally noticing behaviour and combining it with emotional vocabulary so that the language of feelings becomes embedded in your everyday interactions can be a useful way to practise this: for example, 'I'm *delighted* you were able to answer those questions so well', 'I'm *excited* to read this new story with you', 'I can see how *frustrated* you are that you weren't able to finish'. However, describing feelings will only make a difference in enabling your learners to be more fully engaged and more likely to behave in prosocial ways, if you express them:

> *Authentically:* being sufficiently self-aware and knowledgeable about your own and others' internal world to be able to identify what the feelings are, and communicate them with honesty and integrity.
> *Appropriately:* using language that is suitable for the situation and the learner(s) and making sure your body language is congruent with the message you are giving.
> *Safely:* in a way that does not leave you or your learners vulnerable or harmed.

Being *compassionate* means not only understanding what another person is feeling but also acting out of a desire to help them (Goetz *et al.*, 2010). It is often analogous with empathy although being empathic does not always result in action and it is possible to behave compassionately without necessarily experiencing the feelings of the recipient. Gilbert (2010) argues that a compassionate response can have far-reaching effects for both the giver and receiver, including increased confidence, lowered anxiety and hostility, and better physical and mental health. In a typical day, it is likely that you are contributing to these good effects through unwittingly performing numerous acts of compassion for the children you teach. These might be: when a child is too shy to answer a question in front of the whole class and you change your approach, using talk partners and one-to-one questioning instead; when a child is getting frustrated about not being able to stay on task and you let them spend some time in a quiet, calm space in your classroom to refocus; when a child is frightened of going into the hall at lunchtime and you accompany them, spending time trying to find out what they are scared of; all these everyday responses are acts of compassion. However, whilst showing compassion towards a child who is receptive to your help is easy; it is much more challenging to persist compassionately when a child rejects your assistance, especially if their behaviour is rude, abusive, angry, aggressive, uncommunicative or ungrateful. But your capacity for compassion need not be diminished in the face of this rejection if you remember these realities in the moment:

- The child's brain has been emotionally hi-jacked: they are in fight/flight/freeze mode and are unable to think clearly

- The child's behaviour is a response to unmet needs

- The child's behaviour is secondary to the initial source of unmet need

▓ If you focus on the child's needs, rather than your own, you can restore their equilibrium

▓ How you decide to respond is up to you (the child does not have that choice)

▓ As you are the adult here you have greater knowledge and life experience than the child

▓ You can afford to be compassionate

We will consider this in greater detail later in the next section of this chapter, on limit-setting.

Being *kind* and recognising acts of kindness runs parallel to compassion and is one of the most effective ways of promoting and developing positive learning behaviour in your classroom. Phillips and Taylor (2010) assert that living kindly is our natural state and acts of kindness are a common occurrence, particularly amongst young children. However, they also believe that children's natural kindness is rarely given recognition or credence and can easily be sabotaged by a competitive, adult view that success is only achieved through being self-centred. Fortunately there is extensive evidence to counteract this view. Over 20 years ago, V.G. Paley, a successful author of highly influential books about children and education, wrote a seminal work, *The Kindness of Children* (1999) in which she describes how even very young learners can transform themselves and others through exploring narratives of kindness and other acts of goodness. She demonstrates that knowing how to be kind, and receiving kindness, enables children to develop socially, morally and behaviourally. Flook *et al.* (2015) also discovered higher levels of social competence and self-regulation in young children who participated in a mindfulness-based 'Kindness Curriculum' which entailed regularly noticing, sharing, and emphasising empathy and gratitude. In another study, with 9–11-year-olds, children who were encouraged to perform just three acts of kindness per week over the course of four weeks, experienced improved feelings of well-being and significant increases in peer acceptance, whilst their teachers reported fewer incidents of disruption (Layous *et al.*, 2012). These and other examples are persuasive in linking kindness with better behaviour, and although recognising and promoting acts of kindness may already be evident in your classroom, it may deserve greater attention to be truly effective as a transformational behaviour tool.

Picture of practice – teaching about kindness: the kindness tree

Frank is a Year 6 teacher in a one-form entry school where most of the children in his class have been together since Reception. He noticed that distinctive friendship groups had developed into factions and almost gang-like behaviour, with some individuals being persistently marginalised and incidents of bullying becoming quite frequent. He wanted to create a more caring atmosphere and decided to explicitly promote acts of kindness, compassion and generosity between children. To kick-start this, Frank read to the class the popular fiction book *Posted* by John David Anderson (2018). The story explores the themes of bullying and broken friendships and unravels the complexities of communication and how words can help or harm. The children enthusiastically engaged with the characters in the story and with guidance, were able to relate it to their own experience and begin to discuss some of the issues going on between themselves in their own class. Once the children agreed that their classroom would be a better place if they were kinder to each other, Frank helped them create a Kindness Tree. The Kindness Tree consists of a large paper silhouette of a tree with bare branches, stuck on a prominent display board in the classroom, with a bag of cut out paper leaves pinned next to it. Anytime someone in the class does anything that is kind to another person, the recipient writes the name of that person, and their action, on a leaf and sticks it on the tree: for example, 'Jasmine helped me when I was stuck on a maths problem'; 'Ben let me play football at playtime when no one else would'. The children are highly motivated to cover each branch with a leaf until the tree is covered with acts of kindness. Although the factions and occasional bullying has not completely disappeared, Frank has noticed how much more positively connected the children are now, and how more willing they are to be kinder to each other and resolve disputes peacefully.

Contrary to popular belief, none of the examples given here will result in classroom chaos, or use up time that would otherwise be spent learning the curriculum: they can easily be integrated into your normal teaching practices. Moreover, there is considerable evidence that investing your time being *affectionate, compassionate* and *kind* will result in children having increased self-regulation, greater levels of attention and engagement, and better social skills; in short, they will have more positive learning behaviour.

2. Limit-setting

However affectionate, compassionate and kind you are, there is no guarantee that children will always respond to you in the way you would like them to. Sometimes a child's desire to please you, and their engagement in the task or activity you have set them, will be overridden by an instinctive desire to have their needs met first. Unmet need is the most common cause for challenging behaviour. Unmet needs can be physical (e.g. being hungry, thirsty, tired, needing the toilet), cognitive (e.g. being confused, distracted, under-stimulated, unmotivated) or emotional (e.g. feeling unsafe, scared, angry, bored, lonely). When unmet needs combine with an inability to self-regulate or suppress those needs in the moment, children will communicate by behaving in ways that are inappropriate or inconvenient to you, or possibly damaging or dangerous to themselves or others. Being a loving teacher means recognising what those needs are, and responding to them as a loving parent would: providing safe boundaries and setting limits in a proportionate way. Moreover, having boundaries is a human need in itself: providing structure and safety in relationships, and helping us to learn to respect others and develop love and respect for ourselves (Perry, 2019). There are two ways in which we hold safe behavioural boundaries for children: by being *proactive* and being *reactive*. The first includes setting up conventions or rules which usually gain rewards if followed, and incur consequences if broken. The second are the spontaneous interactions which occur when we respond to children's actions or behaviours which challenge us in the moment.

Being proactive: rules, rewards and consequences

Wake (2012: 180) advises parents to express the behaviour they want from their children through their values; he cites 'treat others as you wish to be treated' as a value which avoids having numerous rules such as 'don't hit', 'don't tease', 'don't swear'. Our views chime with this in relation to a school context, and we agree with Rogers (2012: 15) when he says: 'The most fundamental rights of a classroom member are those of respect and fair treatment . . . they relate to due responsibility and fair and agreed rules.' Moreover, we believe that when you are creating, revising or upholding behaviour expectations they should be closely linked to your school values and, above all, should prioritise relationships with children, giving care and attention to their needs.

All schools provide some form of description or list of expected behaviours, usually written into a behaviour policy and often explicitly displayed in corridors and classrooms, as advised by government guidance (DfE, 2011, 2016). Some are referred to as 'Golden Rules' (Mosley and Sonnet, 2005), others have a 'Behaviour Agreement' (Rogers, 2012). Schools achieving a Rights Respecting Schools Award (UNICEF, date unknown) are likely to display a 'Class Charter'. In whatever way they are described in your school, when you are designing or revising expectations for behaviour there are four key elements which support a relationship-based approach. These elements can be identified by the mnemonic EPIC: *Explicit, Positive, Inclusive* and *Collaborative*, and apply not just when generating them initially but also when reviewing and revising them, which it is advisable to do at regular intervals.

Explicit: There is a proven correlation between reduced classroom disruption, as well as children's improved sense of safety and well-being, and having clear, explicit behavioural expectations (Porter, *op. cit.*; Swinson and Harrop, 2012). Cooperation is more likely when you describe the behaviour you want explicitly and clearly, using unambiguous, age-appropriate language: e.g. 'we wait our turn to speak'.

Positive: When guidance is framed in positive language, naming behaviours that are desired, rather than their opposite (e.g. 'we walk around the school' rather than 'no running in school') they are also more likely to be followed.

Inclusive: In order to maintain equity, and ensure that expected behaviours are accessible to all children and adults in the school community, they need to be fully inclusive, recognising that some people may need additional support to follow them. This also means that communicating your behaviour expectations needs to be done through a variety of accessible media such as drawings, photographs or stories (Ellis and Tod, 2015).

Collaborative: Several leading authors on behaviour in school provide tried and tested blueprints for constructing behaviour expectations which emphasise a sense of fairness, so cherished by children, and all recommend collaborative models where children have a voice (Hook and Vass, 2012; Rogers, 2012; Chaplain, 2016; Dix, 2017). Conducting authentic consultations with children about your behaviour expectations, leading a fair and focussed discussion, and genuinely reflecting their views in any agreed framework, is essential for success. Furthermore, for a truly whole-school approach, consultation could be extended to include parents, support staff, local community representatives and other stakeholders. When everyone feels that their thoughts have been seriously considered, their investment and support will be that much greater.

In addition to using the EPIC principles, Hook and Vass (*op. cit.*) suggest that behaviour expectations be aligned to four basic rights: the teacher's right to teach, the pupil's right to learn, everyone's right to safety (physical and psychological), and everyone's right to be treated with dignity and respect. Similarly, Rogers (*op. cit.*) and Chaplain (*op. cit.*) encourage interrogating each expectation as to whether it: keeps everyone safe, enables effective learning, and encourages respect for each other. Dix (*op. cit*: 168) refines this even further with three simple words: 'Ready, Respectful, Safe'. All these experts are of the same mind: that however you devise your behaviour expectations, it is advisable to distil them into a short list that can be easily remembered, understood, and followed by every member of the school family.

Rewards

There continues to be much debate on whether rewarding children for following behaviour expectations is necessary or even moral (Kohn, 1999). Often viewed as a form of bribery, the value of rewards in developing intrinsic motivation is highly questionable, and whilst there is evidence that a consistent reward system contingent on specific behaviours can be effective in controlling children, there is little proof that they are learning anything other than compliance (Robins, 2012). Yet despite the overwhelming evidence that the use of tangible rewards is ineffective in achieving genuine behavioural change, the handing out of stickers, star charts, house points, certificates and prizes for following classroom rules is endemic in our schools and it is likely that you practise, or at least observe, its use yourself. Whilst we dispute the usefulness of extrinsic rewards and agree with those academics and theorists who believe that prosocial behaviour, and subsequent positive social attitudes, cannot be achieved through a simplistic behaviourist model of cause and effect, we are realistic about our inability to overthrow a paradigm that is embedded in school culture. So with that in mind, our specific focus here is on the use and effectiveness of positive reinforcement through teacher praise.

Authentic, positive recognition through verbal and non-verbal praise is known to impact on children's self-efficacy, self-esteem and sense of optimism, and can be an extremely effective way to encourage desired behaviour as well as strengthening positive connections within teacher–child relationships (Gordon, 1974; Maines and Robinson, 1998; Rogers, 2012). However, it is also widely agreed that the use of indiscriminate, unfocussed praise is mostly ineffective and can result in children developing a false sense of self and reducing their resilience (Dweck, 2008; Dawson and Ilsley-Clarke, 2009; Dix, *op. cit.*). To counteract this, there is compelling advice that for praise-giving to be successful, you need to include the following features:

- Be authentic: praise behaviour that you are genuinely glad to see

- Use explicit and specific language to describe exactly what you are praising

- Link praise specifically to your agreed behaviour expectations

- Praise a process (in the present) rather than an outcome that has passed

- Personalise the acknowledgement: name the recipient and include your own feelings about the behaviour

- Ensure that your tone of voice, as well as non-verbal clues such as facial expressions and gestures, are congruent with the praise you are giving

- Differentiate praise so that it is commensurate with the achievement for that child, in that moment

Picture of practice: examples of effective positive praise

Mia (aged 6 years) has some impulsive behaviours and is usually quite fidgety and chatty on the carpet, frequently interrupting her teacher, Sally's input and calling out while Sally or others are speaking. Sally and her TA, Justin, have been working with Mia on impulse-control. This morning Sally is ten minutes into the lesson and notices that Mia has not yet called out, which is a significant improvement for her and Sally is genuinely pleased with this progress. She is not sure how much longer Mia will be able to stay quiet so catches the moment, and during an appropriate point in the lesson, gives her a big smile and a thumbs up and says: 'Mia, I'm so glad you're keeping your voice inside you this morning, that's really helping me teach, and helping everyone else to be able to hear what I'm saying, thank you.'

Jack (aged 11 years) is a quiet member of his class who consistently follows the classroom rules; he is polite and respectful to adults and kind to other children. This afternoon he was particularly helpful to another child who was struggling with a maths problem. His teacher, Carey, wants to give him the acknowledgement he deserves. Knowing that he is easily embarrassed, she decides to have a quiet word with him, rather than make a public announcement. She approaches him discreetly, gently touches him on the shoulder, and says:

'Jack, I've noticed how you helped James with his maths this afternoon and I wanted to let you know that I really appreciate how kind you are to others in this class, thank you. I really love being your teacher.'

A note about negativity bias

Negativity bias is a well-recognised psychological phenomenon. It shows that we react more strongly to unpleasant interactions, and experience the feelings they generate more persistently, than to positive interactions. This means that children feel: 'the sting of a rebuke more powerfully than the joy of praise' (Baumeister *et al.*, 2001). You can balance this positive–negative asymmetry through the care and quality with which you praise children for behaving in positive ways, following the suggestions given earlier, by praising more frequently than giving out consequences, and by being mindful of how you deliver consequences (see the following section).

Consequences

Even the most liberal behaviour management styles usually include the use of consequences when children do not follow established expectations for behaviour. A relationship-based approach assumes that using logical consequences for unhelpful behaviour can enable children to understand the effects of their actions, provide opportunities for them to make reparation, and support them in learning how to behave in more prosocial ways. Ellis and Tod (*op. cit.*) advocate a principled approach to delivering consequences, highlighting the need to preserve a child's relationship with themselves as well as their relationships with others. They refer to Hardin's '5Rs of Logical Consequences' (adapted later) as a useful guide which recommends that consequences be:

> *Related*: Logically connected to the initial behaviour, e.g. when Sara had a tantrum and emptied a shelf of books onto the floor, she had to spend her playtime putting them back and tidying the book corner.

Reasonable: Equal in proportion and intensity to the behaviour, e.g. Tom had five minutes quiet time at the 'time-out' table in the classroom for repeatedly chatting on the carpet, but Karl missed all of lunchtime play to attend a reparation meeting after kicking Rashid.

Respectful: Carried out in a way that preserves the child's self-esteem and well-being, using non-blameful language, e.g. when Blake flicked a rubber across the room, Ms Treadgold told him: 'Blake, we have a rule about taking care of our classroom equipment. I need you to go and pick up the rubber, thank you.'

Reliable: Consistency is key; certainty is more important than severity; empty threats are ineffective and counterproductive. When you state there is to be a consequence, then see it through.

Revealed: Consequences should be clear, with language that is explicit and unambiguous. NB having a displayed list of agreed consequences alongside the behaviour expectations can sometimes be helpful.

(Adapted from Hardin, 2008 cited in Ellis and Tod, 2015: 96)

We would add a sixth 'R' to this list:

Repairable: Designing consequences that aim to repair any harm or damage caused by the behaviour.

Dix (*op. cit*: 118) includes 'repair' as the final step in a five-step plan which he describes as: 'a stripped down set of steps that are focussed on small but certain consequences and a restorative, not punitive, ending: reminder, caution, last chance, time-out and repair'. We discuss this in greater detail in the next chapter, Chapter 6 – 'Repairing Relationships'.

Being reactive – responding to unmet needs

When carefully constructed and practised, explicit behaviour expectations combined with authentic praise and clear consequences can provide a strong and supportive framework to follow when you feel challenged by children's behaviour; sometimes all it takes is a quick reminder of an agreed rule for an unhelpful action to be halted. However, as indicated at the beginning of this section on setting limits, sometimes children's unmet needs override their ability to follow agreed rules. There are several theoretical models describing human needs, probably the most well known being Maslow's Hierarchy (1943) which proposes an order of priorities where physiological needs (food, water, air, shelter) have to be met first, followed by safety, a sense of belonging, and self-esteem needs, if personal potential (or 'self actualisation' as coined by Maslow) is to be achieved. Nelmes (2019: 97) argues that human needs are not hierarchical and depicts them as a wheel with six segments: Social, Physical, Communication, Emotional, Fun, play and hope, and Academic. Whereas Dawson and Ilsley-Clarke (*op. cit.*) refer to three 'human hungers' which, if not met, will result in unhelpful, dysfunctional behaviours: a need to feel alive (stimulated), acknowledged (recognised), and safe (certain). Whatever model of human needs you subscribe to, in order to react well to any spontaneous unhelpful behaviours, and prevent them from escalating, you have to become a skilled interpreter, and be able to quickly recognise the need being presented and how best to respond to it. The way in which you respond to children's behaviour will have a significant effect on the outcome (Davis, 2003).

Bernstein (2013) drawing on the original work of Diana Baumrind (1971) states that when parents feel challenged by their child's behaviour they tend to respond in one of four ways named: authoritarian, permissive-neglectful, permissive-indulgent and authoritative. Gottman and DeClaire's work (1997) reinforces this view with a greater focus on the emotional element to parents' responses. Further research undertaken by Rose *et al.* (2015) recognised the same four responses being played out in schools by adults reacting to children's challenging behaviour, using Gottman and DeClaire's labels: disapproving, dismissive, laissez-faire and emotion coaching. We also found some links between the practices they identified and the assertions of Nelmes (*op. cit.*) who refers to four modes of teacher interaction: facilitative, authoritative, authoritarian and rejection. For the purposes of this chapter, we have combined the qualities of these identified responses under the following four headings: *control, deflect, indulge, support.* By examining each one you could identify the style of response you most commonly use and consider its effectiveness in your own attempts at transforming challenging behaviour into positive learning behaviour (see Table 5.1).

The control response (described as 'disapproving' by Gottman and DeClaire, *op. cit*: 22) is by its nature judgemental and critical, with the use of reprimands, discipline or punishment indicative of this style. Any negative feelings or opinions you may have about the child's behaviour (or even about the child themselves) is apparent in your language, tone, and expression, indicating your disapproval. If you find yourself shouting at children, or using threats, then you may fall into this camp, but equally you can apply this response in a calm, quiet way without a raised voice or the use of intimidation. Whether being loud or not, you are using an authoritarian manner to try to (re)gain control of the situation. It can look like a strong, commanding response, and if you are trying to create a powerful classroom presence it can appear effective, especially if the challenging behaviour of the child immediately stops. Other adults, including parents, are often reassured by teachers who use this response as it can show authority and decisiveness, and some children like the feeling that you are in control. However, it may be driven by your fear of seeming weak or powerless, and the results are often short-lived, with the risk of potential damage to the child's well-being, and to their relationship with you.

The deflect response (described as 'dismissive' by Gottman and DeClaire, *op. cit*: 22) appears much more caring than the control response. If you are using strategies such as: tactical ignoring, offering an alternative activity, or promising a reward if the child stops the undesired behaviour then you are practising the deflect response. It is often used with very young children to distract them out of tantrums or distress, and some children can easily be re-directed by a shift of focus or the promise of a treat. As with the control response, it can have the advantage of being quick and simple to apply and it can feel quite satisfying when your redirection has the desired effect. However, again it is only a short-term solution and whilst it avoids confrontation, it also avoids the opportunity for any longer-term change in the child's behaviour to occur. It can actually increase the likelihood of them repeating the behaviour or escalating it to even more challenging ones. Moreover, by your not addressing the underlying needs causing the behaviour, the child only learns to avoid, rather than face, their difficulties.

The indulge response (described as '*laissez-faire*' by Gottman and DeClaire, *op. cit*: 22) is characterised by an affectionate, caring and extremely tolerant reaction, with you focussing time and attention on a child whose behaviour is challenging or disruptive, to the point of prioritising their needs over your own or other children's. If you repeatedly stop your lessons to attend to one child, giving them your full attention without addressing that they have disrupted the learning taking place, then you are using the indulge response. You may feel that by responding in this way you are developing a close, empathic relationship with the child, and may experience a strong connection with them. They may also feel a connection and understanding from you which is enough to stop their unhelpful behaviour in that moment. This response is not unusual when you have a child in your class who has suffered harm or abuse and you want to nurture them and not let them experience any harshness from you. However, if this empathic approach is not also accompanied by limits being set, this response can result in the child having a false sense of what is appropriate, being confused, and ultimately not building the resilience they need for their well-being. They are unlikely to change their behaviour patterns in the longer term, in fact they are more likely to repeat them if they are always rewarded by a positive feeling of recognition from you. You are also putting yourself at risk as you may become over involved to such an extent that you identify with the child's needs, even experiencing what they are feeling and making yourself emotionally vulnerable.

The support response (described as 'emotion coaching' by Gottman and DeClaire, *op. cit*: 22) is characterised by a calm, clear and assertive reaction without being authoritarian or indulgent. It is a combination of explicitly acknowledging a child's feelings and directing them to a desired behaviour, opposite to the one they are displaying. A typical statement might be: 'I can see how furious you are, I know you're angry because you've missed your playtime, and I need you to sit down now and take a breath.' The key to this response being successful is that by immediately recognising what the child is feeling, in an empathic way, you are engaging their parasympathetic nervous system and helping their brain to be more receptive (Porges, *op. cit.*). Also, by combining empathy with a clear directional statement, you are reinforcing the desired, prosocial behaviours you want to see, and increasing the

Table 5.1 Summary of the four responses to challenging behaviour.

Response	Characteristics	Learning outcome
Control	Authoritative: use of disapproval, discipline and punishment.	Child learns shame and powerlessness.
Deflect	Avoidance: use of distraction and redirection.	Child learns not to trust their own experience.
Indulge	Accepting all emotional expression and behaviour.	Child learns limitless boundaries.
Support	Acknowledges feelings: provides clear guidance and problem-solving.	Child learns self-regulation and self-efficacy.

likelihood of them occurring. If you are using the support response then you will follow up the incident later with a problem-solving conversation (preferably one to one) when the child is calmer, exploring what they were feeling at the time and the source of their distress, reiterating desired classroom behaviours, and sharing ideas about what they could do differently next time. Evidence shows that when used consistently and persistently it can be extremely effective and result in long-term behavioural transformation (Gottman and DeClaire, *op. cit.*; Gottman *et al.*, 1997; Havighurst *et al.*, 2013; Rose *et al.*, 2015).

Once you are familiar with the four responses to challenging behaviour, you may discover that you have a predominant style, or you may recognise that you use a combination of all four. However, it is our view that the support response, as well as proven to be the most effective over time, is also the most respectful and compassionate way to react to unhelpful behaviour. It can achieve the desired result whilst at the same time preserving the integrity and dignity of both you and the child. We recognise that this response does not always work immediately and takes time, persistence and patience on your part to be successful. It also takes commitment and consistency from most, if not all, of the adults in the child's life at school so a collegiate, whole-school approach works best.

Picture of practice: using the support response

Gemma is a Year 3 teacher in a large primary school with a mixed demographic. Fiona is an experienced teaching assistant who works full time in Gemma's class. Tristan is a seven-year-old boy in the class whose angry outbursts would often disrupt teaching and create an atmosphere of anxiety and fear amongst the other children. He has struggled with behaviour problems throughout his school career and, while he does not have a diagnosis of an attachment disorder, his mum is very open about her difficulties in bonding with him as a baby and describes him as 'uncontrollable' at home. Knowing Tristan's history, both

Gemma and Fiona tried to establish a positive relationship with him from the outset, and the first term went quite well with only a few minor incidents; but soon more challenging behaviour patterns began to emerge. He started having outbursts of frustration, such as tearing up his writing, throwing equipment on the floor, shouting at other children, or running out of the classroom. Typically, when Tristan had an outburst, Fiona would use the deflect response which occasionally worked; but when he couldn't be distracted Gemma would step in and use the control response: usually telling him firmly that his behaviour was unacceptable and imposing one of the class consequences such as losing time from Golden Time or staying in at playtime. Unfortunately, this began to enrage Tristan further, in one instance resulting in him ripping down a whole classroom display from the wall and throwing a chair across the room. This was considered sufficiently dangerous, as well as frightening for the other children, for the head teacher to be called. She sent Tristan home and imposed a one-day exclusion. On his return it was decided that a different approach was needed. So Gemma and Fiona agreed to try using the support response whenever Tristan's behaviour was challenging: validating his feelings and directing him to a desired behaviour, followed up with a problem-solving conversation once he was calmer. They began by watching for early signs of Tristan becoming agitated and when this hap-pened one of them (usually Fiona) would try to intervene quickly, naming his emotions verbally and offering to talk it through with him by saying, 'Tristan I can see you're getting frustrated and upset right now. Let's go and talk about how you're feeling and what might help you.' When the intervention was prompt he would calm down almost immediately and after just a few minutes talking through his frustrations, would get back to his task. When neither Fiona or Gemma spotted the signs early enough to intervene and Tristan had a big outburst, one of them (whoever was situated nearest to him at the time) would approach him calmly and immediately name his feelings in an empathic way:

'Tristan, I can see how frustrated and angry you are, I know you're overwhelmed – it's all feeling too much for you right now …' followed by redirection, using a descriptive 'I' statement: 'and I need you to come and sit down with me'. She would repeat these two statements if necessary, staying close, attentive and empathic. Once Tristan had calmed down completely and was able to think again, Fiona or Gemma would have a problem-solving chat with him, reinforcing that it's ok to have feelings but not ok to hurt others or damage things, and thinking together with him about what might help stop those harmful behaviours. Tristan also learned a few calming down techniques and practised them with Fiona. If a consequence was still required, they would choose one related to the behaviour such as mending a book if he had ripped up his writing, helping clean or tidy the classroom if he had deliberately made a mess, or helping someone with a task if he had been unkind. Using the support response did not eliminate Tristan's problems completely, but there was a significant reduction in the frequency of his outbursts and he was soon able to recognise for himself when his frustra-tions were getting the better of him and would try a calming technique or seek out Fiona or Gemma to help him. His relationship with them grew increasingly strong and he became more trusting of them than he had with any other adults in the school previously.

A note about having an aversive emotional reaction

It may be that you experience an aversive emotional reaction to certain behaviours which can result in you responding in a disproportionate way to the behaviour being displayed. This will be unique to you and could be the result of nonconscious brain patterns set during your own childhood, or as a result of later trauma. This explains why some adults have a bigger reaction to certain behaviours than others; it largely depends on what your triggers are. We all have a 'window of tolerance' (Siegel, 2020: 341) and can find ourselves experiencing strong emotions in reaction to specific triggers. For example, an adult with an unpleasant childhood memory of being ridiculed or belittled within their family, may feel intimidated by a child who seems to be laughing at them when they are reprimanding them, whereas another adult who was brought up in a family where banter was encouraged and making fun of each other was a comfortable part of their family culture, will be unaffected by such behaviour. Some adults feel extremely angry when children lie to them, whilst others do not react adversely to lying but are distraught when a child rips up their writing or drawings in front of them. These emotional triggers happen fast and are accompanied by a feeling of urgency. They can have a strong effect on our responses to children's behaviour, so it can be really helpful to know what your triggers are, and to identify how it makes you feel, so you can learn how to avoid being emotionally hi-jacked and, instead, respond in your most adult, appropriate, and loving way.

3. Learning and development

It is now accepted practice for teachers to explicitly teach learning skills and to intentionally refer to internal learning processes, bringing them to light by referring to the *way* in which children are learning as well as *what* they are learning. As well as explicit teaching, these skills are sometimes identified during or after a lesson. For example, praising a child after a science experiment, Kate's teacher says: 'Kate, well done for using your memory and problem-solving skills to work out how to get the ice to melt using salt.' This use of meta-cognition is a key component of popular teaching theories such as Claxton's (2011) *Building Learning Power* and Dweck's (2017) *Growth Mindset* and its practice is now widespread. However, less well practised is teaching children about the internal processes that underlie behaviour, especially about the connection between emotions and behaviour. There is considerable evidence that by incorporating this meta-emotion philosophy as well as meta-cognition in your teaching you can have a significant impact on children's motivation, self-efficacy and learning behaviour (Goleman, 2006; Gottman *et al.*, 1997; Perry *et al.*, 2019). As with learning skills, social and emotional skills can be explicitly taught and can also be identified during lessons. For example, after a tricky maths lesson Abi's teacher says: 'Abi, you nearly gave up on that last sum and were getting really irritated that you couldn't work out the answer, but you managed to stay calm and didn't let your anger get the better of you, well done.' With that in mind, this section is a brief signposting to ways in which you can boost children's motivation to behave in prosocial ways through explicitly teaching them about feelings and behaviour (emotional literacy).

In the first decade of the twenty-first century, teaching children about feelings was seen as a crucial element in promoting positive learning behaviour in schools, as theories linking emotional literacy with better learning and behaviour were popularised by leading figures such as Mayer and Salovey (1993), Goleman (*op. cit.*) and Weare (2003). Their views were endorsed by government guidance, through initiatives such as Social and Emotional Aspects of Learning (SEAL) (DfES, 2005) and Promoting Alternative Thinking Strategies (PATHS) (Kusche and Greenberg, 1994). These and other whole-school emotional literacy programmes develop children's skills in five main areas: self-awareness, managing feelings, motivation, empathy and social skills. Emotional literacy has been widely examined and evaluated and, despite its critics (Furedi, 2004; Craig, 2007; Ecclestone and Hayes, 2009), there is ample evidence that by explicitly teaching about feelings you can make a positive difference to children's well-being and consequent behaviour, producing aspiring, optimistic and resilient learners (Weare and Gray, 2003; Kelly *et al.*, 2004; Coppock, 2006; Curtis and Norgate, 2007; Banerjee, 2010). In the light of this, we support emotional literacy as a fundamental strand of relationship-based teaching and suggest that resources such as SEAL and PATHS are worth revisiting.

Other well evaluated methods to incorporate teaching about feelings and behaviour include: using circle time (Cefai *et al.*, 2014), circle of friends (James and Leyden, 2010) and peer mentoring (Cowie and Hutson, 2005); practices which can result in improved self-esteem, self-confidence, empathy and friendship skills for the participants (Coppock, *op. cit.*). The deployment of emotional literacy support assistants (ELSAs) has also shown to be effective in supporting children to change established patterns of unhelpful behaviour (Hills, 2016; Kay 2018; Wong *et al.*, 2020).

Whilst there has been little in the way of popular discourse on an affective curriculum in recent times, we believe that the imperative for one has never been greater and are encouraged that, at the time of writing, key aspects of PSHE education have now become compulsory in England, and mandatory programmes of study at Key Stage 1 and 2 on relationships education and health education include mental and emotional well-being. This means you are now required to include lessons that 'enable pupils to be taught about positive emotional and mental well-being' and to know 'the characteristics of . . . mutual respect, truthfulness, trustworthiness, loyalty, kindness, generosity, trust' (DfE, 2019: 20–21). Moreover, the document provides links to excellent resources provided by the PSHE Association to support these lessons, which include many aspects of emotional literacy, such as: understanding the range and scale of different feelings, how to recognise and talk about emotions, and having a varied vocabulary of words to use when talking about our own and others' feelings (PSHE Association, 2019). This gives you, and your school, a mandate to incorporate social and emotional teaching into your everyday practice with readily available materials to support you.

Whilst explicitly teaching children about feelings and behaviour has proven to be a powerful tool in promoting positive learning behaviour, you need the right conditions if it is to be successful (Antidote, 2003; Weare and Gray, 2003). You need a commitment from school staff, especially from the leadership team, that they value social and emotional competencies as highly as other curriculum areas. You need to have a willingness to use non-traditional teaching methods such as circle time and peer mentoring, where processes such as self-awareness and self-confidence are more important than producing visible, displayable outcomes. You need to be comfortable with allowing children to express their thoughts and feelings openly and have the skills to listen to them in a non-judgemental, open-hearted way. And you need honest, open and trusting relationships with colleagues so you can support each other, particularly if you are affected by children's or your own emotional responses to some of the learning experiences that occur. With these conditions in place, and drawing on the resources available, you can confidently teach about feelings and behaviour, and use meta-emotion as an everyday tool, to support an environment where positive learning behaviour can develop and thrive.

Prompts for reflection

■ In the light of the framework described in this chapter, consider each of the three key elements: love and commitment, limit-setting and learning and development. How might you include new practices into your classroom that reflect these elements to promote positive learning behaviour?

■ Consider your current school behaviour policy. How are behaviour expectations communicated in your school and how could this be improved using the framework?

■ In what ways can you extend your use of an emotional vocabulary when communicating with children?

■ What can you do differently to promote greater compassion and kindness in your classroom and throughout your school?

■ Reflect on your use of rewards and consequences and to what extent they motivate children to behave in prosocial ways.

■ How do you most commonly react to behaviour that you find challenging, and how effective is it? Consider how you might use the support response more frequently.

■ Which resources will you draw on to integrate social and emotional learning into your teaching?

Shared language

Positive learning behaviour: Ellis and Tod (2009) coined the term 'learning behaviour' to highlight that behaviour is indivisible from learning, and to describe all types of behaviour which occurs in learning situations, in a school context. We have prefaced it with the word 'positive' to enable you to specify observable behaviour that best facilitates focussed learning.

Prosocial behaviour: This describes behaviour that facilitates socialisation such as friendship skills, cooperation and kindness (Dunfield and Kuhlmeier, 2013). It is the sister to positive learning behaviour, although it may not relate directly to a learning situation and can apply outside of a school context. It is a useful way for you to describe children's behaviour that may not have a direct learning outcome (in the narrow sense of curriculum learning), but nevertheless supports the development of essential qualities and human characteristics.

Challenging behaviour: We use this to describe behaviour that challenges you and necessitates the need for intervention. By using 'challenging' rather than words like 'naughty' or 'disobedient' you avoid labelling children, and take responsibility for your part in the process, recognising that all interactions are relational.

Emotional literacy: This describes the practice of recognising and identifying your own and others' feelings, and using that understanding in a considered and thoughtful way to inform your actions and decisions (Weare and Gray, 2003). Although the term has dropped out of usage in recent times, it is still highly relevant to a school context, and can help you define emotional and social competencies in children and in your teaching.

Chapter summary

In this chapter we have introduced a framework with three key elements, to guide you in how to encourage positive learning behaviour in your school. We have considered how you can demonstrate *love and commitment* to children through affectionate, compassionate and kind practices; we have examined how you can *set behavioural limits* through the use of clear expectations, positive praise and relevant consequences, and have described the four different reactions to challenging behaviour, proposing the support response as the most effective and humane one to use. Finally, we have promoted the explicit teaching about feelings and behaviour to support children's *learning and development* and enable them to understand how to act in more prosocial ways.

Further reading

Dix, P. (2017) *When the Adults Change Everything Changes: Seismic Shifts in School Behaviour.* Carmarthen: Independent Thinking Press.

Paul Dix is a renowned advocate of clear, consistent and compassionate ways of encouraging positive learning behaviour in schools. This book provides a realistic, down-to-earth approach on how adults can help children with behaviour, and includes authentic and lively anecdotes to illustrate this.

Robins, G. (2012) *Praise, Motivation and the Child.* Abingdon: Routledge.

Written by a former deputy headteacher, this highly accessible book draws on a range of theoretical models that underpin the use of extrinsic and intrinsic rewards to motivate children. Reflecting on the purpose and effectiveness of different reward systems, Robins brings theory to life and provides practical examples of how and why they continue to be used so extensively in schools.

Gottman, J. and DeClaire, J. (1997) *The Heart of Parenting: How to Raise an Emotionally Intelligent Child.* London: Bloomsbury Publishing.

If you would like to know more about how we respond to challenging behaviour, this is Gottman's seminal work in which he explains the four different parenting styles he identified in his research, and promotes the use of emotion coaching as the best way to support children's social and emotional development and well-being.

References

Anderson, J. D. (2018) *Posted.* New York: Walden Pond Press.

Antidote (2003) *The Emotional Literacy Handbook: Promoting Whole-School Strategies.* London: David Fulton Publishers.

Banerjee, R. (2010) Social and Emotional Aspects of Learning in Schools: Contributions to Improving Attainment, Behaviour, and Attendance. A Report on Data from the National Strategies Tracker School Project. *British Educational Research Journal*, **40** (4), pp. 718–742.

Baumeister, R. F., Finkenauer, C. and Vohs, K. D. (2001) Bad Is Stronger than Good. *Review of General Psychology*, **5** (4), pp. 323–370.

Baumrind, D. (1971) Current Patterns of Parental Authority. *Developmental Psychology Monographs*, **4** (1, part 2), pp. 1–103.

Bernstein, D. A. (2013) Parenting and Teaching: What's the Connection in Our Classrooms? Part One of Two: How Teaching Styles Can Affect Behavioral and Educational Outcomes in the Classroom. *Psychology Teacher Network.* Available at: www.apa.org/ed/precollege/ptn/2013/09/parenting-teaching [Accessed 21.9.2020].

Cefai, C., Ferrario, E., Cavioni, V., Carter, A. and Grech, T. (2014) Circle Time for Social and Emotional Learning in the Primary School. *Pastoral Care in Education*, **32** (2), pp. 116–130.

Chaplain, R. (2016) *Teaching Without Disruption in the Primary School* (2nd Edn). Abingdon: Routledge.

Claxton, G., Chambers, M., Powell, G. and Lucas, B. (2011) *Building Learning Power.* Available at: www.buildinglearningpower.com [Accessed 14.11.2020].

Coppock, V. (2006) It's Good to Talk! A Multi-Dimensional Qualitative Study of the Effectiveness of Emotional Literacy Work in Schools. *Children and Society*, **21** (6), pp. 405–419.

Cowie, H. and Hutson, N. (2005) Peer Support: A Strategy to Help Bystanders Challenge School Bullying. *Pastoral Care in Education*, **23** (22), pp. 40–44.

Craig, C. (2007) *The Potential Dangers of a Systematic, Explicit Approach to Teaching Social and Emotional Skills (SEAL): An Overview and Summary of the Arguments*. Centre for Confidence and Well-Being. Available at: https://img1.wsimg.com/blobby/go/9c7fd4e5-3c36-4965-b6d8-71c83102ff94/downloads/SEALsummary.pdf?ver=1620125160707 [Accessed 05.9.2021].

Curtis, C. and Norgate, R. (2007) An Evaluation of the Promoting Alternative Thinking Strategies Curriculum at Key Stage 1. *Educational Psychology in Practice*, **23** (1), pp. 33–44.

Davis, H. A. (2003) Conceptualizing the Role and Influence of Student – Teacher Relationships on Children's Social and Cognitive Development. *Educational Psychologist*, **38** (4), pp. 207–234.

Dawson, C. and Ilsley-Clarke, J. (2009) *Growing Up Again: Parenting Ourselves, Parenting Our Children* (2nd Edn). New York: Simon and Schuster.

Department for Education (DfE) (2011) *Getting the Simple Things Right: Charlie Taylor's Behaviour Checklist*. Available at: https://assets.publishing.service.gov.uk/government/uploads/system/uploads/attachment_data/file/571640/Getting_the_simple_things_right_Charlie_Taylor_s_behaviour_checklists.pdf [Accessed 8.11.2020].

Department for Education (DfE) (2016) *Behaviour and Discipline in School: Advice for Headteachers and School Staff*. Available at: https://assets.publishing.service.gov.uk/government/uploads/system/uploads/attachment_data/file/488034/Behaviour_and_Discipline_in_Schools_-_A_guide_for_headteachers_and_School_Staff.pdf [Accessed 8.11.2020].

Department for Education (DfE) (2019) *Relationships Education, Relationships and Sex Education (RSE) and Health Education: Statutory Guidance for Governing Bodies, Proprietors, Head Teachers, Principals, Senior Leadership Teams, Teachers*. Available at: https://assets.publishing.service.gov.uk/government/uploads/system/uploads/attachment_data/file/908013/Relationships_Education__Relationships_and_Sex_Education__RSE__and_Health_Education.pdf [Accessed 20.11.2020].

Department for Education and Skills (DfES) (2005) *Excellence and Enjoyment: Social and Emotional Aspects of Learning (Guidance)*. Nottingham: DfES. Available at: https://webarchive.nationalarchives.gov.uk/20110812101121/http://nsonline.org.uk/node/87009 [Accessed 20.11.2020].

Dix, P. (2017) *When the Adults Change Everything Changes: Seismic Shifts in School Behaviour*. Carmarthen: Independent Thinking Press.

Dunfield, K. A. and Kuhlmeier, V. A. (2013) Classifying Prosocial Behavior: Children's Responses to Instrumental Need, Emotional Distress, and Material Desire. *Child Development*, **84** (5), pp. 1766–1776.

Dweck, C. S. (2008) The Perils and Promises of Praise. *Best of Educational Leadership*, **65** (2), pp. 34–39.

Dweck, C. S. (2017) *Mindset: Changing the Way You Think to Fulfil Your Potential* (Revised Edn). London: Constable and Robinson.

Ecclestone, K. and Hayes, D. (2009) *The Dangerous Rise of Therapeutic Education.* London: Routledge.

Elliott, L. (2019) *What 'In Loco Parentis' Means to You.* Available at: www.lawandparents.co.uk/what-in-loco-parentis-means-you.html [Accessed 22.7.2020].

Ellis, S. and Tod, J. (2009) *Behaviour for Learning: Proactive Approaches to Behaviour Management.* Abingdon: Routledge.

Ellis, S. and Tod, J. (2015) *Promoting Behaviour for Learning in the Classroom: Effective Strategies, Personal Style and Professionalism.* Abingdon: Routledge.

Flook, L., Goldberg, S. B., Pinger, L. and Davidson, R. J. (2015) Promoting Prosocial Behavior and Self-Regulatory Skills in Preschool Children Through a Mindfulness-Based Kindness Curriculum. *Developmental Psychology,* **51** (1), pp. 44–51.

Furedi, F. (2004) *Therapy Culture: Creating Vulnerability in an Uncertain Age.* London: Routledge.

Gilbert, P. (2010) *The Compassionate Mind: A New Approach to Life's Challenges.* Oakland, CA: New Harbinger Publications.

Goetz, J., Dacher, K. and Emiliana S. T. (2010) Compassion: An Evolutionary Analysis and Empirical Review. *Psychological Bulletin,* **136** (3), pp. 351–374.

Goleman, D. (2006) *Emotional Intelligence: Why It Can Matter More Than IQ* (10th Anniversary Edn). London: Bantam.

Gordon, T. (1974) *Teacher Effectiveness Training.* New York: David McKay.

Gottman, J. and DeClaire, J. (1997) *The Heart of Parenting: How to Raise an Emotionally Intelligent Child.* London: Bloomsbury Publishing.

Gottman, J., Katz, L. and Hooven, C. (1997) *Meta-Emotion: How Families Communicate Emotionally.* Mahwah, NJ: Lawrence Erlbaum Associates.

Hardin, C. (2008) *Effective Classroom Management.* Upper Saddle River, NJ: Pearson.

Havighurst, S. S., Wilson, K. R., Harley, A. E., Kehoe, C., Efron, D. and Prior, M. R. (2013) 'Tuning into Kids': Reducing Young Children's Behavior Problems Using an Emotion Coaching Parenting Program. *Journal of Child Psychiatry and Human Development,* **44** (2), pp. 247–264.

Hills, R. (2016) An Evaluation of the Emotional Literacy Support Assistant (ELSA) Project from the Perspectives of Primary School Children. *Educational and Child Psychology,* **33** (4), pp. 50–65.

Hoghughi, M. and Speight, A. N. P. (1998) Good Enough Parenting for all Children: A Strategy for a Healthier Society. *Archives of Disease in Childhood,* **78** (4), pp. 293–296.

Hook, A. and Vass, P. (2012) *Teaching with Influence* (2nd Edn). Abingdon: Routledge.

James, A. and Leyden, G. (2010) Putting the Circle Back into Circle of Friends: A Grounded Theory Study. *Educational and Child Psychology,* **27** (1), pp. 52–63.

Kay, L. (2018) Searching for Dumbledore: A Reflection upon the Outcomes of a Tailored Emotional Literacy Programme on Three Key Stage 2 Children. *Support for Learning,* **33** (2), pp. 122–141.

Kelly, B., Longbottom, J., Potts, F. and Williamson, J. (2004) Applying Emotional Intelligence: Exploring the Promoting Alternative Thinking Strategies Curriculum. *Educational Psychology in Practice,* **20** (3), pp. 221–240.

Kohn, A. (1999) *Punished by Rewards: The Trouble with Gold Stars, Incentive Plans, A's, Praise and Other Bribes.* New York: Houghton Mifflin Harcourt Publishing.

Kusche, Â. C. and Greenberg, M. (1994) *PATHS; Promoting Alternative Thinking Strategies.* South Deereld, MA: Developmental Research Programs Inc.

Layous, K., Nelson, S. K., Oberle, E., Schonert-Reichl, K. A. and Lyubomirsky, S. (2012) Kindness Counts: Prompting Prosocial Behavior in Preadolescents Boosts Peer Acceptance and Well-Being. *PLoS One,* **7** (12), pp. 1–3.

Maines, B. and Robinson, G. (1998) *Punishment: The Milder the Better* (2nd Edn). Bristol: Lucky Duck Books.

Maslow, A. H. (1943) A Theory of Human Motivation. *Psychological Review,* **50** (4), pp. 370–396.

Mayer, J. and Salovey, P. (1993) The Intelligence of Emotional Intelligence. *Intelligence,* **17** (4), pp. 433–442.

Mosley, J. and Sonnet, H. (2005) *Better Behaviour Through Golden Time.* Cambridge: LDA.

Nelmes, P. (2019) *Troubled Hearts, Troubled Minds: Making Sense of the Emotional Dimension of Learning.* Carmarthen: Crown House Publishing.

Paley, V. G. (1999) *The Kindness of Children.* Cambridge, MA: Harvard University Press.

Perry, J., Lundie, D. and Golder, G. (2019) Metacognition in Schools: What Does the Literature Suggest About the Effectiveness of Teaching Metacognition in Schools? *Educational Review,* **71** (4), pp. 483–500.

Perry, P. (2019) *The Book You Wish Your Parents Had Read (and Your Children Will Be Glad That You Did).* London: Penguin.

Phillips, A. and Taylor, B. (2010) *On Kindness.* London: Penguin Books.

Porges, S. W. (2011) *Clinical Insights from the Polyvagal Theory: The Transformative Power of Feeling Safe.* New York: Norton and Co.

Porter, L. (2014) *Behaviour in Schools: Theory and Practice for Teachers* (3rd Edn). Maidenhead: Open University Press.

PSHE Association (2019) *Teacher Guidance: Teaching About Mental Health and Emotional Wellbeing.* Available at: www.pshe-association.org.uk/curriculum-and-resources/resources/guidance-teaching-about-mental-health-and [Accessed 17.9.2020].

Reyes, M. R., Brackett, M. A., Rivers, S. E., White, M. and Salovey, P. (2012) Classroom Emotional Climate, Student Engagement, and Academic Achievement. *Journal of Educational Psychology,* **104** (3), pp. 700–712.

Robins, G. (2012) *Praise, Motivation and the Child.* Abingdon: Routledge.

Rogers, B. (2004) *Behaviour Recovery* (2nd Edn). London: Sage.

Rogers, B. (2007) *Behaviour Management: A Whole-School Approach* (2nd Edn). London: Sage.

Rogers, B. (2012) *You Know the Fair Rule* (3rd Edn). London: Sage.

Rogers, B. (2015) *Classroom Behaviour: A Practical Guide to Effective Teaching, Behaviour Management and Colleague Support* (4th Edn). London: Sage.

Rose, J., Gilbert, L. and Licette, G. (2015) Emotion Coaching: A Universal Strategy for Supporting and Promoting Sustainable Emotional and Behavioural Well-Being. *Educational and Child Psychology,* **32** (1), pp. 31–41.

Siegel, D. (2020) *The Developing Mind: How Relationships and the Brain Interact to Shape Who We Are* (3rd Edn). New York: Guilford Press.

Swinson, J. and Harrop, A. (2012) *Positive Psychology for Teachers*. London: Routledge.

UNICEF (date unknown) *Rights Respecting Schools Award*. Available at: www.unicef.org.uk/rights-respecting-schools/ [Accessed 8.11.2020].

Van der Kolk, B. A. (2014) *The Body Keeps the Score: Brain, Mind, and Body in the Healing of Trauma*. New York: Viking Press.

Wake, A. (2012) *The 'Good Enough' Parent: How to Provide for Your Child's Social and Emotional Development*. Melbourne: Palmer Higgs.

Weare, K. (2003) *Developing the Emotionally Literate School*. London: Paul Chapman.

Weare, K. and Gray, G. (2003) *What Works in Developing Children's Emotional and Social Competence and Wellbeing*? Nottingham: DfES.

Wong, B., Cripps, D., White, H., Young, L., Kovshoff, H., Pinkard, H. and Woodcock, C. (2020) Primary School Children's Perspectives and Experiences of Emotional Literacy Support Assistant (ELSA). *Educational Psychology in Practice*, **36** (3), pp. 313–327.

6 Repairing relationships

Chapter objectives

■ To acknowledge repair as a fundamental aspect of strong and healthy relationships.

■ To understand the neurobiological response to perceived threat, and to have the tools to teach this to children.

■ To recognise self-regulation as fundamental to the process of repair and consider how to co-regulate with those children who need it.

■ To be familiar with restorative practices including peaceful conflict resolution and peer mediation.

■ To present the theory and principles of relational resilience.

The lens of the authors

Throughout our teaching careers we have experienced many disruptions: between adults and children, between children and between adults. We have witnessed and been part of conflicts in educational settings that have not only interrupted learning, or halted it completely, but have also caused connections between people to be broken, sometimes irrevocably. Equally, we have been in situations where the problems were assiduously resolved and the relationship was not only repaired but became even stronger than before as a result of the process of restoration and reconnection. We consider repairing relationships to be part of a wider world view of peace-making, and regard this as a desired common cause. We also hold a feminist perspective which approaches peace-making and conflict resolution as 'essentially different to, and qualitatively better than, mainstream (or male-stream) perspectives' (Sharoni, 2017: 1). We believe that as teachers we have a moral purpose and a responsibility to recognise, model and practise how to repair relationships effectively. We are champions of restorative approaches, including peaceful conflict resolution, to encourage better citizenship and social cohesion, as well as

DOI: 10.4324/9781003120537-6

better educational outcomes. Learning how to repair relationships is for life, not just for school!

Our approach throughout this chapter is underpinned by the following key principles:

> *Disruptions and conflict in relationships is normal:* A school context is no different from our out-of-school lives in that all relationships are fluid and subject to occasional disagreements and clashes. We believe in being open and honest with children about this reality and not being afraid to address it.
>
> *All disrupted relationships in a school context are repairable:* We believe that in school it is always possible to repair disrupted or broken relationships when you use a non-blameful, restorative approach.
>
> *It takes time and commitment to repair relationships:* There is no quick fix to repairing a broken relationship: participants have to feel motivated to let go of being right and be willing to see another's perspective. This means a shift in brain chemistry which can only happen successfully with dedication, patience and persistence.
>
> *When conflict is safely resolved it results in better connectivity:* The experience of resolving conflict peacefully, and repairing disrupted relationships, improves connections between people. Moreover, everyone becomes better problem-solvers and more relationally resilient as a result.

Introduction

As we outlined in Chapter 4, connectivity is at the heart of a relationship-based approach, and the way you connect with children has a profound effect on their cognitive, emotional and social learning and development. Establishing positive connections with all the adults in your school family is equally important and can make a powerful difference to your teaching and the children's learning. However, it is normal and natural for relationships to be interrupted at times and for disconnections to occur. From minor disagreements to major disputes, disrupted social interactions are an inevitable part of a healthy relationship and, although sometimes distressing, these disconnections provide opportunities for greater self-awareness, cognitive growth and social and emotional competencies (Schneider, 2016). As Perry says (2019: 18), 'It is not the rupture that is so important, it is the repair that matters'. In a school context, there is a range of potential disconnections in relationships, some of which you are directly involved in: e.g. a disagreement between you and a child or between you and another adult (a colleague or parent), and others where you are trying to resolve disputes, e.g. between children, between a child and an adult, or sometimes between adults. There are also variations in the intensity of a disruption and the degree to which it has an impact, as well as how quickly you can restore a state of safety, equilibrium, social cohesion and learning back to your classroom. However, whatever the particular circumstances, or the age of the participants, there are common processes at work when it comes to ruptured relationships and we begin by exploring what happens inside your brain and body.

The neurobiology of disconnection

When your relationships are harmonious, and you feel connected to others, your brain and body are in a parasympathetic vagal state, experienced as calm alertness which we discussed in Chapter 4 in relation to being *affecting* as a way of securing connectedness. We also referred to how a perception of threat or danger plunges you into a sympathetic vagal state, and you feel disconnected from others (Porges, 2011). The mental and physical reactions to perceived threat are universal: the oldest and most primitive part of our brain, the reptilian brain, responds by shutting down the frontal cortex where rational thinking presides, our bodies are flooded with the necessary chemicals to activate faster oxygen intake and a higher heart rate, our pupils dilate, and our blood is redirected away from our internal organs in order to support increased muscle activity in our arms and legs (Harris, 2008). Sometimes referred to as emotional hijacking (Goleman, 2006) this results in a fight response (being destructive, aggressive or violent), a flight response (emotional withdrawal, running away or removing yourself), or a freeze response (being unable to think or act). Ekman (2004) suggests that one of the most common triggers for an emotional hijack is being thwarted; when you do not get what you want or need, your brain registers it as a threat and activates a visceral response to remove the obstacle in your way. In a school context, we believe this is the cause of most disruptions to relationships.

Picture of practice: examples of being thwarted

Corey is a particularly skilful football player and was on the team last week when he scored the winning goal in a match against a neighbouring school. He is confident that he will be picked again for the team for the upcoming game this week. However, the teachers have recently decided that, in order to give everyone a chance to play in the school sports teams, there will be a fair rota, with all children having a turn. When his teacher announces this week's team and Corey is not on the list he feels thwarted by her and is overcome with rage. He stands up suddenly, knocking his chair over, sweeps everything on his table onto the floor, and shouts at her loudly and furiously.

Trace and Ryan have been close friends since they began school together in Reception, they are now in Year 3. They always play together at playtime and often go to each other's homes after school. When a new girl, Logan, joins their class from another school, Trace and Ryan are asked by their teacher to welcome her and to help her settle in. This works well until Logan is invited to tea at Trace's house and Ryan is not invited. The next day at school Trace and Logan are sitting together at lunchtime in the dining hall, talking and giggling about something that had happened the evening before, and Ryan feels excluded. In an attempt to win Trace's favour back, Ryan asks Trace to come out and play a ball game with her that they had invented together and which only needs two players. Trace replies that she will come out with her if Logan can play too. Ryan, feeling thwarted by her friend, reacts by running fast from the hall and out to the farthest end of the playground. She hides behind a bench and sobs.

Fred is a creative and energetic teacher in a Year 6 class, and is under a lot of pressure to improve this year's SATs levels in English. Charlie is a capable child in his class who is particularly skilful in writing and could achieve a high level in the upcoming assessment. However, Charlie sometimes seems quite anxious and Fred is pleased that Charlie has recently become more popular in the class, partly as a result of being a good basketball player. Charlie's parents ask to meet with Fred to discuss how to improve Charlie's academic achievements. The meeting does not go well as the parents' focus is particularly on the SATs assessments and, although Fred tries to communicate to them his concerns about Charlie's well-being and that he believes Charlie's popularity and sporting prowess are equally as important as his English assessments, he finds himself unable to bring them round to his way of thinking. The parents then tell Fred that they have hired a private tutor to help Charlie improve his levels in the English assessments. Fred feels thwarted by them, his whole body goes cold and his mind goes blank. Charlie's parents leave the meeting early, having made their point, and Fred sits very still for several minutes feeling powerless and at a loss, convinced that Charlie's parents have no confidence in him as a teacher.

In these scenarios, Corey, Ryan and Fred feel disconnected from others as each perceive them to be obstructing, or getting in the way of their needs and desires. In neurobiological terms, recognising a threat to themselves, their reptilian brains have been activated, their frontal cortex has shut down, and their bodies flooded with adrenaline and cortisol, so Corey fights, Ryan flees and Fred freezes. None of the protagonists could have articulated in the moment exactly what it was they wanted or needed before the feelings of frustration, anger and disempowerment overwhelmed them. Their reactions were immediate because the perception of threat came from a deeper place than each trigger suggested, unique to each individual and influenced by embedded, nonconscious memories. Corey's desire to be in the football team came from a need to feel accepted; Ryan's desire to have Trace back as her best friend came from a fear of abandonment; and Fred's desire to persuade Charlie's parents to agree with him came from a need for approval. The inward feeling of dissonance and disconnection will persist for Corey, Ryan and Fred, and the interruption to their respective relationships may even escalate, unless they are able to self-regulate, or experience co-regulation with a supportive other, and begin the process of repair.

Self-regulation and co-regulation

In infancy, when a child is in distress and is more often than not soothed and restored to a feeling of safety by a loving and attuned caregiver, a neurobiological blueprint (an 'internal working model') becomes established and the child gradually learns to self-soothe, eventually being able to calm themselves without adult support; this is self-regulation. Repetition of this experience throughout childhood enables us to normalise what was previously perceived as frightening and threatening, and paves the way for managing future stress in our lives (Bergin and Bergin, 2009). The positive consequences of self-regulation are that we grow up recognising and understanding our emotional and physical states and are able to make good decisions and judgements, manage strong emotions and have trust in the world. Research shows that in a nurturing learning environment children who can self-regulate are not only able to understand and manage their own emotions, but are also unlikely to be overwhelmed by other people's feelings. Moreover, their teachers perceive self-regulating children to be socially competent, popular and capable learners (Music, 2017).

In 1972 Walter Mischel devised the now famous, *Marshmallow Test* to examine self-regulation in young children. In the test, a marshmallow is placed in front of a child who is told that if they can resist eating it for ten minutes they will receive two marshmallows. This test has been adapted and repeated many times over the years to demonstrate how children manage their feelings and whether they can regulate their desires. The children in Mischel's original experiments were followed up 40 years later in 2012, and a clear correlation emerged showing that those who could self-regulate, and resist eating the marshmallow, were in employment, in stable relationships and had supportive and reliable friendship groups (Music, *op. cit.*). As our ability to self-regulate carries us into adulthood, and children learn to self-regulate from their relationships with the adults around them, it follows that by being skilful at self-regulation yourself you are providing the best conditions for children to be able to regulate themselves. As well as modelling it in your behaviour, there is also evidence that the skills of self-regulation can be taught (Joliffe, 2017). Dr. Dan Siegel, a clinical psychiatrist and well-known educator and author, has developed a range of tools to help us understand and manage our emotions and self-regulate. One is the popular Hand Model of the Brain which children can easily relate to (Siegel, 2020). By using this model you can demonstrate what is happening in your brain when you feel out of control and disconnected from others:

1 Hold your hand in a fist with your thumb tucked inside. Explain that your hand is your whole brain and your thumb represents the oldest, most primitive or 'downstairs' part of it. This is covered up by your fingers that represent your thinking or 'upstairs' brain, which is in charge most of the time.

2 Suddenly open your fingers, to expose your thumb. Explain that you have 'flipped your lid' and your 'downstairs' brain is now in charge which means you can no longer think straight, and are in fight, flight or freeze mode. Note: You could also use images and examples to illustrate what each of these states feel like.

3 Slowly return your fingers back to their original position, covering your thumb. Explain that by calming yourself, or being helped to calm down by someone you trust, you can bring the lid back down to return to a feeling of safety with the 'upstairs', thinking, brain back in control.

You can find a video explanation of this model on Dan Siegel's website, available at: https://drdansiegel.com/hand-model-of-the-brain/

There are also visual models you can use to help children recognise the signs that they are about to 'flip their lid' and which use a scaling system. One of the first ones to become popular in schools was the Emotional Barometer which was provided with the resources for Social and Emotional Aspects of Learning (SEAL) (DfES, 2005). More recently, Olson (2014: 47) suggests a 10-point scale, with 1 being 'relaxed and learning' and 10 being in a state of high arousal, and unable to think straight. There are several ways you can use the scale, but typically, scaling techniques work by asking what number someone thinks they are on, and helping them move to a lower number. Other scaling models include *The Incredible 5-Point Scale* (Buron and Curtis, 2012), a cognitive-behaviour approach originally designed for children with autism but which has proved successful in mainstream classes. It is colour coded and starts at 1 with 'calm and relaxed' with number 5 being: 'I am going to explode!' The materials for this are available at www.5points-cale.com/. A number of primary schools have also recently adopted The Zones of Regulation (Kuypers, 2011) which also uses colours to represent different states. There are four zones: blue for 'moving slowly' e.g. feeling sad, tired, bored; green for 'ready to learn' e.g. feeling calm and alert; yellow for 'loss of some control' e.g. feeling frustrated, worried, excited; and red for 'out of control' e.g. feeling angry or terrified. There is a wide range of resources to support using the zones available at: www.zonesofregulation.com/.

As well as teaching children about how their brains work, and helping them to recognise different states of arousal, it can also be helpful to teach them some calming down strategies.

Self-management techniques for children are designed to be used in the moment, and are a key component of many anger-management resources. Several ideas are available in published books and on websites such as www.elsa-support. co.uk/ and https://copingskillsforkids.com/. Most include focussing on the breath and sensations in the body. Regulating your breath so that it becomes slower and deeper will help reduce your heart rate and there are imaginative ideas that you can teach children such as 'dandelion breathing' or pretending to blow out candles on a birthday cake. Becoming aware of sensations in your body, and gently rubbing your tummy, or massaging your arms and legs as if kneading dough, can redirect blood flow and help restore the body to a state of balance. Other physical activities such as counting aloud (forwards or backwards), singing, stamping or clapping a rhythm can sometimes refocus attention away from distress and into a calmer state. There is also a popular technique called 'tapping' which involves tapping particular places on your body repeatedly; it can trigger the vagus nerve and quickly decrease levels of cortisol (Ortner, 2018). For more sustainable change, Olson (*op. cit*: 158–172) advocates having a regular mindfulness practice in schools and cites several studies to support the view that it can redirect neural pathways in the brain and improve self-regulation. Children's yoga is also a popular way to teach children how to calm themselves, and there is some evidence that it can make a difference to classroom ethos as well as improving children's mental health and well-being (Eggleston, 2015).

Picture of practice – Dante learns how to self-regulate

Dante was in a Year 4 class in a large urban primary school and frequently got into disputes with other boys. He wasn't always the perpetrator, but was very sensitive to signs of criticism from others (or what he perceived to be criticism), and would suddenly retaliate without thinking, which could quickly escalate into a physical fight. Rather than single Dante out, his teacher decided to work with the whole class on self-regulation. He taught them about how the brain works, using Siegel's Hand Model (*op. cit.*) and explored 'flipped lids' further by using large whole-body outlines for children to mark with coloured pens the areas on their bodies where they experience the sensations of feeling out of control. Dante used a red pen (to show feeling hot) to colour in his head and hands, and a blue pen (to show feeling cold) to colour in his tummy. His teacher discussed this with him, trying to help him talk about what triggered those feelings and what the experience was like. The teacher then introduced an image of an emotional barometer, similar to the Zones of Regulation (Kuypers, *op. cit.*), and helped the children to identify how feelings in our bodies can change from being calm and relaxed (at the bottom of the barometer), to being unable to think straight (the top of the barometer). He also used a guided visualisation, music and images to help the children reflect on what helped them feel calm and relaxed. When the class shared their ideas, many of them mentioned being with their pets, and Dante said, 'when I smooth my dog, Tyrone, I feel happy'. His teacher then suggested that the children bring in photos or small items that could remind them of what helped them to feel calm. Dante brought in a photo of Tyrone and his teacher stuck a small piece of fake fur to the back of it which he was allowed to keep in his drawer and go to whenever he felt his mood changing. (He had a small version of the emotional barometer stuck to his desk, to refer to.) Over the weeks that followed, with the help of his teacher, Dante tried to notice when he was starting to feel sensations that signalled he was about to 'flip his lid' and would go to his drawer, look at his photo of Tyrone and stroke the fake fur. Remarkably, this strategy worked really well for him, and by the end of that term his record of fighting was significantly reduced.

In addition to teaching children about self-regulation, and giving them opportunities to practise it, there will be times when they are unable to regulate themselves, particularly for those with a disordered attachment style or who have experienced early trauma, and you need to co-regulate with them to bring them back to a state of calm. Co-regulation is part of the support response mentioned in Chapter 5 and includes identifying what the child is feeling in that moment to engage their parasympathetic nervous system and reverse the flow of adrenaline and cortisol which has flooded their bodies (Porges, *op. cit.*). You have to be focussed, attentive and above all, empathic when you are co-regulating with a child, and you need to communicate that you know what they are going through, and that together you will soon feel calm and safe again. This requires you to be in a calm, self-regulated state yourself which also means recognising and managing your own levels of stress.

It is now well recognised that teaching can be an extremely stressful profession (NFER, 2019; Nuffield Foundation, 2020) and there are a number of techniques you can practise outside of school that can help with stress management. From yoga, meditation and mindfulness training, to creative writing, dancing and art therapy, there are ways to look after your mind and body, and maintain a lifestyle that supports self-regulation. However, we agree with Cowley (2019: 12) that well-being isn't just 'massage, meditation and mindfulness', and we acknowledge that your capacity to manage stress is affected by school-based factors beyond your control such as government, or local, policy demands, a challenging workload, the leadership style in your school, and the availability of support. Additionally, at the time of writing, this has also been exacerbated by having to cope with the pressures of the Covid-19 pandemic: keeping safe at school, and the challenges of home learning. We believe teacher well-being is a shared responsibility and whilst we urge school leaders to prioritise teacher well-being, and we continue to campaign for change on the wider issues that increase teachers' stress levels, we also encourage you to recognise where you want to place your attention and energy and what you can do to be in the best possible mental and physical state to help co-regulate the children in your care.

Restorative practices

So far we have addressed states of arousal which lead to ruptures in relationships, and how to regulate and de-escalate the feelings associated with them. Now we will consider how disputes can be discussed, conflicts peacefully resolved and relationships repaired without the need for blame or punishment. First though, it is important to note that it can take time to fully readjust after an emotional hijack, and any attempt to facilitate a process of restoration that requires calm, rational thinking will only be successful once all parties have had the opportunity to regulate their feelings first. This sometimes only takes a few minutes but can take several hours, even days. There is also a 'post-crisis depressive phase' which can occur after an event, when each participant can experience a feeling of exhaustion, hopelessness and remorse; in this phase, they appear calm but are still unable to think straight (Wolf and Knight, 2014). Giving sufficient time for everyone (including yourself) to be ready to engage in a restorative practice is crucial to the success of the process.

There are a number of approaches in schools that offer a non-blameful process to repair ruptured relationships which we identify here under the broad banner of 'restorative practices'. Often recognised in relation to restorative justice, which was designed for the criminal and youth justice services; these practices may include: a one-to-one restorative enquiry, or conversation, a third-party mediation, a restorative conference, or a family group conference (Hopkins, 2004). Many schools have introduced one or more restorative practices as part of their behaviour policy as an alternative to a punitive response to harmful behaviours, and have discovered new insights about themselves and the children as well as improved relationships and friendships throughout the school. There is considerable evidence that a restorative approach improves social and emotional competencies for all: children have an improved sense of self-efficacy, and there is greater respect for each other throughout the school community (Sellman *et al.*, 2013). All restorative practices use the following key questions: What happened? Who has been affected? How can we put it right? And, what have we learnt so we can make different choices next time? The phrasing of each question is carefully designed to be non-blameful, encourage the expression of feelings, imply a shared responsibility, offer possibilities for joint problem-solving, and provide learning opportunities for the future. A restorative conversation, or a conference which involves everyone who has been affected, uses the key questions to enable all parties to feel heard and tell their side of the story. Often when two parties are in dispute it is hard to establish an obvious perpetrator and victim, but when it is clear that harm has been done to one person by another, this process empowers the person who has been harmed, and helps the harmer to make reparation. There is also considerable evidence that providing a positive alternative to punishment is far more likely to repair the ruptured relationship than disciplining the harmer (Hopkins, *op. cit.*). Children who have been hurt and have engaged in a successful restorative process state that it has made a significant difference to be listened to by the harmer, to share the extent and impact of the harm done, to give them a chance to put it right, and to have reassurance that it won't happen again. Whilst the harmers explain that hearing the harm they have caused has helped them understand themselves better, and motivated them to make amends and move forward, knowing that there will be no continued resentment or likelihood of revenge (Hopkins, *op. cit.*). Guidance on how to use restorative practices in your school is available from a number of organisations including Restorative Justice 4 Schools (available at: www.restorativejustice4schools.co.uk/) and Transforming Conflict (available at: https://transformingconflict.org/).

Peaceful conflict resolution

In a dispute where there is no clear perpetrator or victim, a third-party mediation is the most appropriate way to restore the relationship. Peaceful Conflict Resolution is a mediation process devised as part of the HighScope approach to early childhood education (HighScope Educational Research Foundation, 2021). It provides a blueprint for the restorative practice of a third-party mediation. It has been adopted in schools throughout the world and continues to afford adults a non-blameful process for helping to repair disruptions in relationships between children. There are six steps which although they are more directive than the key questions in a restorative conversation, echo the same principles:

1 Approach calmly and with an open mind: 'We seem to have a problem here.'

2 Acknowledge children's feelings: 'I can see how upset you both are.'

3 Gather information from both sides: 'What happened?'

4 Restate the problem: 'So the problem is . . .'

5 Ask for ideas for solutions and choose one together: 'What can we do to solve the problem?'

6 Be prepared to give follow-up support: 'Well done, you found a solution. I'll be here for you if you need any more help.'

(Evans, 2016)

As well as the steps facilitating the process of repair, each step enables children to develop skills in self-regulation, perspective-taking, active listening, self-expression and problem-solving, each of which can be broken down and taught independently of the process.

Using the conflict resolution steps, and restorative practices in general, may initially seem to take up a lot of time. However, there is ample evidence that once it is embedded in your practice the time taken to resolve issues becomes significantly reduced. Moreover, children learn competencies which last a lifetime (Cremin, 2007).

Trying to go it alone

Any conflict in school, however minor or insignificant the disagreement may seem, is worth repairing, and children and adults alike are often motivated to attempt to 'make it up' themselves, without help. However, trying to resolve a rift on your own can be extremely challenging and often results in another emotional hijack if one or other parties still harbours strong feelings, or an unmet need persists. So we would always recommend that, where possible, a neutral third party is asked to facilitate a restorative process.

Peer mediation

All children, and especially very young children, have the capacity for compassion, empathy and problem-solving and from our experience we know that, with support, they can become capable facilitators of peaceful conflict resolution themselves. Peer mediation is a recognised programme for teaching children how to practise this, and many schools in the UK have adopted it. The principles of peer mediation are the same as for all restorative approaches in school; the difference here is that the third-party facilitators are children, trained in how to guide other children who are in conflict to find a win-win solution, through active listening and helping them to communicate with each other. Participation is voluntary and the mediators cannot impose their will to find a solution onto the conflicted parties, and as Cohen (2005) states, this is one of the strengths of mediation as the parties in conflict receive focussed assistance whilst still having control of the outcome.

> ### Picture of practice: peer mediation in a primary school
>
> The staff at an urban primary school were concerned about the amount of time being taken up in the Key Stage 2 playground to resolve disputes between children. The lunchtime staff were exasperated by the number of low-level arguments they were getting involved in, and the teachers were frustrated by how many of these conflicts spilled over into the classroom. It was decided that they would introduce peer mediation in an attempt to address the issue, and Surinda became the designated teacher to coordinate it. She devised a training programme of ten one-hour sessions and was released from her classroom to run them. Surinda decided to offer the training to children in Year 5 only, considering them to have a sufficient level of competence and experience, and out of a desire to give them some status and responsibility. Although the whole of Year 5 (58 children) were keen to start the programme, they were given the chance to opt out after each of the ten sessions, and by the end of the training 20 committed peer mediators remained. Once the training was completed, these mediators then chose a name for themselves (they decided on 'Playground Buddies'), how to be visible (they chose to have yellow baseball caps), and gave an assembly, using role-play, to inform the whole school community (including lunchtime staff and parents) how peer mediation would work. During the first week, there was so much interest in the Playground Buddies that the

mediators were overwhelmed with the number of disputes they had to deal with, some of which were bogus but children were curious to experience the process. By the end of the month this had calmed down to two or three disputes a day (and only genuine ones), and by the end of the term this had reduced to approximately one a day. Surinda met with them regularly to discuss how it was going, and it was out of these meetings that it was suggested there be a dedicated space in the school for mediation, partly because the mediators were finding it hard to mediate in a busy playground, but also because this space could then be used as a calm area for children needing it during lesson times. The mediators recognised that they were being used less and less in the playground and wanted to keep up their profile so arranged to do another assembly on peace-making at the beginning of the following term and devised a simpler version of peer mediation for the children in Key Stage 1. Towards the end of Term 6, they also contributed to the training programme to train the next cohort of Year 5s to be peer mediators, and to hand over their responsibilities to the next group of Playground Buddies.

This example is supported by evidence from a report by Cremin (2002) on the findings from 15 primary schools that practise peer mediation. The report notes that a peer mediation programme is more likely to be successful and sustainable when all staff understand and value the humanist principles behind it, and are willing to promote it and give it a high profile in their school. The research also emphasises that, for children to become successful mediators, they need a high-quality training which goes beyond just teaching them how to facilitate the basic conflict resolution steps and also includes activities that deepen their understanding and knowledge of the nature of conflict and its consequences. It also helps develop and extend their social and communication skills (Cremin, *ibid.*). If you are considering implementing peer mediation in your school there are a number of published training programmes and resources available for you to refer to (see Further Reading at the end of this chapter for two examples). From our experience, it is worth exploring the available materials and creating a bespoke course that takes account of the particular ethos of your school community, and the prior knowledge and experience of your children. On a practical note, peer mediation clearly requires commitment in terms of time, resources and staffing. However, data collected in 2014 from a sample of primary schools who practise it, reported staff experiencing a positive impact on their schools overall, with mediators feeling they had improved academically as well as having increased confidence (Healthy Minds London, 2015). Moreover, Chittooran and Hoenig (2010) show that, when successfully implemented, as well as reducing the number of incidents of conflict and the need for adult intervention, peer mediation can significantly improve the climate of a school, increase a feeling of safety, and strengthen the whole learning community.

Relational resilience

Research tells us that one of the consequences of experiencing restoration after disruption is that it can help build resilience (Olson, *op. cit.*). This capacity is often referred to in relation to children's mental health and well-being and definitions of resilience continue to evolve as new research and theories emerge. Rutter (1979: 3) first identified a resilient person as someone who 'overcomes misfortune, survives stress, and rises above disadvantages', while Yeager and Dweck (2012), in considering the benefits of developing resilience in learning situations, cite resilient children as those who are able to seek new strategies, exert greater effort, or use problem-solving skills to overcome difficulties. More recent research suggests that being resilient is not just the ability to recover from adversity but to respond to challenges in a way that prevents harm to ourselves or others and results in positive personal growth (Ungar *et al.*, 2019; Siegel, *op. cit.*). All of which resonates with our experience of the outcomes of successful restorative practices.

Although the concept of resilience is now fairly commonplace in schools, the theory of relational resilience is relatively recent and rarely mentioned in educational contexts. We will address it here as it is particularly pertinent to repairing relationships and broadens the more familiar view of resilience. The relational resilience concept proposes that 'resilience resides not in the individual but in the capacity for connection' (Jordan, 2013: 73) and focuses on how the bonds between people are developed and strengthened. As with the research on individual resilience, it also suggests that disruptions in relationships, when addressed and repaired empathically, provide unique opportunities for growth. However, rather than just focussing on personal growth, relational resilience highlights how the process of repair supports *inter*personal growth and facilitates better connections between people. When relational resilience has been purposefully applied it has proven to be particularly powerful when used between adults in mentor–student relationships in higher education (Jordan, 2004, 2013) and is worthy of consideration in terms of how you might approach any disrupted relationships you have with other adults in school. Table 6.1 illustrates different responses to supporting someone through a crisis or conflict by comparing the perspective of individual resilience with that of relational resilience. In the table, the left-hand column identifies the features associated with supporting resilience in an individual and the attitude, or thinking behind each attribute (in italics), while the right-hand column does the same for promoting relational resilience. It demonstrates how there is an inequity of power when there is a focus on individual resilience, whereas relational resilience emphasises a shared experience and the potential for growth on both sides.

Although originally designed with adults in mind, we believe this model can be successfully applied to primary-aged children and used as a guide in how you approach reconnection and repair. Much of the rhetoric on how to build resilience in children is based on individual, or 'within-child', resilience as well as a

Table 6.1 Reframing resilience through a relational lens.

Individual resilience	Relational resilience
Control dynamics	Supported vulnerability
You can get through this by managing your feelings and behaviour better, and I can show you how	*We are in this together and can help each other*
One-directional support	Mutual empathy
I am here to help you	*I understand what you're going through and have felt it too*
Self-esteem	Relational confidence
You will feel better about yourself after this	*We trust each other and can get through this together*
Power dynamics	Mutual growth and constructive conflict
I can help because you are vulnerable right now and I am stronger than you	*We can both learn through this experience even if we disagree*
Self-awareness	Relational awareness
You will know more about yourself through this experience	*We will know each other even better through this experience and have a closer connection*

Source: Adapted from Jordan (2004: 32).

popular notion that when you are resilient, you are tough and unbreakable whatever life throws at you (Neenan, 2018). However, by reframing resilience through a relationship-based lens, you can examine the different messages you are communicating when there is conflict, and observe how a relational resilience perspective could transform your approach. In practice, when a child in your class is involved in a conflict, either with yourself, another adult or with another child, it is likely that once you have ensured everyone's safety, your reaction, understandably, mirrors the attributes associated with individual resilience as shown in the left-hand column: being supportive, encouraging and directive. However, although your actions may be driven by a desire to help, and your motivation is to repair and restore the relationship without causing harm, you are also maintaining the *status quo* in terms of power and control, and reducing the potential for a more equitable relationship. We suggest you consider moving towards a relational approach to resilience, allowing yourself to express your own vulnerabilities and to be alongside children in their difficulties (within safe boundaries), as shown in the right-hand column of the table. This means using language that encourages mutuality and a shared experience. Although this may feel as though you are relinquishing your role as 'more knowledgeable other' and the power that comes with it, the evidence is that the relational resilience approach not only increases children's capacity to come back from feeling disconnected more easily and help them develop greater empathy for others, but will also improve your own capacity for resilience (Olson, *op. cit.*).

Prompts for reflection

■ To what extent do you notice disconnected or disrupted relationships in school? How might you increase your awareness of it?

■ How do you react to conflict? How does it make you feel? How do you communicate that?

■ How might your knowledge of the way the brain and body react to perceived threat and danger impact on how you respond to conflict?

■ Which aspects of self-regulation might you incorporate into your teaching? How does it apply to you, and how do you manage your stress levels?

■ Consider how using restorative practices, such as the peaceful conflict resolution steps might increase your confidence at addressing disrupted relationships and conflict.

■ What could be the benefits of introducing peer mediation into your school?

■ What is your response to the principles of relational resilience? How might you put it into practice?

Shared language

Self-regulation: This is about recognising and managing your emotional state and being able to self-soothe or calm down when you need to without harming yourself or others. It is established in infancy as a result of being soothed by attuned, empathic carers and persists into adulthood.

Restorative practices: This refers to a collection of non-blameful approaches that are used in schools to repair ruptured relationships. Based on key questions that enable shared responsibility, empowerment and reparation (if appropriate), restorative practices can range from one-to-one conversations to large group 'conferences'.

Peaceful conflict resolution: This describes the non-blameful, six-step approach devised by Evans (*op. cit.*) designed to be used by a trained facilitator to restore rifts in relationships between children. It employs the use of emotional literacy and problem-solving skills to restore connections.

Peer mediation: A third-party mediation process applied by children for children. Following a series of training sessions in the appropriate skills, peer mediators volunteer to help resolve conflicts in school, usually during playtimes.

Relational resilience: A paradigm for resilience that focuses on the capacity for connection and how bonds can be strengthened between people. A relational resilience lens centres on shared vulnerabilities and openness, providing opportunities for interpersonal development and growth.

Chapter summary

In this chapter we have used neurobiology as a starting point to consider what happens in our brains and bodies when we are thwarted, and how this disables our ability to connect with others. We address the need for self-regulation, or co-regulation with a trusted other, to restore us to a place of safety and equilibrium and discuss how this can be taught. We then consider restorative practices, including the conflict resolution steps and peer mediation, to support non-blameful relationship repair. Finally we suggest relational resilience as a potential lens to promote a mutually shared approach to repairing ruptures in relationships.

Further reading

Brummer, J. (2020) *Building a Trauma-Informed Restorative School*. London: Jessica Kingsley.

This compelling book combines restorative approaches and trauma-informed practice with the first part providing up-to-date theory on both. The second part presents practical examples of how schools can use strategies such as circle time, respect agreements and restorative dialogues to help all children to understand and repair relationships.

Thorsborne, M. and Blood, P. (2013) *Implementing Restorative Practices in Schools: A Practical Guide to Transforming School Communities*. London: Jessica Kingsley.

In this book the authors demonstrate how adopting restorative practices in school can transform children's behaviour and improve teaching and learning. They argue that a relational school culture needs to underpin restorative practices, and provides realistic and pragmatic guidance on how to achieve this.

Peer Mediation (Practical Guides): Stacey, H. and Robinson, P. (1997) *Let's Mediate*. London: Sage Publications.

This comprehensive guide for teachers provides detailed steps on how to introduce, teach, support and maintain peer mediation processes for children in primary schools. Reprinted several times due to its popularity, it is now available as an e-book and includes permission to copy activity sheets for use when training children to become peer mediators.

Cohen, R. (2005) *Students Resolving Conflicts: Peer Mediation in Schools* (2nd Edn). Culver City, CA: Goodyear Books.

Written by Richard Cohen, the co-founder of School Mediation Associates, this book explains, step by step, how to set up peer mediation in schools. Although this is an American publication and designed for high school students, it is easily adaptable and contains useful sample mediation session transcripts and 12 conflict resolution lessons with permission to copy them.

References

Bergin, C. and Bergin, D. (2009) Attachment in the Classroom. *Educational Psychology Review*, **21** (2), pp. 141–170.

Buron, K. and Curtis, M. (2012) *The Incredible 5-Point Scale: The Significantly Improved and Expanded Second Edition: Assisting Students in Understanding Social Interactions and Controlling Their Emotional Responses* (2nd Edn). Shawnee Mission, KS: AAPC Publishing.

Chittooran, M. and Hoenig, G. (2010) *Peer Mediation: A Guide for Educators*. National Association of School Psychologists. Available at: www.nasponline.org›assets›documents › Handouts › nasp_peermediation [Accessed 4.3.2021].

Cohen, R. (2005) *Students Resolving Conflicts: Peer Mediation in Schools* (2nd Edn). Culver City, CA: Goodyear Books.

Cowley, A. (2019) *The Wellbeing Toolkit: Sustaining, Supporting and Enabling School Staff*. London: Bloomsbury Publishing.

Cremin, H. (2002) Pupils Resolving Disputes: Successful Peer Mediation Schemes Share Their Secrets. *Support for Learning*, **17** (3), pp. 138–143.

Cremin, H. (2007) *Peer Mediation: Citizenship and Social Inclusion Revisited*. Maidenhead: Open University Press.

Department for Education and Skills (DfES) (2005) *Excellence and Enjoyment: Social and Emotional Aspects of Learning (Guidance)*. Nottingham: DfES. Available at: https://webarchive.nationalarchives.gov.uk/20110812101121/http://nsonline.org.uk/node/87009 [Accessed 18.2.2021].

Eggleston, B. (2015) The Benefits of Yoga for Children in Schools. *International Journal of Health, Wellness and Society*, **5** (3), pp. 1–7.

Ekman, P. (2004) The Universality of Emotion. In D. Goleman (Ed) *Destructive Emotions and How We Can Overcome Them*. London: Bloomsbury Publishing.

Evans, B. (2016) *You Can't Come to My Birthday Party* (2nd Edn). Ypsilanti, MI: HighScope Press, HighScope Educational Research Foundation.

Goleman, D. (2006) *Emotional Intelligence: Why It Can Matter More Than IQ* (10th Anniversary Edn). London: Bantam.

Harris, R. (2008) *The Happiness Trap: Stop Struggling, Start Living*. London: Constable and Robinson Ltd.

Healthy Minds London (2015) *Peer Mediation Makes a Positive Difference to Thousands of London's Young People*. Conference Presentation, The Mayor's Education Conference. Available at: www.healthymindslondon.co.uk [Accessed 17.2.2021].

HighScope Educational Research Foundation (2021) *Our Approach*. Available at: https://highscope.org/our-practice/our-approach/ [Accessed 24.2.2021].

Hopkins, B. (2004) *Just Schools: A Whole School Approach to Restorative Justice*. London: Jessica Kingsley.

Joliffe, W. (2017) Effective Learning. In W. Joliffe and D. Waugh (Eds) *NQT: The Beginning Teacher's Guide to Outstanding Practice*. London: Sage.

Jordan, J. (2004) Relational Resilience. In J. Jordan, M. Walker and L. Hartling (Eds) *The Complexity of Connection: Writings from the Stone Center's Jean Baker Miller Training Institute*. New York: Guilford Press.

Jordan, J. (2013) Relational Resilience in Girls. In S. Goldstein and R. B. Brooks (Eds) *Handbook of Resilience in Children* (2nd Edn). Boston: Springer.

Kuypers, L. (2011) *The Zones of Regulation: A Curriculum Designed to Foster Self-Regulation and Emotional Control*. San Jose, CA: Social Thinking Press.

Music, G. (2017) *Nurturing Natures: Attachment and Children's Emotional, Sociocultural and Brain Development* (2nd Edn). Abingdon: Routledge.

National Foundation for Educational Research (NFER) (2019) *NFER Comment on the Teacher Wellbeing Index*. Available at: www.nfer.ac.uk/news-events/press-releases/nfer-comment-on-the-2019-teacher-wellbeing-index/ [Accessed 19.2.2021].

Neenan, M. (2018) *Developing Resilience: A Cognitive-Behavioural Approach* (2nd Edn). Abingdon: Routledge.

Nuffield Foundation (2020) *More Teachers Reporting Mental Health Problems Than Ever*. Available at: www.nuffieldfoundation.org/news/more-teachers-reporting-mental-health-problems-than-ever [Accessed 19.2.2021].

Olson, K. (2014) *The Invisible Classroom: Relationships, Neuroscience and Mindfulness in School*. New York: Norton and Company Inc.

Ortner, N. (2018) *The Tapping Solution for Parents, Children and Teenagers: How to Let Go of Excessive Stress, Anxiety and Worry and Raise Happy, Healthy, Resilient Families*. CA: Hay House.

Perry, P. (2019) *The Book You Wish Your Parents Had Read (and Your Children Will Be Glad That You Did)*. London: Penguin.

Porges, S. W. (2011) *The Polyvagal Theory: Neurophysiological Foundations of Emotions, Attachment, Communication and Self-Regulation*. New York: Norton and Co.

Rutter, M. (1979) Protective Factors in Children's Responses to Stress and Disadvantage. *Annals of the Academy of Medicine*, **8** (3), pp. 324–338.

Schneider, B. (2016) *Childhood Friendships and Peer Relations: Friends and Enemies* (2nd Edn). Abingdon: Routledge.

Sellman, E., McCluskey, G. and Cremin, H. (Eds) (2013) *Restorative Approaches to Conflict in Schools: Interdisciplinary Perspectives on Whole School Approaches to Managing Relationships*. Abingdon: Routledge.

Siegel, D. J. (2020) *The Developing Mind: How Relationships and the Brain Interact to Shape Who We Are* (3rd Edn). New York: Guilford Press.

Sharoni, S. (2017) Conflict Resolution: Feminist Perspectives. *International Studies*, 30.11.2017. Available at: https://doi.org/10.1093/acrefore/9780190846626.013.130 [Accessed 8.2.2021].

Ungar, M., Connelly, G., Liebenberg, L. and Theron, L. (2019) How Schools Enhance the Development of Young People's Resilience. *Social Indicators Research*, **145** (2), pp. 615–627.

Wolf, K. and Knight, M. (2014) *The Assault Cycle and Verbal Diffusion Handout*. Online Webinar. Available at: www.ala.org/pla/sites/ala.org.pla/files/content/onlinelearning/webinars/Assault_Cycle_Rev.pdf [Accessed 22.2.2021].

Yeager, D. and Dweck, C. (2012) Mindsets That Promote Resilience: When Students Believe That Personal Characteristics Can Be Developed. *Educational Psychologist*, **47** (4), pp. 302–314.

7 The changing nature of relationships

The lens of the authors

As mature adults we have experienced a great deal of change both in our personal and professional relationships and have developed a view of change as a positive and transformational process. As educators we have witnessed, and been party to, some enormous upheaval in children's lives and have been impressed by the way they have navigated this and been inspired by the competent and loving way in which adults have provided a safe pathway to continuity and stability. We believe that any type of change in a school context, be it an everyday transition in the classroom or the 'big move' to secondary school, can have a profound effect on children's relationships with adults and each other. Equally, supportive loving relationships within school can have a powerful and positive effect on how children experience change, and help them learn to embrace it. We claim that harnessing the emotional impact of change in relationships, combined with respect for the ever-changing cycles of the natural world, can offer a positive and purposeful meaning to this inevitable, and sometimes seemingly unmanageable, part of school life.

DOI: 10.4324/9781003120537-7

Our approach throughout this chapter is underpinned by the following key principles:

Change is inevitable but not always predictable: Accepting the inevitability of change in our lives can be liberating, and when you enable children to notice and respond to change with trust, empathy, respect and love, they become better equipped to experience sudden or unpredictable changes when they occur.

Change generates a range of emotions and behaviours: Acknowledging the emotional impact of changing relationships is crucial to understanding and supporting the process children go through in school. Recognising and responding lovingly to any expression of emotion, whilst at the same time encouraging prosocial behaviour, is both desirable and achievable during these times.

Expected transitions are worthy of positive, compassionate attention: There are a number of predictable transitions within a school day, a year and throughout the overall time a child spends at a school. Each transition can affect children's relationships and offer invaluable opportunities for learning and building relational resilience. Teachers have a responsibility to pay attention to even the smallest change in a child's life, and when it is a predictable one, prepare for it with love and compassion.

Changes in relationships deserve honesty: A school context is no different from our out-of-school lives in that all relationships are fluid and subject to discontinuity, whether it be a temporary break or a permanent loss. We believe in being open and honest with children about this reality and not being afraid to address it.

Change can make us stronger: The benefits of going through a life-changing event with loving, compassionate support is incalculable. It can reverse a negative experience of separation, provide a feeling of competence, confidence and empowerment, enhance resilience and help establish a blueprint for welcoming future life changes.

Introduction

The natural world is in a constant state of movement and change: day into night, the cycles of sun and moon, ever-changing weather, the turn of the seasons. Our lives are also in a continuous state of flux, affected by the natural rhythms of passing time, of birth, growth, ageing and death. So too are our relationships with others, as connections begin, develop, flourish, fade, revive or end. However, we often resist, or try to ignore, the inevitability of change, possibly driven by fear of an unknown future or unresolved, sometimes painful, experiences of loss. In a relationship-based approach we give value to all types of change, recognise its impact, and support the process so that fear and loss are balanced with feelings of comfort, safety and joyful anticipation.

Change, transfer or transition?

In this chapter we use the word *change* in its broadest sense, referring to the extensive range of life changes that affect our relationships. This includes changes in health, family circumstances and important life events, such as the birth of a new sibling or the death of beloved granddad. We also recognise that relationships are affected by everyday changes in school life and we use the word *transition* to refer to the many times throughout a school day, term and year when children move from one activity to another, one location to another, and experience any number of different adults and children to connect and reconnect with. Unquestionably though, one of the biggest changes in children's lives is moving schools and we use the word *transfer* to refer to the times when children leave one educational setting to attend a different one, typically from an early years setting to a Reception class, Year 6 to Year 7, or when relocating to a different school for other reasons.

Theoretical perspectives

Many of the theories related to change acknowledge the psychological impact it has on individuals or groups of people, even when the focus is not specifically on the relationships between them. Kurt Lewin is recognised as one of the original pioneers of change theory and his model consists of three stages: *unfreezing*, which involves becoming ready for change and unlocking the motivation to move away from the current status; *moving*, which is the actual state of transition when the change is happening; and *freezing*, when the changed state is being established (Burnes, 2019). Subsequent theorists also replicate the three stages, although with varying emphases. William Bridges, well known for creating the *Bridges Transition Model*, refers to: *endings, a neutral zone*, and *new beginnings*. In this model the experience of loss is acknowledged in the first stage, confusion and distress in the neutral stage, and new energy and fresh identity in the final stage (Bridges and Bridges, 2017). These models and others like them are frequently used by leaders and managers to guide them when implementing a process of change in their organisations. They can also be used to help explain what the experience of change feels like in any circumstance. In a school context, the same three-stage principles apply, whether it be on a macro scale such as the systemic restructuring when becoming an academy, or the micro scale of a child moving from their group table to the carpet for a plenary. Although the speed and impact may differ, the process is always the same: moving away, moving through and moving on. From a relationship perspective this translates as: disconnecting, being unconnected, and (re)connecting and, as we have described in Chapters 4 and 6, this process has a significant emotional element.

The emotional impact of change

Michael Fullan, Director of New Pedagogies for Deep Learning, has written and spoken extensively on organisational change in education, particularly in terms of school improvement. Although he predominantly addresses the managerial aspects of change, and is mainly addressing school leaders, we have found that significant aspects of his work resonate with our knowledge of the emotional impact of change and the importance of relational support during times of adjustment. He recognises that change can arouse powerful emotions and identifies a six-stage cycle suggesting that moving through change in school provokes: loss, doubt, discomfort, discovery, understanding and integration, and these apply equally to children and adults (Fullan, 2008). We are also reminded of the emotional 'change curve' defined by Elisabeth Kubler-Ross in her seminal work *On Death and Dying* (1969) where she describes the five stages of grief. Although originally designed to help explain the grieving process, it is now widely agreed that the identified emotions of denial, anger, bargaining, depression and acceptance, can apply to any process of change (Kubler-Ross and Kessler, 2005). These models give a flavour of the emotions that the experience of change can generate and can help prepare you for some of the feelings you are likely to encounter in school. However, from our experiences with children going through changes we know that their emotions rarely follow a pattern that neatly fits a theoretical pathway. Moreover, we would also add to these lists, feelings of excitement, anticipation, joy and hopefulness! We also recognise that sometimes children appear to show no emotions and can be indifferent to even a big change in their life. We would advise you to be particularly aware of those individuals as, paradoxically, they may need more time and attention than others to thrive during a change. Your role is to be open and accepting of all, and any, emotions expressed by children during times of change, and to be their safe haven, offering understanding and empathic support.

Although most of this chapter addresses children's experience of change and offers some suggestions on how you might offer them appropriate emotional support, we begin with an example from adults in a school facing change in their professional lives.

> **Picture of practice: using a life map activity to identify times of change in our lives**
>
> A small rural primary school was about to become part of a multi-academy trust and the close-knit staff team, many of whom had worked at the school for several years, were feeling a mixture of excitement and anxiety about the forthcoming changes. To help explore, and share how they were feeling with each other, they used one of their staff meetings to do a life map activity which led to some honest and heartfelt conversations. Each member of the team drew a personal 'map' of their life on large paper, beginning

with their birth, identifying all the times they had encountered a major change in their life such as moving house, changing schools, getting a new job. They had free reign to design and illustrate their maps and, although it was not intended to demonstrate their artistic skill, they all enjoyed being absorbed in a creative activity together. Some used a linear design with a road or river representing their life, others used a tree or an island. To illustrate the major changes, they used a range of words, images, colours and shapes. As the activity was voluntary, the choice of change events was personal to each individual, and whilst some felt comfortable to include their divorce or the death of a loved one on their map, others preferred to keep some of their more distressing memories private. Once their maps were completed, they shared them with a partner, briefly talking through the changes they had chosen and highlighting the most memorable ones. They focussed on identifying the feelings they had at the time, and who, or what, helped them through the process. These thoughts were then shared with the whole team. The resulting list of emotions included: afraid, worried, angry, nervous, confused, excited, surprised, pleased, glad and relieved. They recognised that some of these emotions were relevant to the imminent change they were now facing, and that they resonated with their current feelings. The recollections of what, or who, helped them through the change ranged from practical suggestions, such as maintaining a daily routine, to emotional support, such as being able to cry on a friend's shoulder. From these lists, everyone was supported in acknowledging the emotional impact they were experiencing and identifying ways in which they could seek support and help each other through the weeks ahead.

In this example, recalling past experiences helped to inform a current situation, and it is often useful to draw on your own understanding of change when supporting children through theirs. It also helps to know something of children's own experience of past changes in their lives, and to use that knowledge to inform how you relate to them.

One emotional aspect of change that is well understood is separation anxiety. It is used to describe the emotional outbursts which infants and toddlers express when their main attachment figure(s) leave them in the care of someone else. Typified by crying, wailing, screaming, reaching out, or clinging, it can be very distressing and concerning to be part of, either as the leaving adult or the receiving one, let alone what the child themselves may be experiencing. However, this obvious suffering is considered to be not only a normal part of healthy development but also a clear sign of a baby's strong attachment to their main caregiver (O'Connor, 2018). Experts believe that the anxiety is based on the infant's fear of abandonment and subsequent loss of safety, as well as a lack of trust in strangers. This usually begins to occur around 6–8 months old, when babies' brains have developed a nonconscious understanding of their dependency, combined with an already existing instinctive reaction to perceived threat or danger (Gerhardt, 2004).

Although children are believed to grow out of separation anxiety, with leading authorities on child development claiming it will end when a child is between one to three years old, the nonconscious emotional memories it establishes can have a powerful impact on future experiences of separation and loss (Read, 2014). Moreover, as young children's responses to separation, and being reunited, with their main caregiver, are used as an indicator of their attachment style, it has considerable significance in terms of how they will respond to changes in their relationships throughout their lives. There is a good deal of advice for parents and early years educators on how to help children when they are experiencing separation anxiety, including the use of transitional objects, having a ritual leave-taking, talking about feelings, etc. (Dunlop and Fabian, 2007). Although this guidance is designed to help very young children, much of it is relevant to any age or stage of development, including adults. So in the rest of this chapter we consider how the recommendations for managing separations can be applied to enable change to be experienced positively for your whole school family, at any time while they are with you.

Everyday transitions

In the course of an ordinary school day there can be innumerable transitions. Children physically move between home, playground, corridor, classroom, school hall and sometimes a small group room or designated learning area, and cognitively they have to adjust to a variety of learning activities and tasks. From a relationship perspective, they experience different combinations of children and adults throughout a single day, individually and in small and large groups, some familiar, some unknown to them. For every transition, everyone involved or affected by it experiences an internal adjustment and a re-configuration of brain circuitry (Music, 2017).

In Chapter 4, we suggest that if relationships between people were visible we would see a complex web of connecting threads in the room. Imagine now if each transition in your classroom was also made visible by a light being switched on and off: the effect of lighting up all the threads would be almost strobe-like at certain points in the day! When you recognise the ramifications of this, it is inspiring to know just how relationally resilient children seem to be in the face of such continuous adjustments, and how apparently willing they are to repeatedly move between relationships throughout any given day. However for some children, particularly those with attachment disorders or who have experienced early trauma, the smallest transition can be a source of immense turmoil. As O'Connor (2018) reminds us, these individuals not only struggle to leave their main carer in the morning, and yet resist reuniting with them at home time, but can also experience a feeling of threat or danger every time they are expected to relate to a different person throughout their school day. In Chapter 4 we also consider the neurobiology of disconnection in relationships and describe the powerful effect of an emotional hijack when this happens, and how disturbing it can be. It follows, therefore, that if everyday transitions are a common source for such disruptions it is worth addressing how to minimise their effect and find ways to transform them into positive experiences. Although this apparently may only seem necessary for those children who are very vocal and physical about showing you their reactions to transitions, you cannot assume that they are the only ones in your class experiencing discontinuity and disconnection and, as we will demonstrate, what works for those with the greatest need improves life for everyone.

Picture of practice: Shelley notices all the transitions in her day

Shelley is a competent, confident and well-loved eight-year-old who also happens to be visually impaired. Although it is necessary to mention her impairment for the purposes of this illustration, she does not identify herself by this disability, nor is she defined by it by her family, friends, or teachers. However, she does rely on sensory information other than sight to distinguish who is with her, and to recognise the connection between them. Every time Shelley has to adjust to a different person in school she takes slightly longer than others to (re)settle into the relationship, even if it is someone she is already familiar with. Shelley wanted to make these transitions quicker and easier for herself so she asked her support worker, Pascal, to write down her words each time she had to adjust to a different person during the course of an ordinary day. These are the words recorded from her arrival at school in the morning until playtime:

> Mum said bye and left me in my usual spot on the playground. I waited on my own for a while but Janey and Lee have come up and want to play with me.
>
> Janey and Lee took me into the cloakroom and then walked down the corridor with me to our classroom, now other children are around me – I'm sitting on the carpet, I think it's Billie and Shania sitting next to me.
>
> I wait for Ms Taylor to take the register but it's a different voice, he says he's Mr Richards and Ms Taylor is coming later, he doesn't say when.
>
> It's after register Mr Richards tells us what's going to happen this morning and then to get ready for assembly, I always go behind Hodan and in front of Roisin who puts her hands on my shoulders as we go down the corridor.
>
> In the hall there's a lot of different people I don't know but I'm ok with Hodan and Roisin next to me. The person taking assembly is Ms Lambert I think, she didn't say her name but she used to be my teacher last year, is it her?
>
> It's after assembly, I hold hands with Roisin and we go back to our classroom. She sits next to me on the carpet. Mr Richards tells us what to do and I go to my group table for writing. I'm sitting next to Blake today, I know it's him because of his voice, and he talks a lot. You're on the other side, Pascal, helping me write my characters for my story.
>
> In the middle of creative writing, someone comes in, I work out it's Ms Taylor and she's talking to Mr Richards. Ms Taylor is our teacher again but I don't hear Mr Richards going out. Is he still here? Ms Taylor says thank you for being good for Mr Richards.

> *When it's nearly playtime, Ms Taylor asks us to come back to the carpet and talk about the characters in our stories. Ms Taylor chooses two people to read theirs out. She chooses Troy and Devon. I know it's them because she says their names.*
>
> *We get ready for playtime. Roisin and Janey want to play with me.*

In this example, Shelley adjusts to nine transitions and 14 different people in less than two hours. Pascal's record of the whole day showed that this number had risen to over 20 transitions and Shelley had connected with as many as 30 different people by home time. Although Shelley's visual impairment was the impetus for recording her experiences, her teacher was stunned to discover the volume of transitions every child in her class goes through on a daily basis, and it made her reflect on her expectation that they engage fully with each person they encounter, every time. This revelation prompted her to look more closely at the processes happening each time a transition occurred and the impact it had on the children's relationships with her and each other. When she opened the topic up for discussion, the children suggested a number of modifications to the way transitions happened in their class which were then tested and further adjusted. The subsequent alterations made a significant difference to everyone, including Shelley. Below are a few examples from their experiences as well as some additional suggestions drawn from the literature on transitions in school.

Say your name

In order to help Shelley connect more easily with whoever was speaking, rather than have to work it out for herself, the class adopted a pattern of saying their name first before saying anything else. This quickly developed into a habit in all their interactions whether Shelley was there or not. Saying their name first applied whether it was a direct question: 'Roisin here, Shelley do you want to play with me?', part of teacher information: 'Ms Taylor here, everyone it's time to come to the carpet, thank you', or during lively discussion: 'Hodan here, Janey, I think the character in your story could be more colourful'. 'Janey here, Hodan, I don't agree with you!' Although it seemed a bit laboured at first, and visitors to the class were intrigued, it soon became a familiar way of speaking and the rest of the school were encouraged to adopt it too. It was significant that, as well as saying their own name, Shelley's class also chose to name whom they were speaking to. Hearing your own name said aloud, whether it is you or another person saying it, is shown to activate a unique neural pathway in your brain related to self-perception and self-representation (Carmody and Lewis, 2006). Consequently, saying children's names frequently, particularly before and after a transition, helps you maintain continuous connections with them by reinforcing each child's sense of self.

Moreover, saying your own name aloud, and encouraging children to say theirs, is self-affirming and is shown to have a positive and calming effect on the brain (Cascio *et al.*, 2016) which is noticeably beneficial when navigating any transition. Although there are numerous guides available, from how to learn and remember names easily to games you can play to help children learn each other's names, many of these are practised at the beginning of a school year and then discontinued as everyone becomes familiar with each other. However, research from a range of disciplines has proven that when your own name is spoken aloud frequently and over time, you feel continuously acknowledged and included (Bernardin and Russell, 2013; Sternheimer, 2016). Furthermore, studies show that when children hear their name spoken regularly by their teacher they feel valued by them, more interested in learning, more comfortable to ask for help, and believe that their teacher cares about them (Cooper *et al.*, 2017). Crowe (2012) also discovered that when children habitually refer to each other by name, they develop greater empathy towards each other, value differences more, and have a better understanding of the importance of friendship. The reference to frequency is crucial here: only when naming is used in nearly every interaction, as in Shelley's class, will it support continuity in relationships during transitions.

Say what has happened, what is happening, and what is about to happen

Shelley's teacher was struck by how often a timetabled transition, particularly a change of staff, went unacknowledged. Shelley's record demonstrated that she was often momentarily confused during these times and it also helped to explain why several other children became distracted, and less connected to others, in the hiatus between activities. Research shows that when we are in a learning situation, our executive functioning, or brain management system, depends heavily on what is known as 'working memory' to carry out even simple tasks (Gathercole and Alloway, 2008). However, this function is located in the prefrontal cortex which, as we have described in previous chapters, is an area of the brain that can quickly become hijacked by our emotions when we experience a perceived threat, resulting in feelings of being overwhelmed and unable to relate to others (Goleman, 2006). Any disruption to a state of 'flow' (Csikszentmihalyi, 2002) when our working memory is in full swing can create the same destabilising effect and generate feelings of confusion, resentment and distress. This is particularly noticeable in younger children when they are so immersed in an activity that any suggestion of moving to a different task results in an emotional outburst. There are tried and tested methods for strengthening, and stabilising, our working memory which can help prevent an emotional hijack during a transition. One of which, as Shelley's teacher discovered, is what Rogers and McPherson (2008: 24) describe as 'transition clarity'. This includes breaking down information into bite-size chunks, using clear, straightforward language, and minimising background noise when giving your message. There are three elements to a transition communication which are essential to help children feel safer. They need to know: what has happened, what is happening and what is about to happen. More importantly they need to know who will be there so that there is a continuity between relationships, which means including and naming the people involved in all parts of the transition. In Shelley's class, the adults introduced these three-part transition messages throughout the day, for example saying: 'Ms Taylor here, everyone, I have completed doing the register with you, thank you. Now Pascal is going to take you to the hall for assembly. When you get to the hall Ms Lambert will be there and is going to tell you a story.' As with the introduction of saying their names first, this way of giving information seemed somewhat contrived and effortful at first, but soon became absorbed into the classroom culture and was accepted by everyone. It also made a significant difference to some of the children who had previously felt confused and distracted during transition times.

Visual timetables

An extension of the three-part messages described here is the use of visual timetables which many teachers have adopted in their classrooms to give clarity to transitions, and to improve children's working memories. Although originally designed for children with autistic spectrum disorders (ASD), they have proven to be useful for children of all ages and capabilities and are seen in many primary classrooms (Hanley *et al.*, 2017). Typically, they are displays with a sequence of removable pictures on a timeline, which is referred to at points of transition throughout the day. Teachers use them to include children in noticing what has happened, removing the picture that illustrates it, and identifying what the next activity will be. When you also include the names of those involved in the activity accompanied by a photograph or drawing of them, you can make an important difference to relational continuity. Recent research into the use of visual timetables has revealed that they do indeed ease transitions, resulting in reduced anxiety, confusion and frustration and an increase in positive peer interactions (Rutherford *et al.*, 2020). That said, the children who participated in the study identified the need for teachers to consult with them more fully on how to design and implement the timetables. They wanted to ensure that it was referred to frequently and consistently and preferred to have responsibility for managing it themselves without being reliant on their teacher (*ibid.*).

Children's autonomy

The investigation here highlights another key factor in creating positive transitions, that of giving children greater ownership and choice. This chimes with one of our core values explained in the first chapter of this book: that we see children as capable and competent who have the right to be involved in all decision-making that affects them. Symonds (2015), in equating autonomy with well-being, considers it to be a necessary component of successful transitions. She states that when children are given some choice in decision-making they are more engaged and feel motivated to support the shift or movement expected of them. In a relationship-based approach this means consulting with children about who they are with, as well as how frequently they are expected to connect and reconnect from one person or group of people to another. In many early years settings each child is allocated an identified key person from the outset. This is a named member of staff responsible for all aspects of the child's well-being, development and learning who often becomes a close attachment figure for them (Elfer *et al.*, 2012). In moving through an open, free-flowing environment with a number of adults available to guide and support them, it is not unusual for a child to form an attachment to an adult who is not their allocated key person. With this in mind, staff use careful observations and shared reflections to determine the child's preferences and will reallocate the key person roles accordingly. It is noteworthy that the care taken to elicit the child's view is a serious pursuit and nearly always results in better and closer relationships between children and their key persons (Read, 2014). Although the child-to-adult ratio is higher in the primary phase, it is worth considering how adults are assigned to a class, group or individual in your school, and whether children could have more say in which adults they are learning with, particularly when they experience a frequent change of adult throughout their school day. Children could also be consulted on the frequency of transitions occurring throughout the day as Shelley did and, in particular, notice how often their relationships with you and each other are disrupted. It is worthwhile identifying together the times in a day when you expect children to relate to a person or a group for one activity and then move on to a different person or group for the next activity. We suggest you try to minimise those that cause the biggest interruptions and lengthen the times between transitions in order to facilitate greater social cohesion and to help deepen the connections between everyone.

Sense of belonging

Anthropologists find that tribal groupings provide protective factors from external dangers which, interestingly, is also cited as the rationale for teachers giving prominence to a sense of belonging during transitional periods in school (Anna Freud National Centre for Children and Families, 2018). In Chapter 3 we consider the notion of a 'tribal classroom' as developed by Cozolino (2013) which offers the familial comfort of a safe, loving and supportive school family and also enables children's neural networks that are essential for learning to flourish. We suggest that everyday transitions run more smoothly when children feel they belong to your 'tribe'; so recognising and maintaining the group connectedness as described in Chapters 3 and 4 has an important role to play here. Attending to a sense of belonging throughout your school day means providing a recognisable, cohesive narrative that offers continuity for everyone in your class. This narrative ranges from the imagery that makes your class identifiable to the regular timetabled activities that everyone joins in with. However, as we have already mentioned, these, and the other elements commonly found in classrooms that are designed to give a sense of belonging and familiarity, are only truly successful when children experience ownership of them. One way of achieving this is to co-create the story of your classroom tribe with the children, providing a literal class narrative. This could be a physical book or a display which provides a tangible way for everyone to recognise themselves as a member of your class. It could include a pictorial representation of each child and adult, showing how everyone is connected; words and images showing shared experiences; and descriptions of what makes your class special and unique. Whatever format it takes, the essential features are: that it be the children's own class story, devised by them, that everyone is included and that it is accessible to all. Cozolino (*ibid.*) reminds us that creating a personal narrative facilitates memory storage, emotion regulation and social cohesion. So having a tangible classroom story created by the children will not only provide a group identity but will also help to establish positive neural pathways for each person. Referring to the class story at times of transition, for example expecting any new adult such as a supply teacher to read and acknowledge it, can help children feel more confident and self-assured. It is also important to continually revise and update your class story so that it remains current and relevant, reflecting the changes that happen in children's lives throughout the year.

Held in mind

Transitions that are caused by absence can have a significant impact on some children, and it is not unusual for a child's behaviour to noticeably change when their familiar teacher is absent and a different adult is teaching the class. When a child has formed a relationship with you, they need to know that you 'hold them in mind' when you are away from them (Read, 2014: 72). Finding ways to communicate this to children can significantly help with separation anxiety and improve the transition from one teacher to another. Knowing that you are continuing to think of them is important for children of any age. Therefore, when you, or another familiar adult, knows you are going to be absent for a period of time, it can be helpful to follow these three steps: tell children before you leave that you will be thinking of them while you are away; leave a familiar object or article of clothing, such as a scarf, easily visible and accessible to indicate that you will be coming back; and on your return tell them you had been thinking of them. In this way you can provide reassurance, continuity and safety. It is equally important that when a child is away, and you are thinking of them, that you express this openly and model to the rest of the children that the absent child continues to be a valued member of your class, even when they are not there. You can do this by, for example, making a positive comment about them at registration, making sure their places (peg, drawer, chair) remain unused to show you are anticipating their return, and wondering aloud about them throughout the day. When there is an extended absence, sending messages home and giving children the opportunity to as well, shows that you are thinking of them and they are important to you.

Everyday hellos and goodbyes

When school begins each morning everyone is bringing with them their experiences of the day so far, since they woke up. If it is the first day back after a weekend, or a longer break such as a school holiday, there could be a series of experiences or unresolved feelings and thoughts accompanying each person's arrival. This applies to yourself as well as the children, and it is helpful to have your own ritual for letting go of any 'emotional baggage' and being fully present and ready to receive the children before they enter the classroom. Your role is to provide a warm welcome that acknowledges whatever emotional state children arrive in, to give them opportunities to discharge any unhelpful feelings, and to support them in beginning their new day in the best way for them. We suggest you greet every child with a smile and an acknowledgement, showing that you know them as individuals and care about them. It is also important to provide opportunities for them to 'offload' their feelings. Sometimes this is done through a system such as a *feelings board* where each child places their name or photo beside a picture or illustration of an emotion, including 'don't know', on an easily accessible display board, alternatively a *feelings tree* where each child chooses a coloured egg, with each colour representing a different emotion, to hang on a branch-like structure in a pot. If you use a system like this we advise caution: children need to know this is an optional activity, that all feelings are acceptable and that whatever emotion they choose, or not, they will be taken seriously. It is a vehicle for you to acknowledge that there is always an emotional element to the start of each day and for you, or another adult, to follow up with anyone who has arrived showing that they need help to ease them into their day in a positive way. Having music playing can also encourage the mood of the room, whether it is to calm or stimulate. Overall, taking time every morning to create a safe space, and communicate that everyone is welcome and belongs there, reconnects you with each child and sets the scene for the rest of the day.

Taking time to end each day well is equally important and worth preparing for. Giving children opportunities to share their feelings about their day, and to celebrate what they have enjoyed, is a helpful ritual. Communicating your gratitude and pleasure at having spent the day with them, expressing your anticipation at seeing them again, and letting them know that you will be holding them in mind in the meantime, will also reinforce the connections between you.

Annual transitions

A common feature of most primary classrooms is that regular events in the calendar, whether they are religious festivals such as Christmas, Diwali, Easter or Eid, or more secular traditions such as Father's Day or World Book Day, are occasions for celebration and commemoration. Children experience them repeatedly during their time in school and each event represents an easily identifiable transition point in every school year. These recurring rituals can offer stability and continuity which can be very reassuring for children. You could also use these as opportunities to reflect with your class on previous times and consider what has changed and what is the same. By using already existing transitions to highlight the process of change you can help deepen children's understanding of it. Changes in the natural world, and in particular new seasons, are also often recognised in school with writing, artwork and displays reflecting the time of year. Again, you can use the cyclical nature of the changing seasons to reinforce continuity, and help build children's confidence when faced with a transition. You can also focus on aspects such as the different moods or feelings we have when seasons change, for example when the days are getting longer or shorter, and consider the emotional impact it has on each of us and how it affects our relationships with each other. Connecting with the emotional and relational aspects of predictable, annual transitions and reflecting with children about these characteristics can help develop their knowledge and skills, enabling them to be better equipped when faced with unexpected or unpredictable transitions.

One of the most important and predictable annual transitions in school is moving on to the next class. We believe this deserves particular attention and care so that children experience continuity and safety in their relationships. To maximise this, one of the first things to consider is who the change of adult will be and whether it would be possible for teachers to follow the children, rather than the other way around. Known as 'looping', there are numerous studies to show that this can have significant benefits, particularly for children with attachment disorders who have experienced early trauma (Forsten, 1999; Orvalle, 2004). Hume (2010) argues that relationships between children, teachers and parents are considerably improved when looping happens, with greater respect and confidence evident. Moreover, at the time of writing children have been home learning for long periods due to the pandemic Covid-19 and there is renewed interest in looping as a way of ameliorating their enforced isolation from school and providing reassurance and stability by (re)connecting with the same teacher for a further year. If looping is not appropriate in your school, and the teacher cannot move with the class, then another familiar adult such as the classroom teaching assistant may be able to move with them instead, and this could provide invaluable emotional and relational continuity for children. At the same time, you can help develop children's relationships with their next teacher by setting up opportunities for them to get to know each other during terms five and six, prior to their move. In one school, for example, each teacher covers the planning, preparation and assessment (PPA) time for the class of children they will be teaching the following year, so they are building relationships with them long before they become their everyday teacher.

When it gets closer to the end of the school year, it is invaluable to be able to spend time with the current teacher of the children you will be welcoming into your class in September. This is a time to discuss the children's needs, characteristics, friendships and learning styles and is often more important than the necessary paperwork that comes with transfer. No amount of assessments or data can replace the first-hand knowledge of the person who has developed a relationship with them for the past year. They can share with you individuals' little idiosyncrasies: for example, how to reassure the child who is hyper vigilant, how to praise the child who hates a public acknowledgement, and explain why one child needs to be physically close to you most of the day. Of course, some of the previous teacher's experiences and perspectives will not be yours, and some children will want a fresh start with you; so we suggest that you use this prior knowledge with care and sensitivity as a starting point to building your own unique relationships with the next class of children in your care.

With regards to passing on knowledge about themselves, children can take responsibility for creating their own *transition passports*, similar to the *all about me* booklets which very young children's parents are encouraged to complete prior to their child starting in an early years setting. These passports can include drawings, photos and written information that children are comfortable sharing with their next teacher, such as: their likes and dislikes, who they are friends with, what they do outside of school, and what they enjoy in school. The metaphor of a passport can be extended so that it is described as a document that gives them *permission* to enter their next class, and they have to hand them over to their next teacher for a light-hearted *inspection*.

To support continuity, and to help children feel a sense of belonging as quickly as possible in their next class, it is worth having a specific moving day before the end of the year when children physically move their most recent learning and belongings into their next classroom and stay there for the remainder of the term. This is particularly important for children who have specific equipment or a tailor-made learning station to take with them, although everyone will find having their familiar things around them reassuring. As their next teacher, by continuing their learning in the same books, journals and folders, and through your interest in what they have brought with them, you are giving value to their achievements and respecting what matters to them.

Before moving day, each class can also create a welcome message for the next group of children who will be learning in their classroom. Similar to the class story previously described in this chapter in relation to a sense of belonging, this is typically a display or a class book designed to celebrate and showcase some of the best experiences of being in that class for the past year. Created by the children themselves, it could include particular aspects of being in that year group, or with that teacher, as well as their wishes and hopes for the incomers. As the receiving teacher, giving value and significance to this welcome message when the next cohort of children arrive is another indication that you hold children in mind when they have moved on and your care and attention is continuous.

Life changes

Many of the transitions in school are predictable and, although you cannot guarantee how children will respond to them, you can do some degree of planning to preempt the reactions you are most likely to encounter, and to prepare for the impact on your relationships. When a change occurs in a child's life outside of school, which you had not anticipated or had no prior knowledge of, it can have an unexpected effect on your relationship and deserves attention in order for you to take steps to reconnect with them. Major life changes that can affect children include: birth, illness, accidents, adoption, moving house, leaving home, marriage, divorce and death. Some of these may be anticipated, although often not, and especially not by children. The first knowledge you may have that a child has experienced a major life change is when you notice a change in their behaviour and, although it is common practice to ask parents to inform you of any significant changes that might affect their child in school, it is not always possible or comfortable for them to do so. This is where your ability to be attuned and empathic is vital, as we discussed in Chapter 4, so that you are aware of children's needs and can act appropriately and promptly to support them.

To help alert you to changes in children's lives, you can provide regular opportunities for your class to share their experiences and feelings through activities such as circle time, or in small discussion groups, with prompts that help them reflect on whatever has happened in their life recently, or whatever is important to them. Having a dedicated time, with safe boundaries, and allowing for open-ended talk can sometimes give children the opportunity they need to explore their thinking about, say, a new sibling, or moving house. Sometimes this will be cause for celebration, although you cannot assume that children are completely happy about the change they are experiencing, and in most cases they are likely to be feeling a mixture of emotions, all of which are valid and deserve acknowledgement. Some teachers also offer regular one-to-one times which individual children can sign up for and use to talk about whatever is on their mind, knowing that they will be undisturbed and have your full attention.

Above all, your role at a time of change in a child's life is to help them to: feel safe enough with you to explore their experience; be acknowledged by you for their openness, and sometimes courage; and be reassured by your empathy and compassion. It is also worth noting that absorbing and integrating a life change can sometimes take a long time and children may need to revisit their experience of it several times. Each time it emerges for them, they deserve your time and loving attention.

One of the most challenging changes anyone has to face is the death of a friend or loved one, which we will now consider in the light of a class bereavement. Please be aware that the following example gives an account of a child dying of cancer.

Picture of practice: supporting a class through grief

Chrissie was a newly qualified teacher in a mixed Reception/Year 1 class. The school was part of a fairly close community with most of the families living locally, so many of the children in Chrissie's class already knew each other before getting to know her. Leo had been diagnosed with cancer before he arrived at the school, and because he was well known in the neighbourhood, Chrissie was keen to become as familiar with him and his family as others were. Leo's transition into Reception included a considerable amount of information being passed on to Chrissie about his treatment and medical needs. Chrissie also had several early meetings with Leo's family, especially his mum, to establish how to include Leo as a full member of the class while at the same time keeping him safe, and to agree what knowledge about his condition could be shared with the other children. This relationship became vital for both Leo's family and Chrissie, and helped Chrissie to feel confident that she was doing the best for Leo as well as supporting the whole class through what proved to be quite a challenging year. It was quickly apparent to the other children that Leo had particular needs so Chrissie was as open as possible with them about his illness, answering their questions and helping them to understand what he needed when he was with them, and why he was away from school so much. When he was absent, Chrissie referred to him frequently, reminding children that he still belonged to their class and supporting them in fully including him on the days he was able to attend. When he was in school, Leo's physical appearance was usually altered from the previous time, due to the progression of his disease and his treatment, and he became less able to join in with class activities, but the children all accepted him without exception. Chrissie continued to model compassion and sensitivity whenever they were curious about his illness or long absences. She kept in regular contact with Leo's family, and after several months Leo was too unwell to attend school; so Chrissie told the children that they would no longer be able to see him, but that they could stay connected with him through letters, drawings and other messages, and she continued to talk about him as part of their class. As is normal in any Reception class, Chrissie had already read to the children stories which included death and she acknowledged their everyday comments and questions about it. So by the time Leo was receiving end-of-life care, talking about death was not exceptional. She kept all the children's parents informed and, as it was understood that Leo was dying, she was open with them about her approach. At the point when Leo died, Chrissie was relatively well prepared for telling the children. She did it by gathering them together and explaining gently and honestly, with empathy and authenticity, acknowledging that they might experience different feelings, including sadness. Chrissie offered lots of opportunities for children to share their memories and feelings. They could write and draw messages to Leo's family, if they wanted to, and help to choose flowers for Leo's funeral. She also set up other activities: writing messages about Leo, tying them to helium balloons and letting them go, and putting different coloured beads in a 'rainbow' jar to represent their different feelings, such as blue for sad, red for angry. She continued to enable children to include Leo in everyday chat and tasks for several weeks, and kept Leo's name on his peg and drawer, right through until the end of the school year. Even today Leo is still remembered at the school, and especially by the children and staff who knew him during the brief time he was there. For Chrissie, he will always hold a special place in her heart.

The death of a child is undoubtedly one of the most difficult and distressing events any teacher might have to face. What is so heartening about this account is the openness and honesty which Chrissie demonstrates in her relationships, not only with Leo and his family, but with all the other children in her class, and their parents. She made sure that throughout his time at the school, Leo was included at every opportunity regardless of his long absences; she treated him with the same love and respect as any child in her class, which continued after his death. She did not shy away from talking about illness and death with the children, and by making it an available topic for questions and discussions she enabled them to feel comfortable and safe about being curious. Chrissie also gave ongoing opportunities for the children to share their thoughts and feelings after his death, again providing a respectful, non-judgemental space for them to express what they were experiencing. By being proactive, and preparing for an inevitable ending, she allowed the natural process of grief to happen; Leo was remembered in a loving way and the children who knew him were lovingly nurtured through a life-changing event.

There are a number of books you can use with children to support their understanding of death and bereavement and we have listed two recommendations under further reading at the end of the chapter. The following organisations also offer useful help and advice in the event of the death of a child: Winston's Wish, available at: www.winstonswish.org/; Child Bereavement UK, available at: www.childbereavementuk.org/ and Grief Encounter, available at: www.griefencounter.org.uk/.

Transfer

Undoubtedly transferring from one educational setting to another is one of the biggest life changes children and their parents have to face. As a teacher in a primary school you will be aware of the care and attention given to receiving new children into their Reception class every September as well as the efforts made to ensure that when children leave at the end of Year 6 they experience a successful move to their secondary school. You will also be aware of the occasional arrival or departure of some children part way through a school year and their need for particular support. Whatever the type of transfer, one of the most important aspects of your role is to enable children to thrive during the experience. There are count-less books, articles and websites giving advice on how to make school transfer as smooth and seamless as possible and we do not wish to replicate here the valuable guidance already available to you. However, we will highlight those aspects which we think are particularly salient in a relationship-based approach.

Picture of practice: supporting the transfer to Year 7

Every September in this large primary school the majority of children in Year 6 transfer to a popular local secondary school. However, despite its popularity, the data over a number of years was showing a significant dip in academic progress following the move to Year 7; so the schools decided to work together to come up with creative solutions to try and 'bridge the learning gap'. This involved consultations with staff from both schools, as well as discussions with the children from both year groups, resulting in a transfer project which proved so successful that it has been repeated every year since its incep-tion. Whilst the adults were concerned with the *what* and *how* of learning, the children were significantly interested in *who* they would be learning *with*; so the project focussed as much on staffing and relationships as it did on curriculum content and teaching styles. From early on in term five (just after the Easter break) the teachers from the secondary school with the greatest capacity, typically those who were Year 11 tutors whose stu-dents were mostly now 'off timetable' doing self-study in preparation for GCSEs, began to plan and teach with their Year 6 colleagues in the primary school. They began by lead-ing some of the maths and English teaching, gradually including science, art, PE and music over the course of terms five and six. Although continuing to teach their subject special-ism, the visiting teachers, inspired by their observations in the primary classrooms, soon began adapting their pedagogy to include more holistic and democratic practices typical of the school and quickly became part of the school family, involving themselves in other aspects of school life beyond just coming to teach their subject. In addition, as a result of the relationships they had developed with the Year 6 children, rather than incrementally increasing the amount of subject-based teaching as intended, they chose instead to reor-ganise the proposed timetable for Year 7. They included cross-curricular learning as well as the skills- and group-based activities more suited to their learners transferring from the primary school ethos. When the children were asked their views at the end of the project, they commented on how much they had enjoyed the challenge and excitement of learning new things in the safe, familiar space of their primary school home. They also liked getting to know some of their new teachers before moving on to the secondary school and found having different people to teach them throughout their day was more fun, and less scary, than they thought it would be.

As well as having the desired effect of shrinking the gap in academic pro-gress between Years 6 and 7, this project had a transformational impact on all the teachers, children and parents involved. By moving into the children's learning space prior to their transfer, the secondary teachers developed a better understanding of their learners' considerable competences, as well as greater respect for the pedagogical practices of their primary colleagues, than they would have if they had only met the children at the usual transfer visits previously undertaken in the secondary school at the end of term 6. Moreover, making connections with their prospective students over several weeks prior to their transfer had a discernible effect on their future relationships with them. The children felt reassured and more confident to begin their next school knowing that at least some of the teachers were friendly! From an organisational point of view this project was relatively straightforward for the primary school as the majority of children transfer to the same secondary school. In situations where children transfer to several different schools the logistics may be more complex, but engaging with staff from all of the schools, and encouraging them to form a collaborative partnership with you, is likely to reap benefits for everyone. If the children can experience being taught in their Year 6 home by at least one teacher from their prospective school, and feel a connection with them, it can make a significant difference to all their relationships with the adults in their future school. The headteacher who initiated the transfer project believed that part of its success was the amount of time given to it. By beginning early in term 5, children and teachers had the chance to build their relationships slowly over several weeks, getting to know and trust each other. Also, by seeing each other outside of the classroom, e.g. at the school gate in the morning and in the playground at playtime, there were additional opportunities to make authentic connections that are not always afforded secondary school staff or their prospective Year 7 learners.

Another key aspect to children's relationships when transferring to their next school is peer friendships. Evangelou *et al.* (2008) found that, when asked, the majority of children stated that staying with their friends was the most important factor in choosing a secondary school, and indeed those that were able to maintain their old friendships tended to settle in much more successfully than others. Jindal-Snape and Miller (2010) comment on the state of flux which occurs during this time, and how some children who have known each other for years can become strangers. Galton *et al.* (2003: 77) suggest: 'if teachers and children worked more on what constitutes friendship and what it means, the positive effects of it . . . things would improve, not just socially but academically as well. . . . Raising the profile of friendship would raise achievement.' Your role, therefore, is to reassure children that some friendships will continue, even if they no longer attend the same school, and some will end, even if they go into the same Year 7 together and to help children understand, acknowledge and feel at peace with, the potential changes ahead. One of the most successful ways of helping to prepare children for the different possibilities that can occur in their peer relationships is by exploring it through arts activities of poetry writing, painting, photography, puppetry, drama or dance. McLellan *et al.* (2012) demonstrate that, by offering children a range of creative opportunities to express their thoughts and feelings about their changing friendships, they become more open and resourceful and feel greater confidence at how to navigate those changes. Using group discussions and circle-time activities to consider and act out potential scenarios can also be a powerful way to help children explore their changing relationships with each other. The resource 'Changes for Years 5 and 6' from the *Social and Emotional Aspects of Learning* materials (DfES, 2005) has some particularly useful suggestions. Equally, offering a range of reading materials, fiction and non-fiction, which address the impact on peer relationships during transfer can give children further ideas and reassurance. We offer a small selection in the further reading section at the end of this chapter.

Galton and McLellan's research (2015) showed that, although children were worried about losing old friends, they also felt excited to make new ones and revealed the extent to which children have more and new friendships as an important indicator of a successful transfer. Some secondary schools facilitate this with a range of cooperative and collaborative activities to help children from different primary schools to get to know each other during induction events at their schools, and in some cases set up a 'buddy' system (Newman and Blackburn, 2002). You could also support this by setting up meet and greet opportunities in collaboration with other feeder primary schools during terms five and six, bringing children together who will be transferring to the same secondary school. This could enable them to begin to get to know each other, and focus on friendships, in a familiar environment without the pressure of meeting for the first time in their next school when so much other new information is being presented to them.

Giving children the right to participate

As already mentioned, giving children greater ownership and choice about transitions makes a significant difference to their engagement and experience of it and this is no less important, possibly even more so, when it comes to transferring from one school to another. Giving children a voice at such a significant time in their lives when change can feel imposed and unnecessary can help them make some sense of it, feel more empowered, and identify the aspects they can have some control over. Rudduck and McIntyre (2007) are among several advocates for consulting with children during the transfer from Year 6 to Year 7, highlighting how it supports children's well-being. Using creative activities and opportunities for open discussions, as described in the previous section, can also enable children to express what they would like to happen and how they would like to be supported through transfer. As well their current teachers listening and acting on their suggestions, these messages can be shared with their prospective teachers in their next schools, thus continuing a democratic and inclusive approach. Studies that sought the views of children after they had transferred to secondary school found participants were deeply reflective about their experience, particularly about peer friendships, and were able to offer helpful guidance (Galton *et al.*, 2003; Evangelou, *op.*

cit.). Inviting Year 7 children to come and share their experiences and advice for your Year 6 transferees could be valuable to both sets of children: acknowledging and valuing the Year 7s as well as providing a useful source of support for the Year 6s. You could also connect Year 6 children with a Year 7 counterpart, if they wish to, in a 'buddy' system as an alternative, or in addition to, the one described in the previous section between Year 6s from different schools (Symonds, *op. cit.*). They can choose to be in contact during the summer and re-connect with each other when they arrive in September. Having someone familiar and friendly to refer to when facing a strange, new environment can make a significant difference to children's self-efficacy and well-being.

Revisiting and reconnecting

Returning to the concept of being 'held in mind', an essential component of a successful transfer to their next school is children knowing that you still think of them and care about them. Sending children messages during the summer break, particularly just prior to the first week in their next class or school, can be very reassuring as it reminds them that they are known and understood at a time when they are surrounded by the unfamiliar. Also, making the effort to visit children in their 'new home' shows that you still value them as well as providing a feeling of safety and continuity which, rather than being destabilising, is known to have a calming and supportive effect. We suggest you liaise with colleagues, whether in your own school or a different one, to arrange these visits or to find other ways to continue the invaluable threads of connection between you and your learners which, as we demonstrate in our final chapter, can have a deep, lasting and powerful effect that can endure for a lifetime.

Prompts for reflection

- Consider the three stages identified in change theory. Can you identify when one stage ends and another begins? How can this help inform your practice?

- Draw a life map described in the first picture of practice and focus on one of your own experiences of change. What feelings did you have at the time? Who or what helped you?

- Using your knowledge of separation anxiety and attachment theory, reflect on those children who have particular needs during times of change. How might you support them?

- Consider all the everyday transitions that occur in your classroom, particularly when there is a change of adult. How can you minimise these?

- How can you give children greater autonomy and choice when it comes to daily transitions?

▓ When children move between year groups in your school, in what way do you enable continuity of relationships?

▓ How do you know when children are experiencing a major change in their life? How do you support those who are?

▓ What resources can you access to support children's understanding of grief?

▓ How does your school support children's transfer from early years to the Reception class, from Year 6 to Year 7, and for children moving from one school to another for other reasons? What more could you do to help children thrive through transfer?

Shared language

Change: This is a broad term to describe all types of experiences which involve moving out of, through and into an altered state which has a physical, cognitive and/or emotional impact.

Transition: We refer to transition to describe the everyday changes experienced in school when children move from one activity, space and/or relationship to another.

Transfer: This term is used to refer to the times when children leave one educational setting to attend a different one, typically from an early years setting to a Reception class, Year 6 to Year 7, or when relocating to a different school for other reasons.

Chapter summary

In this chapter we have considered some aspects of change theory and how it relates to a school context, with a particular focus on the emotional impact on children's relationships. We have used our knowledge of child development and successful transitions in early years settings to inform pedagogy for older children. We have explored change from the perspective of small daily transitions in school, larger life events, and transfer from one school to another, offering suggestions on how to provide a sense of safety and continuity for all children.

Further reading

Books on bereavement

Varley, S. (2013) *Badger's Parting Gifts* (35th Anniversary Edn). London: Anderson Press Ltd.

This multi award-winning picture book, suitable for younger children, provides a sensitive narrative about losing a loved one. This edition features a helpful reading guide from Child Bereavement UK that provides tips for reading *Badger's Parting Gifts* with children and helping them understand grief better.

Rosen, M. (2008) *The Sad Book*. London: Walker Books.

Written by the much-loved children's author Michael Rosen following the death of his son, this book offers a moving combination of sincerity and simplicity. It acknowledges that sadness is not always avoidable or reasonable and describes complex feelings in a straightforward and accessible way. With beautiful illustrations by Quentin Blake, it is suitable for children of all ages.

Books for children on transfer

Camden, S. (2018) *Everything All at Once*. London: Macmillan.

This collection of poetry captures the pictures, tastes, smells and feelings encountered during the first week at a secondary school. Finding friends, falling out, worrying, getting lost and recovering are all addressed in a lively, humorous and heart-warming way which will appeal to children in Year 6.

Howard, C. (2018) *Splash: Your Best Friend or Your Biggest Dream?* London: Nosy Crow.

The protagonist in this story is a girl in her last year of primary school with a secret dream. The changes and challenges she encounters, not least the tension between her and her unsupportive 'best friend', offer useful starting points to talk about friendship and self-identity as children face secondary transfer.

Burton, M. (2020) *Go Big: The Secondary School Survival Guide*. London: Hachette Children's Group.

This non-fiction guide is written by the headteacher from the popular television series 'Educating Yorkshire' and offers useful information that is funny and engaging including encouragement and support on how to navigate new friendships and not be afraid of the 'terrifying-looking' older students.

References

Anna Freud National Centre for Children and Families (2018) *Relationships and Belonging*. Available at: www.mentallyhealthyschools.org.uk/risks-and-protective-factors/school-based-risk-factors/relationships-and-belonging/ [Accessed 4.3.2021].

Bernardin, H. J. and Russell, J. E. A. (2013) *Human Resource Management: An Experiential Approach* (6th Edn). New York: McGraw Hill, Irwin.

Bridges, W. and Bridges, S. (2017) *Managing Transitions: Making the Most of Change* (4th Edn). London: Nicholas Brearley Publishing.

Burnes, B. (2019) The Origins of Lewin's Three-Step Model of Change. *The Journal of Applied Behavioral Science*, **56** (1), pp. 32–59. Available at: https://doi.org/10.1177/0021886319892685 [Accessed 13.3.2021].

Carmody, D. P. and Lewis, M. (2006) Brain Activation When Hearing One's Own and Others' Names. *Brain Research*, **1116** (1), pp. 153–158. Available at: www.sciencedirect.com/science/article/abs/pii/S0006899306022682?via%3Dihub [Accessed 7.3.2021].

Cascio, C., O'Donnell, M., Tinney, F., Lieberman, M., Taylor, S., Stretcher, V. and Falk, E. (2016) Self-Affirmation Activates Brain Systems Associated with Self-Related Processing and Reward and Is Reinforced by Future Orientation. *Social Cognitive and Affective Neuroscience*, **11** (4), pp. 621–629. Available at: https://academic.oup.com/scan/article/11/4/621/2375054 [Accessed 7.3.2021].

Cooper, K. M., Hanley, B. and Krieg, A. (2017) What's in a Name? The Importance of Students Perceiving That an Instructor Knows Their Names in a High-Enrolment Biology Classroom. *Life Sciences Education*, **16** (1). Available at: www.ncbi.nlm.nih.gov/pmc/articles/PMC5332051/# [Accessed 7.3.2021].

Cozolino, L. (2013) *The Social Neuroscience of Education: Optimising Attachment and Learning in the Classroom*. New York: W.W. Norton and Company.

Crowe, C. (2012) *How to Bullyproof Your Classroom*. Turners Falls, MA: Northeast Foundation for Children Inc.

Csikszentmihalyi, M. (2002) *Flow: The Classic Work on How to Achieve Happiness*. New York: Harper and Row.

Evangelou, M., Taggart, B., Sylva, K., Melhuish, E., Sammons, P. and Siraj-Blatchford, I. (2008) *Effective Pre-School, Primary and Secondary Education 3–14 Project (EPPSE 3–14) What Makes a Successful Transition from Primary to Secondary School?* London: Institute of Education. Available at: www.ucl.ac.uk/ioe/research/featured-research/eppse-publications [Accessed 3.3.2021].

Department for Education and Skills (DfES) (2005) *Excellence and Enjoyment: Social and Emotional Aspects of Learning. Changes Years 5 and 6*. London: Crown Publications. Available at: https://webarchive.nationalarchives.gov.uk/20110810110916/http://nsonline.org.uk/node/65856 [Accessed 13.3.2021].

Dunlop, A. W. and Fabian, H. (2007) *Informing Transitions in the Early Years: Research, Policy and Practice*. Maidenhead: Open University Press.

Elfer, P., Goldschmeid, E. and Selleck, D. (2012) *Key Persons in the Early Years: Building Relationships for Quality Provision in Early Years Settings and Primary Schools* (2nd Edn). Abingdon: Routledge.

Forsten, C. (1999) *The Looping Evaluation Book*. Peterborough, New Hampshire: Crystal Springs Books.

Fullan, M. (2008) *The Six Secrets of Change: What the Best Leaders Do to Help Their Organizations Survive and Thrive*. San Francisco, CA: Jossey-Bass.

Galton, M., Gray, J. and Ruddock, J. (2003) *Transfer and Transitions in the Middle Years of Schooling (7–14): Continuities and Discontinuities in Learning*. Queen's Printer: National Foundation for Educational Research. Available at: www.

researchgate.net/publication/242587990_Transfer_and_Transitions_in_the_ Middle_Years_of_Schooling_7-14_Continuities_and_Discontinuities_in_Learning [Accessed 15.3.2021].

Galton, M. and McLellan, R. (2015) *The Impact of Primary-Secondary Transition on Students' Wellbeing: Final Report*. Cambridge: Nuffield Foundation. Available at: www.educ.cam.ac.uk/ [Accessed 12.3.2021].

Gathercole, S. and Alloway, T. (2008) *Working Memory and Learning: A Practical Guide for Teachers*. London: Sage.

Gerhardt, S. (2004) *Why Love Matters: How Affection Shapes a Baby's Brain*. Hove: Routledge.

Goleman, D. (2006) *Emotional Intelligence: Why It Can Matter More Than IQ* (10th Anniversary Edn). London: Bantam.

Hanley, M., Khairat, M., Taylor, K., Wilson, R., Cole-Fletcher, R. and Riby, D. M. (2017) Classroom Displays – Attraction or Distraction? Evidence of Impact on Attention and Learning from Children with and Without Autism. *Developmental Psychology*, **53** (7), pp. 1265–1275.

Hume, K. (2010) Academic Looping: Problem or Solution? *Education Canada*, **47** (2), p. 63. Available at: www.edcan.ca/articles/academic-looping-problem-or-solution/ [Accessed 14.3.2021].

Jindal-Snape, D. and Miller, D. (2010) Understanding Transition Through Self-Esteem and Resilience. In D. Jindal-Snape (Ed) *Educational Transitions: Moving Stories from Around the World*. London: Routledge.

Kubler-Ross, E. (1969) *On Death and Dying*. New York: The Macmillan Company.

Kubler-Ross, E. and Kessler, D. (2005) *On Grief and Grieving: Finding the Meaning of Grief Through the Five Stages of Loss*. New York: Scribner.

McLellan, R., Galton, M., Steward, S. and Page, C. (2012) *The Impact of Creative Partnerships on the Wellbeing of Children and Young People*. Newcastle: Creativity, Culture and Education (CCE).

Music, G. (2017) *Nurturing Natures: Attachment and Children's Emotional, Sociocultural and Brain Development* (2nd Edn). Abingdon: Routledge.

Newman, T. and Blackburn, S. (2002) *Transitions in the Lives of Children and Young People: Resilience Factors*. Edinburgh: Scottish Executive Education Department.

O'Connor, A. (2018) *Understanding Transitions: Supporting Change Through Attachment and Resilience* (2nd Edn). Abingdon: Routledge.

Orvalle, R. (2004) Why Isn't Looping a More Common Practice? A Leadership Case Study. *International Journal of Educational Reform*, **13** (2), pp. 136–142.

Read, V. (2014) *Developing Attachment in Early Years Settings: Nurturing Secure Relationships from Birth to Five Years* (2nd Edn). Abingdon: Routledge.

Rogers, B. and McPherson, E. (2008) *Behaviour Management with Young Children*. London: Sage.

Rudduck, J. and McIntyre, D. (2007) *Improving Learning Through Consulting Pupils*. Abingdon: Routledge.

Rutherford, M., Lahood-Kullberg, B., Baxter, J., Johnston, L. and Cebula, K. (2020) Pupils' Views on Visual Timetables and Labels in Mainstream Primary Classrooms. *Good Autism Practice (GAP)*, **21** (2), pp. 11–22.

Sternheimer, K. (2016) *Tips and Tools for the Art of Experiential Group Facilitation* (2nd Edn). Bethany, OK: Wood N. Barnes.

Symonds, J. (2015) *Understanding School Transition: What Happens to Children and How to Help Them*. Abingdon: Routledge.

8 The legacy of love

The lens of the authors

As classroom teachers we found it far too easy to lose sight of the things we were doing well. We tended to dwell on the areas that we wanted to improve, or the criticisms directed rightly, or sometimes wrongly, our way. It is only later in our careers that we have felt more confident to recognise the value of our role, the part we play in delivering social justice, the opportunity to inspire a love of learning and the nurturing of critical, curious and courageous minds. We have therefore spent the latter phases of our careers encouraging teachers to recognise themselves as the impassioned and compassionate leaders they are. Despite our best intentions, however, we know that the greatest accolade comes not from well-meaning consultants, teacher trainers and headteachers, but from the children (and their parents) themselves. It is the heartfelt messages written at the end of term or the pictures brought into school after the weekend that have given us most pleasure and to which we have attributed most value. What a privilege it is that, of all the people in a child's life, they choose to share their feelings and offerings with us. It is the moving and inspirational aspect of our practice that we don't take for granted!

This chapter encourages you to appreciate the things that the children and their parents say about what you do well. We explore ways to use this 'evidence' in your professional development and to consider the nature of your teaching 'legacy', the way you would like to be remembered. Our assertion is that it is the loving, respectful, trustworthy and empathic teachers who will be held in the highest regard. This view is shared by Carl Jung (1954: 144) who suggests 'one looks back with appreciation to the brilliant teachers, but with gratitude to those who touched our human feelings'.

Our approach throughout this chapter is underpinned by the following key principles:

> *Education is concerned with the what if, the what could be and the what should be, rather than with the what has always been:* Teachers have an obligation to reflect on their own practice and the school context and to be open to new ideas, continually adapting their methods and approaches in the light of experience, knowledge and dialogue.
> *We need to look critically at the conditions we are creating for children and childhood:* Children require teachers to widely champion their rights to learn, to participate and to form loving relationships.
> *Teaching is both a privilege and a responsibility:* We need to acknowledge and pay serious attention to the role we play in shaping the children's views about themselves and the world around them.

Introduction

The purpose of this chapter is to both provide a vehicle for reflecting on the understandings you have taken from the book and to 'showcase', through the testimonies of teachers and children themselves, the impact of mutually secure relationships rooted in respect and love. Our aim is to inspire you to share with others what you have found interesting about this book and to encourage you to explore these ideas further, informing new practices and conversations.

Key messages

Best practice in any authentic learning situation would usually demand that at the end of a project or lesson the teacher asks a series of open questions to elicit what the learners have taken away with them. In this way the teacher is in a position to assess how successfully the learning intentions have been met and whether there has been a gap between what the teacher had intended the outcomes to be or any additional and unexpected 'happy accidents' that have actually enhanced the learning experience. We find ourselves in a curious position when, at the end of this 'learning' encounter, we are merely regaling the messages that we *hope* you have heard, whilst also expecting that there will be other flashes of inspiration that we had not anticipated! For our part we have taken the overriding messages of this book to be the following:

- We support an enhanced learning context that emphasises mutually respectful and loving relationships as central to children's emotional, social and cognitive development and which provide safety and continuity.

- We promote the importance of your own character development as ethical and empathic human beings as critical to your pedagogic understanding.

- We recognise the significance of the school as a social and connected space where a common cultural identity is celebrated, resulting in an ethos of intimacy and protection.

- We acknowledge the power of recognising and understanding emotions and using the vocabulary of feelings in all aspects of relationship-based development, including rupture and repair.

- We consider how you can support children to act in more prosocial ways through compassionate, kind and loving practices.

- We promote the need to teach self-regulation or co-regulation with a trusted other in order to support you and the children to safely manage your emotions to ensure harmonious and mutually supportive relationships.

- We explore the emotional impact of inevitable breaks and endings in relationships and suggest ways in which you can support the children to manage, and where possible anticipate, these changes whilst ensuring that their trust and emotional well-being remain intact.

- We promote a positive and powerful view of children that acknowledges the importance of their forming their own views, having their ideas heard and where their active participation is valued as a significant part of society's democratic processes.

Next steps

We wonder how these messages have resonated with you and in what ways this book has broadened and challenged your thinking and assumptions? When reflecting on these questions we would remind you of the importance of reflexivity, introduced in Chapter 2, as a force to enable change. As described by Etherington (2004: 23), being reflexive allows us to understand how our 'personal views and beliefs . . . guide our choices between paradigms and methods', and as we have already suggested, being aware of this can open up the way we respond to new perspectives. In many ways this book is testament to the process of reflexivity itself. In Chapter 1 we began by sharing our own particular life stories and, through the feature of the 'authors lens', have further revealed how our own thinking has been stimulated by our experiences, interpretations and innovations. Etherington (*ibid*: 23) also understands the influence of personal accounts and considers that as a reader you might 'be changed and find new meaning in your own life as you resonate with participants' stories of lived experience'. Etherington (*ibid*: 29) further recognises the importance of initiating dialogue with others in order that your own views might be 'extended, challenged and validated'. In the same way that we have advocated the importance of teachers and children co-constructing understanding and shared meaning, we recognise too the power of reflecting critically with others who may offer alternative analysis and opinion. We therefore suggest that your first step in moving your thinking forward could be to ask yourself: *who will I share my thoughts about this book with*? We recommend that you start by choosing someone with whom you have a relationship that is characterised by mutual respect and safety. This will be particularly pertinent when you are thinking about any of the issues raised in the book to do with personal character development. Sensitive ethical issues may be raised for example, when you start to question and check the values or beliefs that you have held unknowingly, or without questioning, since childhood. As Etherington (*ibid*: 23) explains, 'by allowing ourselves to be known and seen by others we open up the possibility of learning more about ourselves in greater depth'. In this way the discussions you initiate with others may support you to generate further action points by asking yourself: *what aspects of 'self' do I need to acknowledge, change and develop?*

How confident you feel in sharing more widely with your colleagues any of the other theoretical and practical issues that have been raised here will perhaps go a long way in determining the nature of the school culture. Does your school promote, for example, a professional community as recommended by the Teaching Schools Council (2016: 10) 'where approaches are changed if existing ones do not work, where teachers are able to take thoughtful risks and learn from the outcomes, and where teachers and leaders consistently look outside their school to find evidence and best practice to learn from'? Pollard and Tann (1993: 288) argue that teachers have both a 'right' and a 'responsibility' to consider and question the approaches and strategies adopted by the school and warn against practices that are 'static', 'routinized' and 'locked into taken for granted conventions'. Blatchford (2014: 18) suggests that the most 'successful schools and their leaders are *restless* (original emphasis) . . . continually looking for ways to change and improve . . . where the teachers are proud to teach with "open doors" . . . and build in rich opportunities for staff to conducting meaningful action research'. We love this description of a school that champions 'challenging conversations' and where talking about the uncomfortable is commonplace. We also welcome and share the positive view of evidence-based reviews of classroom practice, knowing what a difference it can make to children's experiences. However, if your school context does not mirror the description offered by Blatchford, you may feel that your ability to suggest or initiate any changes is hampered by 'your degree of status, power and authority'

(Pollard and Tann, *op. cit*: 294). In that case undertaking classroom based research, either as a part of an academic qualification or as an authentic means to develop new systems, can be a legitimate and appropriate strategy for action to be supported by the leadership team. Moreover, it is also recognised that undertaking such professionally based knowledge can bring a 'sense of reinvigoration or rejuvenation' (Field, 2010: 491) with consequent impact on teacher retention (NFER, 2020).

However you decide to take your new understandings forward we suggest that a third key question for you to consider is: *what changes can I make to my teaching approach and how can I negotiate with colleagues a shared and collective strategy for action?*

Picture of practice: sharing new ideas

In this school, value is placed on robust evidence, external expertise as well as learning from each other. Staff regularly visit each other's classes and indeed weekly staff meetings are 'hosted' by different teachers, with the first standing item on the agenda being recognising innovative practice. The staff are used to the headteacher sharing articles and 'inspirational' quotations and the staff room has a small area dedicated to professional reading. Reena, in her third year of teaching, has taken it upon herself to initiate a monthly meeting with colleagues before school with the aim of sharing best practice. This might be a reading, a new resource, or an opportunity to revisit a current school approach to clarify understanding. All of the staff are welcome to attend and a different person takes responsibility for selecting the area for discussion, as well as providing breakfast! Staff members will sometimes make the headteacher aware of the areas that have been discussed and seek to influence decisions and priorities across the school. The headteacher welcomes the staff's enthusiasm, their focus on reflecting and actively developing practices that will improve the children's experiences and outcomes.

Throughout this book we have upheld the practice in Reggio Emilia as an example of an education system in which an image of the child as capable and competent lies at the heart of its principles and consequent policy decisions. Traditionally aligned with practice in the early years, we have attempted to build a case for the adoption of more respectful views and practices relating to children of all ages. Research based on the opinions of the children themselves tells us this is critical. Outcomes from *The Good Childhood Report* (Children's Society, 2020) show for example, that children and young people have become increasingly unhappy with their lives, with factors like friends, school and bodily appearance all playing a role. At the time of writing we can only speculate as to what impact the current pandemic will have on exacerbating these issues. Even in 2019, Sir Al Aynsley Green (First Children's Commissioner 2005–2010) was making it abundantly clear in his book *The British Betrayal of Childhood* that more needs to be done to improve the

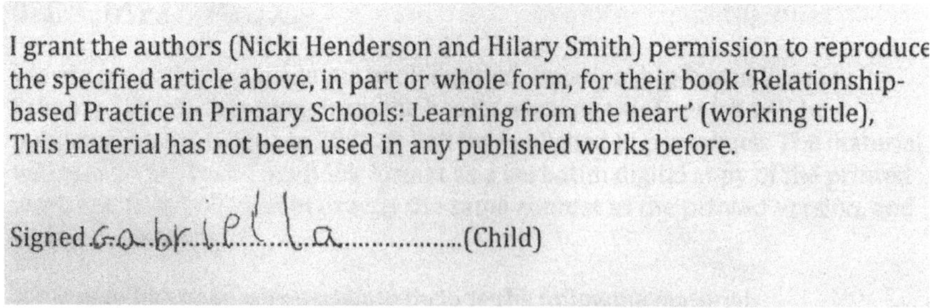

> I grant the authors (Nicki Henderson and Hilary Smith) permission to reproduce the specified article above, in part or whole form, for their book 'Relationship-based Practice in Primary Schools: Learning from the heart' (working title), This material has not been used in any published works before.
>
> Signed Gabriella ....(Child)

Figure 8.1 Child's permission.

conditions for children. He suggests that the attitudes of those living with children, those working *for* children and who provide media representations of children have a particular responsibility and opportunity to reconceptualise both the view and the lot of children in society. Whilst Pollard and Tann (*op. cit*: 312) rightly acknowledge that the 'major structural features of society are extremely resistant to change', we are resolute in our conviction that as teachers we are obliged to use the power and status that comes with the position to act as advocates for our children and, moreover, for childhood itself (Loreman, 2009). We suggest, therefore, a further key question for you to consider is: *how are you promoting a positive image of children and how are you showing in your practices and dialogue with others that children's ideas are valued, respected and acted upon?*

By way of an example, during the process of writing this book we have gathered permissions from the individuals who have kindly contributed their offerings for our final section. Whilst the recognised expectation was that parents would need to authenticate on behalf of their children, for us it was paramount that the children were asked to give this for themselves, with a clear commitment that if they did not give it we would not use it! Our conviction is that children should always be consulted before any of their pictures or photographs are posted on social media, have their learning displayed and, indeed, in any aspect of their lives that involves public scrutiny. In this way we are affording the children the dignity and respect to which they are entitled (see Figure 8.1).

Testaments to teachers

So far we have invited you to reflect on aspects of your practice that you might do differently in response to reading this book. We also encourage you to recognise and catalogue the aspects of your practice that you are proud of, that are working well and that your most discerning critics (i.e. the children and their parents) respect and love about you. The following accolades are born out of the kind of relationship-based pedagogy we are advocating here, and bear witness to the contributors' lasting emotional footprint: the way they have made the children feel, and the consequent impression of themselves and their capabilities. We urge

Figure 8.2 The best teacher

you to keep similar treasures that will have been sent your way and to use them formally (e.g. extracts in letters of application to evidence your 'impact') and, perhaps even more valuably at times, when the job feels too difficult and overwhelming. We guarantee there is nothing more cathartic than returning to a pile of heartfelt messages. The children are quite literally 'gifting' you their praise and endorsement.

Thank you

You got to know me when I was about 3 years old. As a friend of my mum you saw me grow up and loved and spoiled me. Thank you.

As a teacher you were kind and good with all the children. My heart is very sore that you are leaving but I know you will come back one day.

I love you very much and will miss you – lots.

Reconnecting

One former pupil from the very first class I taught contacted me after about ten years to tell me about the impact she felt I'd had on her life – she said that actually, her experiences with me in primary school carried her through difficult secondary years. I was torn by this – on the one hand immensely touched that she would think to get in touch, but also so sad that she had had to keep this primary school experience as a little nugget of hope. I've kept in touch with her – some years later when Facebook kicked off, she found me again and then this generated a little group of former Y4/Y5 whose contacts I hold so dearly to my heart. Just occasionally one of them will post a 'do you remember when we did X with Miss M?' and the group memories start flying in. A few years ago I was visiting the town where I'd taught and we had an impromptu get together – we shared photos, some brought their kids, some brought their mums! We laughed about our shared memories. The relationships between children and teachers at primary school can matter so so much. You are closer to this group of little people than in any other work situation – one mum told me to my horror, 'you know in the years you taught her, she loved you more than she loved me'. That's such a huge responsibility. I'm struggling to find the words to describe the physicality of the emotion I felt on that reunion day: pride (in playing just a small walk on role in their lives), nostalgia (it seemed so simple and clear), immense gratitude to think about how much we had impacted on each other.

When I look back on that first class, I also glance at the conkers I have in my study given to me by a little boy 28 years ago. Most of the children in that class have stayed in their small town: one went to prison, one grew up to be a cage fighter, one became a town councillor, one died of cancer a few years back. I wish I could track them all down – especially the little ones who had such a difficult childhood – the children of alcoholics, the foster kids. Are they ok? It's a lasting relationship, that carries on even now. At the start of the COVID lock-down, another child from the class (hmmm must be 37 now!) contacted me out of the blue through Facebook to ask me about the very first 'topic' I'd taught them – she could remember parts of what we did but wanted some inspiration for homeschooling. She told me that it was the favourite thing she had done in all the things she did at school. I'm sure they weren't the best planned lessons, or even that they had particularly clear learning objectives, but I cared and I loved those children.

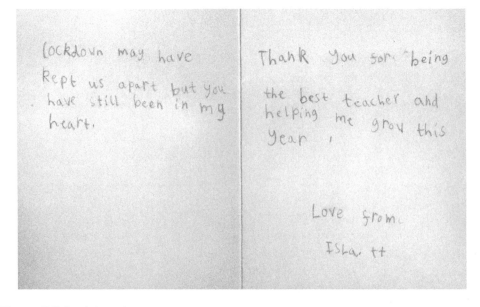

Figure 8.3 Lockdown heart

Inside a book

As an 11-year-old boy wearing my school shorts and dreaming about becoming an England cricket player, I wandered along to an English lesson that has stuck with me ever since.

Almost as soon as we sat down, the teacher told us all to get up from our chairs and follow him outside with no explanation. Once we reached a courtyard, he handed each of us a blindfold and told us to put them on. With hindsight, this seems like an incredibly strange request from a teacher to a group of pre-teen pupils, but we followed the instruction without hesitation. He then proceeded to spin each blindfolded student a few times before announcing that we needed to find our way back to his classroom (which was through a set of doors, down a long corridor, and then up a flight of stairs). Chaos ensued. Screaming, shouting, and the sounds of people bumping into one another rang out, likely irritating the music teachers diligently providing recorder instruction next-door. We were then told to stop and stand still. A few moments passed and instructions began to be given out by two of our classmates who quickly gathered a conga line and led everybody, unscathed, back to the classroom. We removed the blindfolds and flopped down into our chairs, assuming that it was just another one of the teacher's eccentricities, along with his tendency to shout 'have a toffee, boy!' and hand over some sweets when somebody had made a good point. That was until he produced a set of books and told us to turn to one of the pages where we collectively read through a passage from The Day of the Triffids, *recounting the horror of a world in which almost all of the world's population becomes blind overnight, finding their lives turned upside down. By luck, some people retain their sight, and this particular passage sees them leading the blind in chains through the city, just as our classmates had led us back to the classroom.*

I had always loved reading, but I had never been inside a book before. It was a genius twist, and was one of many ways in which the teacher in question made every lesson feel like an event. I continued to be fascinated by literature long after I had moved on to another school, and ultimately went on to study English at University, still inspired by the toffee-wielding maniac who made us blindfold ourselves in a courtyard.

Chocolate lover

You are the best teacher in the world!
I will always remember all the funny things you said and did like 'where is your money honey?'
I will never forget you are a chocolate lover.
I know you will miss us as much as we will miss you.
Thank you for being such a great netball coach, if it wasn't for you we wouldn't have won any matches!
All my love

Emotional connections

I had had an intense year working closely with the family of a boy in my class who had speech and language issues, as we worked to get him a diagnosis and the support he needed. The school and the family were both amazing, putting him first and doing everything we could to help him, but it was an emotional experience both for his parents and for me as we cared about him so much. On the last day of the school year, his mum burst into tears telling me that they couldn't have got through the experience without my support, and telling me that all year she knew her son would be ok at school because I was 'his favourite person in the world'. Even though her words were probably something you just say in an emotional moment, they stuck with me because it meant a lot to me to know that this boy had come to school feeling safe and happy during such a difficult time. It still strikes me that when I look back at all of my highlights in teaching, they are hardly ever to do with educational breakthroughs, and almost always to do with making emotional connections with the children or families I've worked with. I still feel so lucky to be able to make these connections and I look forward to seeing what other moments like this I will get to experience.

Family connections

Max (not his real name) arrived in Y2 completely unable to read and with a track record of behavioural issues. The family were new to the area as well as the school.

I tried to cover a lot of the basics with him and he had additional support from a TA who was a very experienced qualified teacher but he made very slow progress.

I had met his parents and they realised there was an issue but didn't know how to help. They seemed keen to help and I gave them the usual advice about reading together, encouraging him to talk about pictures and stories, practise high frequency words, etc. and they agreed but still very slow progress. I gradually got to know the parents and his family. Max was the eldest of three children. Through the informal contact of trips and events it became clear without them ever actually saying so that neither parent could read well themselves. From then on it was clear that the parents were learning to read with Max. I wasn't experienced enough to immediately know what to do but I adapted my approach a bit, meeting the parents at least once a week and talking about what Max had learned, asking about what he'd done at home and explaining and showing what he could do next. This replaced a mostly written record of Max's reading. We also had regular conversations about activities the family had been involved in and films and tv programmes they'd watched. A real milestone was when he brought in a comic from home and was keen to read it to me.

It wasn't a magic wand, but Max made better progress and his parents' reading improved too so they were more able to help him. Max was still cheeky and preferred physical activities. When I left the school I was surprised to receive hugs from both parents and a thank you letter from Max.

Our teacher

Beautiful and kind
And always help us out
Ready when we need her
Loving and cuddly
Oh what fun we have had
We will miss you very much

Care, conversation and confidence

Picture this: A Level year, school university practise interviews with three outside interviewers and a teenager filled with self-doubt.

I was that teenager and ordinarily I would have leaned on my parents to assuage my worries, but my mother was extremely sick and my father, understandably, distracted. Instead I had allowed myself to get into a right state convincing myself that I was not worthy of a university place so how could I possibly perform well in any interview.

Enter Mrs H., a pocket rocket of a teacher, enthusiastic, inspiring, and caring. Somehow, she saw that this normally confident teenage girl was distinctly wobbly. She simply sat me down and chatted to me about all the things I had achieved in school. Most importantly she commented on a review that I'd written, directed and acted in saying that I would have fitted in so well with the line-up of the iconic 60's satirical show 'That Was The Week That Was'. I was floating on air. I was hoping to study English and Drama and my dream job was to write and act in something similar. Her comment hit the spot and gave me the confidence needed. I smashed the practise and the real interview, and I got that English and Drama degree – I've not yet written and acted in my own TV or radio show but there's still time.

Mrs H. sadly died last year, and I wrote to her sons telling them how much she had meant to me and I thanked them for sharing their mother with so many other children. It will come as no surprise that her sons had received hundreds of letters from her former pupils saying what a difference she had made to their lives. What a legacy!

Your lasting legacy

In this space we encourage you to place the first of many letters from your own children celebrating your virtues, dedication and lasting legacy. It is far too easy to allow yourself to get sidetracked and lost in a world of deadlines, documentation and data: in the end the only thing that matters is the positive impact you have made on the children and their future lives.

Prompts for reflection

▨ How do you recognise, remember and build on the things you do well?

▨ What is your emotional footprint? How do you know?

▨ How is sound professional practice noticed, celebrated and shared at your school?

▨ What opportunities do you have to influence new practices and approaches at your school?

▨ Who can you start a dialogue with?

Chapter summary

In this chapter we have revisited the key messages of this book and invited you to use the process of reflexivity to consider your immediate responses as well as planning next steps for action and development. We have explored opportunities for you to think about the implications for self-development, classroom practice, the school context and wider society. We have shared some wonderful examples from teachers and children that illustrate the very powerful impact and impression that loving connections can evoke.

Further reading

Loe, R. (Ed) (2017) *The Relational Teacher* (2nd Edn). London: Relational Schools.

Loe's book, and the accompanying film, resonates with the messages in this book in that they promote a relational approach to teaching and learning that focuses on the quality of human interactions between a teacher and their students. The scenarios, drawn from the experience of a number of secondary school teachers, offer powerful and thought-provoking examples of this approach as an agent of change. The underpinning principles relayed here could equally apply to practice in primary schools.

Loreman, T. (2009) *Respecting Childhood*. London: Continuum.

Tim Loreman calls for a fresh approach to the way children and childhood are valued in society and seeks to re-examine traditional views observed in child-rearing practices, the structures and practices in schools, and media portrayal. Loreman advocates an approach that respects childhood as a stage in its own right rather than as mere preparation for adulthood.

References

Aynsley-Green, A. (2019) *The British Betrayal of Childhood: Challenging Uncomfortable Truths and Bringing About Change*. Abingdon: Routledge.

Blatchford, R. (2014) *The Restless School*. Woodbridge: John Catt Educational Ltd.

Children Society (2020) *The Good Childhood Report*. Available at: www.childrenssociety.org.uk/sites/default/files/2020-09/PRE022a_Good%2520Childhood%25202020_V6_LR.pdf [Accessed 10.3.2021].

Etherington, K. (2004) *Becoming a Reflexive Researcher: Using Our Selves in Research*. London: Jessica Kingsley.

Field, K. (2010) Continuing Professional Development. In J. Arthur and T. Cremin (Eds) *Learning to Teach in the Primary School* (2nd Edn). London: Routledge.

Jung, C. (1954) *The Development of Personality*. Hove: Routledge.

Loreman, T. (2009) *Respecting Childhood*. London: Continuum.

NFER (2020) *Teacher Autonomy: How Does It Relate to Teacher Satisfaction and Retention?* Available at: www.nfer.ac.uk/teacher-autonomy-how-does-it-relate-to-job-satisfaction-and-retention/ [Accessed 10.3.2021].

Pollard, A. and Tann, S. (1993) *Reflective Teaching in the Primary School: A Handbook for the Classroom* (2nd Edn). London: Cassell.

Teaching Schools Council (2016) *Effective Primary Teaching Practice*. Available at: http://tscouncil.org.uk/resources/effective-primary-teaching-practice-2016/ [Accessed 2.6.2017].

Index

Printed in Great Britain
by Amazon